Ernest Hemingway

A Literary Life

Linda Wagner-Martin

First published in hardback 2007
First published in paperback 2010 by
PALGRAVE MACMILLAN

Palgrave Macmillan in the UK is an imprint of Macmillan Publishers Limited, registered in England, company number 785998, of Houndmills, Basingstoke, Hampshire RG21 6XS.

Palgrave Macmillan in the US is a division of St Martin's Press LLC, 175 Fifth Avenue, New York, NY 10010.

Palgrave Macmillan is the global academic imprint of the above companies and has companies and representatives throughout the world.

Palgrave® and Macmillan® are registered trademarks in the United States, the United Kingdom, Europe and other countries.

ISBN: 978-1-4039-4001-8 hardback
ISBN: 978-0-230-27696-3 paperback

This book is printed on paper suitable for recycling and made from fully managed and sustained forest sources. Logging, pulping and manufacturing processes are expected to conform to the environmental regulations of the country of origin.

A catalogue record for this book is available from the British Library.

A catalog record for this book is available from the Library of Congress.

10 9 8 7 6 5 4 3 2 1
19 18 17 16 15 14 13 12 11 10

Printed and bound in Great Britain by
CPI Antony Rowe, Chippenham and Eastbourne

Dedicated to all the students and scholars who have made my career as an Americanist so satisfying

Contents

List of Illustrations   viii

Preface   ix

Acknowledgments   xi

1   "'Fraid a Nothing"   1

2   Eighteen and Fear—and Agnes   12

3   "Dear Ernesto"   19

4   The Route to *In Our Time*: The Arrival   32

5   Of Babies and Books   46

6   Pauline Pfeiffer and Hadley Richardson Hemingway   56

7   Marriage in the Midst of *Men Without Women*   66

8   *A Farewell to Arms*   77

9   The Bullfight as Center   86

10 Hemingway as the Man in Charge   96

11 *Esquire* and Africa   104

12 Hemingway in the World   112

13 Martha Gellhorn and Spain   121

14 War in Europe and at Home   131

15 The Fourth Mrs. Hemingway   141

16 From Cuba to Italy   149

17 Old Men, Prizes, and Reports of Hemingway's Death   158

18 Endings   165

Notes   174

Bibliography   190

Index   195

List of Illustrations

1 The young family on Walloon Lake   2
2 Hadley Richardson before she became the first
   Mrs. Hemingway   24
3 Hadley and Ernest soon after their marriage   43
4 Pamplona (San Fermin fiesta) during the tense
   summer of 1926   61
5 The newly married Hemingways   68
6 A domestic scene   83
7 Hemingway poses proudly with his sons Patrick,
   Bumby, and Gregory   106
8 Hemingway with Martha Gellhorn soon after
   their wedding   132
9 Mary Welsh Monks on her way to becoming
   the fourth Mrs. Hemingway   147
10 A dinner scene at the Finca in Cuba   169

Cover photo: Mary and Ernest on safari

All photos used by permission of the Hemingway Room, the John F. Kennedy Library, Boston, MA.

Preface

Of all the varied profiles of Ernest Miller Hemingway that already exist here in the twenty-first century, perhaps none does justice to his unusual capacity for adaptation. When Hemingway was with his male friends—during the Michigan summers, in the Paris cafés, in wartime, on his boat *Pilar*—or with other correspondents during the Greco-Turkish War, the Spanish Civil War, or World Wars I and II, he showed a carefully constructed masculinity. When he was with a woman he loved, he reflected at least a part of her empathetic sensuousness. When he felt the floodlight of media scrutiny upon him, he intentionally misbehaved— or at least his behavior fed his celebrity status: he was likely to be, at best, unpredictable. In a lifetime of only 62 years, Ernest Hemingway— whether healthy or ill—seemed proud of his ability to be a chameleon.

Yet, of his important fiction it is frequently said that the principal male character resembles Ernest Hemingway. The judgment is not intended as a joke. The irony of a man who was so often a shape shifter being described as a stable persona in readings of his art has gone largely unremarked. Perhaps one of Ernest Hemingway's most successful creations was himself, as both living person and fictional character.

This biography gets to tackle such an irony. It is the aim of this study to emphasize the fluidity of the author's self as it developed through his relationships with the women he married, and a few of those he did not. Married young, Hemingway was adapting to the influences of particularly his first and second wives, Hadley Richardson and Pauline Pfeiffer. But at the start of his life stood his mother Grace Hall Hemingway, surrounded by his four sisters—and the father Hemingway came later to see as less effectual than he would have desired. While his mother might today be seen as using some "tough love" behaviors with her older son, in Ernest's imagination Grace worked actively to thwart his career. Supportive as his sisters Ursula, Sunny, and others were, aided by such Parisian women mentors as Gertrude Stein and Sylvia Beach, and carefully provided for by particularly his first wife, Hadley, the boyish naïf Hemingway was for years feeding all his energies into becoming the writer he had long dreamed of being. This study pays close attention to Hemingway's progress toward his writerly goals, because it was as writer that Hemingway consistently defined himself.

After his divorce from Pauline and his marriages to both Martha Gellhorn and Mary Welsh, Ernest Hemingway developed an often unpredictable personality. His self as it had been shaped earlier underwent changes that even the most loving partner could neither anticipate nor prevent. The second part of Hemingway's life is, consequently, given a briefer treatment in this biography. The greatness of the man as writer remains the truest biography of Ernest Hemingway.

Acknowledgments

My scholarly life has been full of amazingly wonderful Hemingway scholars and students: there seems to be no end to the work which is possible and, as the decades pass, necessary for younger readers to understand the complex writer and stylist that Ernest Hemingway was. There is little question that Hemingway will be read and loved even into the twenty-second century.

My thanks to the staff at the Bogliasco Foundation for a secluded atmosphere in the beautiful Italian Riviera, and to James Thompson, chair of the English Department at the University of North Carolina-Chapel Hill, for the released time that made the sojourn in Italy possible. I am also grateful to the John F. Kennedy Library for permission to use the photographs in this book.

1
" 'Fraid a Nothing"

From the start, Ernest Miller Hemingway liked to lisp that he was " 'fraid a nothing."[1] As both his fiction and his autobiography show, however, one of America's greatest twentieth-century writers was a complicated blend of bravado and fear, conscious always of the way he was appearing to others, fretful that he could not find, even for himself, the heart of his real character.

It was probably less the fact that he was the first son, the second child, born to Grace Hall Hemingway and Dr. Clarence (Ed) Hemingway; birth order should not have troubled his development. It was no doubt that he was so intuitive about his parents' moods, and their relationship, that he could see unsettled lives everywhere he looked. His mother, with her fine contralto voice and early feminist sensibility, was resentful that she was not singing on stage in New York. His father, unsure of his abilities even in his medical practice, found little satisfaction in ministering to his patients and preferred the supplemental work he did giving insurance examinations for extra money. What Dr. Clarence really preferred was being out of doors and running the Agassiz study group for the young boys of Oak Park, Illinois, his young daughter Marcelline and son Ernest among them.[2]

Much has been made of the fact that his mother occasionally dressed Marcelline, the first born, and Ernest, the second, as twins. Sometimes they were both boys, garbed in overalls and heavy shoes; at other times, they appeared as girls, in ruffles.[3] In the turn-into-the-century late 1890s, gender roles may have been less self-consciously described. It may not have mattered to either Marcelline or Ernest that they swapped identities at their mother's whim—although the pretense of their being twins extended to the children's first grade, where (because Marcelline had stayed at home a year longer) they entered school as twins. It probably mattered more as the third, fourth, fifth, and sixth of the Hemingway children were born—and as more and more of their mother's time was given to instruction in music and her pupils' lavish recitals—that the Hemingway household sometimes seemed rudderless. After the death of Grandfather Ernest Hall, with whom the family had lived while the first three children were small, the sense of randomness—of small bodies rushing to practice their music, do their homework, find a quiet place to read, take a bath—increased. Just as there was more and more pressure for Dr. Clarence to bring in money, so there was for Grace (who in some years made much more than her spouse) to increase her income.

Oak Park, Illinois, was a visibly middle and upper middle-class community. People had things. They wanted to have more and more things, and to have reasons to be in near-by Chicago frequently—for concerts, museum openings, visits to art galleries, lectures. What Oak Park neighbors saw a family doing increased that family's worth, and the respectable

1. The young family on Walloon Lake: Ernest in his mother's arms, Grace Hemingway dressed fashionably, Clarence Hemingway, and Marcelline.

capitalism of this prestigious town marked its residents' behaviors. Oak Park was used to fame of all sorts: Frank Lloyd Wright's scandalous departure, like his scandalous (if interesting) architecture, was the kind of prominence Oak Park admired. Ernest Hall's accumulation of his fortune, like the teaching his daughter did, was the kind of serious success the community venerated—and all success was charted in the type of house the family built, and that house's address. The Hemingway family, for instance, lived in the large, turreted Hall home until they could afford to build a suitably large and imposing house of their own. (Grace Hall Hemingway used her father's bequest, and the proceeds from the sale of his house, to build the house which she had designed, the construction of which she had overseen. The Hemingway house on Kenilworth and Iowa avenues had a large high-ceilinged music room area with wonderful acoustics, an office for the physician's practice, and ample space for the children.) The families were closer than most because, as Marcelline Hemingway pointed out in her family memoir, Grandfather Hall's house (at #439 North Oak Park Avenue) was "directly across the street" from Grandfather Hemingway's smaller home, which was #444.[4]

Another marker of financial success was having a place on a Michigan lake in which to go to escape the city's summer heat. Born on July 21, 1899, Ernest was taken when less than a year old to Walloon Lake, where the family built a modest frame cottage, which his mother called Windemere. The house was surrounded by pine trees, in one group of which was hidden the outhouse. Scarcely populated at that time, Horton Bay on Walloon Lake became Ernest's favorite haunt for the next 20 summers: out of the sight and hearing of his mother, he played on the shore, fished, swam, trapped animals, rowed across the small lake whenever he wanted to go to town (and always for the mail), played adventure games with his sisters, some of the Michigan Indians, and the neighbor boys, and generally just fooled around. The Hemingways traveled without their cook, because even though Grace did not like spending time in the kitchen, Clarence did. Life was orderly in Michigan, but there were few neighbors, and no one paid much attention to the oldest son—provided he did his chores, showed up for meals, and had clean hands.

What Ernest remembered most about those early summers, when he was only five or six or seven, was the time he got to spend with his father. The best wing shot in Michigan, Clarence Hemingway taught his son at an early age to handle guns, and to handle them safely. Rigid enough gender lines existed that the Hemingway sisters—except

Marcelline—were not interested in most of these outdoor sports, so what Ernest remembered as precious was the private time he had with Clarence.[5] His son was clearly his favorite child. By the time Ernest was ten, however, his father seldom summered in Michigan. Bothered with depression (which no one in Oak Park was to know about), the doctor sometimes took rest cures elsewhere (described as studying abroad); sometimes he visited New Orleans, again surreptitiously; sometimes he just stayed home and continued working while the ever-growing family was gone. Whereas Hemingway seldom wrote about his relationship with his father, who was a stern and even brutal disciplinarian, in his 1932 story "Fathers and Sons," he described the best parts of the strangely conflicted man ("a great hunter and fisherman and he had wonderful eyes"[6]); the dialogue is past tense, spoken between the protagonist and his young son, and it is written only a few years after Clarence's suicide by gunshot.

Scott Donaldson and other of Hemingway's earlier biographers have told the story of Clarence's severe depression, which occurred in 1909, when Ernest would have been ten. Just a year after Clarence had closed his practice for six weeks—taking a course in New York that lasted for four, and then spending the two extra weeks in New Orleans—he sent to Grace in Michigan instructions that she was to follow about claiming his insurance pay-offs, if he were to die of blood poisoning. At this time, Clarence was 50 years old. He had taken out policies from 11 different insurance agencies, for varying amounts, and so there would be $50,000 the family could claim, if Grace carefully told the same story to each. Clarence also supplied the names of two doctors who would support his story.[7]

Despite the fact that Clarence and Grace were to have two more children, the family was aware in 1909 that their parents were at odds over Grace's building herself a new, separate cottage on Lake Walloon (rather, across the lake, since one had to row to its location). Part of Clarence's anger over the project stemmed from his suspicion that Grace was planning to live there with her young protégé, Ruth Arnold, a voice pupil only a bit older than Marcelline who had earlier moved into the Hemingway home in Oak Park to help care for the children.[8] Part came from the fact that Grace was spending what remained of her inheritance on the house—and in a family whose coffers were never full enough, even modest expenditures called for unanimity. To watch his wife perform the same machinations with what to him seemed to be an unnecessary Michigan house as she had in building their Oak Park home made Clarence even more anxious. Although years later Ernest was to say that he could not go to college because his mother had spent so much money on the Michigan house, that was only a self-pitying excuse: Marcelline, after all, went to Oberlin, and the family had planned for all their children to be college educated.

The Hemingway children were good in school. Educated in the public schools of Oak Park, considered some of the best in the Chicago area, they were conscientious and, at times, even eager students. Ernest took great pride in his careful drawings for science classes, and some of the papers which his mother saved are those of science experiments, printed in pencil but clearly legible. As the Hemingway family archives at both the Lilly Library at Indiana University and at the Harry Ransom Humanities Research Center at University of Texas, Austin, show, Grace and Clarence saved a number of school papers of all their children. For students with such interests early in the twentieth century, university educations would have been likely, if not mandatory. (Many of Ernest's Oak Park friends went on to college, some to the University of Michigan.)

The Hemingway children were also good at music, and one of their mother's coercive practices was teaching each of them a musical instrument—so that the family could be seen as one of talent, acting out their mother's gifts and ambition. For Ernest, being a cello-playing part of the family ensemble was a mixed blessed; while he later complained that he had had little talent, he had learned much about music, written scores, harmony, precision, tone, and tempo. His playing in the high school orchestra supplemented the home instruction. In later years, in the company of the musical Ezra Pound (and his mistress, the superb violinist Olga Rudge), the talented pianist Alice B. Toklas, and most importantly his talented pianist wife Hadley, Hemingway felt he was an informed part of their lives. Musical education early in the twentieth century had become a marker for the middle and upper middle classes in the States: having a piano in the drawing room was an important manifestation of education and of culture.

So was active membership in a church community. The Hemingways were members of the First Congregational Church in Oak Park, where for many years Clarence taught Sunday school classes. Married there in 1896, Grace and Clarence attended every sort of class; their children were baptized there; and Grandfather Hall was buried from there in 1905. Whereas Hall had led morning and evening prayers, and Grace had assumed the Hall family was about as upstanding as a Christian family could be, the zeal of the Halls was nothing compared to that of Clarence Hemingway. Living life by Biblical principles, Clarence also believed that sparing the rod made little sense, and he gave quick punishment for any infraction—washing out the mouths of the smallest Hemingways for saying bad words or sassing their parents, giving a kind of silent treatment to the older children, who sometimes waited days for their father's forgiveness (or, if not forgiveness, acceptance once again). Leicester Hemingway described Clarence's methods of disciplining his children as a kind of coventry, physical and psychological banishment (methods the younger brother thought affected Ernest for the rest of his life).[9] In the twenty-first century, Clarence's punishments might be called manipulative, because they certainly gave him clear authority, and they certainly taught his family exacting behavior. There was no challenging his law. Grace Hall Hemingway may have found ways around that law while her father was still alive, often joining forces with him against her husband; after Abba Hall died, however, she had little choice but to support Clarence's treatment of the children—even if she would probably not have punished them in the ways he did (if at all). Judging from the scrapbooks Grace kept for each child, she tended to find their misbehaviors amusing.[10]

Sundays in Oak Park, however, were spent within the church and the house: no friends could come to play, no one wasted time or indulged in games, everything was sober and self-improving—and everyone went to prayers and church services. It was also true that Oak Park was a largely protestant community; there was only one Catholic church, and it was more near to Chicago than Oak Park. There was no parochial school. Everything about Oak Park was conservative, protestant, middle class, white, and several generations away from residents' initial immigration. All these considerations were important: the village did not want to be plagued by differences from the main religion, history (many Oak Park women belonged to the Daughters of the American Revolution (DAR), and the DAR was powerful in its social action programs), and heterosexual behaviors.

Everything about the Hemingway children's lives in Oak Park was regulated. They were taught behavior and religion by Dr. Clarence; they were taught music, literature, and the arts by Grace. They were trained to be a well-behaved troop of Oak Park First Congregationalists, middle-class advocates of honor, truth, belief in higher powers, and modesty. Dr. Clarence's forming and teaching the Agassiz nature study group was one manifestation of what he wanted his own children to learn; his teaching Sunday school classes was another. Grace Hall Hemingway's being seen as an expert (and expensive) music teacher, and a person who contributed to all the town's charitable events, was yet another. Learning was what one did: education was somber and serious. In Beegel's essay about Ernest's diligence in preparing his science reports, and charting his science experiments, she noted the high seriousness with which he was preparing himself to become a hunter-naturalist.[11]

The appeal of authority ran through both the Hall and Hemingway lines: successful people, proud of what they contributed to the suitably graceful tenor of Oak Park, Clarence and Grace saw their children as reflections of their own competence. That Grace kept extensive scrapbooks for each child showed how satisfying each was to her sense of success as a mother. There are women who are happy mothers because they watch their children develop into people in their own right; there are others, and Grace Hall Hemingway was more comfortable in this group, who see their children as mirror images of their parents—and then any misbehavior on the child's part is read as a rejection of those parental values. As Ernest began making more and more of his own choices, which often were not the choices his parents would have made, both Clarence and Grace found his behavior inexplicable—and threatening.

It was probably during the second or third year of high school that Ernest found the power of his writing voice. He wrote for the school paper—largely sports stories and humor columns in the vein of Ring Lardner, the Chicago writer. According to Leicester, he brought his irony to bear on many of the school's foibles, and sometimes included his competitive sister Marcelline, whom he saw as "the embodiment of the sanctimonious social belle."[12] He published short stories in the school's literary magazine. To this time, fiction meant unrealistic, if imaginative, plot lines and stereotyped characters. But Ernest was sure he had found what would be his life's calling. Such a commitment was easy to make: thanks to Grace's practice of taking one or another of the children to every Chicago event she wanted to attend herself, Ernest had been to his share of performances, concerts, lectures, operas, and plays—far beyond the experience of most high school students. He knew what an orchestra did during a musical; he knew how to behave as an actor (and he had one of the lead roles in Clyde Fitch's *Beau Brummel*, the senior play—as he had in other plays, beginning with the seventh-grade *Robin Hood*).

Here in the early twentieth century, under the influence of the remarkable Theodore Roosevelt and other fitness gurus, the well-rounded person was also a sports enthusiast: Ernest worked his way up from the junior varsity football team to become a second string varsity tackle; he joined the swimming team and played water basketball; he boxed and taught his friends to box. Under Grace's coercion, and after much argument with Clarence, who did not believe in social dancing, card playing, or drinking, he went to dance class and occasionally took Marcelline, if she didn't have a date, to school dances (he didn't go on his own because he seldom had extra money, and he remained self-conscious about the size and clumsiness of his feet). He kept his paper route, although Clarence drove him for the deliveries when the weather was bad.

He seemed to be a student teachers liked. Not only did he do well in science, Latin, English, mathematics, biology, history, and music, he was the school delegate to the Older Boys Conference in Galesburg, Illinois; and he spoke when he joined the Boys' Club of the First Congregational Church spring of his senior year. When he and Marcelline graduated in May of 1917, Ernest was named Class Prophet, a role that was a tribute to his acknowledged writing talent, while his sister gave a speech about the "new girlhood."

Hemingway's social life to this time in Oak Park had been buried under a daily calendar that kept him running from school to activities to paper delivery to band practice to sports practices. Whether because he was in the same class as Marcelline, or because he was shy, he had his first date when he was a junior in high school.[13] In Michigan, however, his time was more his own, and he spent long hours doing adolescent boy things with Jim Dilworth, whose home in Horton Bay became a kind of refuge for him. Then, the summer before his junior year in high school, he met the brother and sister who were to become some of his best friends—Bill and Katy Smith. Staying with their aunt, Mrs. Joseph Charles, in Horton Bay on Lake Charlevoix, Bill at 21 and Katy at 25 were sophisticated, well educated, witty, and used to having fun in their home town of St. Louis. Just two miles away from the Hemingway cottage, the Smiths liked to do things with the handsome young—and sometimes charmingly naïve—Hemingway. Katy treated him with a mixture of flirtatiousness and motherliness; she was an avid reader and brought new books to both the boys. Bill was a congenial buddy.

Ernest's willingness to return to Windemere for summers late in his high school years, even for the summer following his graduation, stemmed from his friendship with the Smiths, and the almost nightly swims at Horton Bay. He also kept up friendships with some of the itinerant Cherokee Indians who lived near the far edge of Walloon Lake. While his relationship with Prudy Boulton, the beautiful Indian girl from "Ten Indians" and other stories, was never confirmed, the possibility of a flirtation with the exotic girl—and his understanding that any close relationship with an Indian would have him banished from his Oak Park family—made Ernest consider such a relationship desirable. Already aware that he would need to leave his coercive family if he were to escape Oak Park—and its stolid conventions—Ernest took his time in making key decisions.

One of those decisions was his conviction that he was not going to college. Instead he wanted to get a job on a major U.S. newspaper and learn to be a real journalist. Because the United States had entered World War I, both Hemingway parents were happy that Ernest was not inclined to volunteer—although they hoped his weak eyes would keep him out of war even if he had tried to enlist. So after his summer in Michigan in 1917, during which he and Clarence with some hired hands made the recently purchased land across the lake into the start of a working farm, in October, Ernest went to Kansas City. First he lived with Uncle Tyler Hemingway who had helped him get an internship on the *Star*. Eventually, when he was hired on at the newspaper, he roomed for $2.50 a week with the man who had been courting Katy Smith. From October, 1917, to early spring of 1918, Ernest absorbed everything there was to know about journalism—some nights he slept in the city room on a couch. He pushed for more and more assignments, and he took seriously the paper's style sheet—use simple sentences and short first paragraphs; use no unnecessary words. The phrases were prescient of the principles of Imagist poetry which he was to hear again in Paris from the American poet Ezra Pound.

Hemingway met a variety of people in the quasi-frontier town of Kansas City, people he would have had no way of running into in Oak Park, Illinois. Because he told his parents that he was frantically busy, he wrote home less and less often. The occasional boxes of cookies from Grace, which Hemingway shared with his newspaper friends, did little to bridge the ever-widening gap between Oak Park and Kansas City. Grace's requests for copies of his stories went unanswered. It was time to break out of the kind of writing that could be pasted into the family scrapbook.

And Hemingway did break out. Much of his journalism was marked, perhaps unexpectedly, with insistent descriptions of character—but this time, real character, observed from the real people (whether prostitutes, prize fighters, law men, bankers, clergymen, prison guards, cooks, journalists, politicians, waitresses, housemaids) he was meeting. These figures were linked with the events the *Star* wanted covered. In an age of journalism that was less rigidly codified than it was to become during the 1920s and the 1930s, Hemingway's journalism-as-story was close enough to the standard "take" on happenings to be permissible—and also to add flavor to the newspaper page.

Surrounded as he was with both news and people who recognized its importance, Hemingway was learning a lot about not only journalism but also about the war. One of the other reporters at the *Star* was Ted Brumback, who had just returned from four months as a volunteer in France with the field service. He was planning to re-enlist: Ernest's weak eyes would not keep him out of such service, even though they might keep him out of the regular military. In January, 1918, just a few months after beginning work for the *Star*, Hemingway applied to the American Red Cross as an ambulance driver; in April, he gave notice at the *Star*. Early in May, after a few weeks at home and in Michigan, he was called to New York for his physical examination.

Oak Park kept track of its patriots. It announced the young Hemingway's imminent departure, and the Hemingway family too became newsworthy. Sent off to France with enthusiastic blessings from particularly his mother (Clarence prayed nightly for his son's safe return and could find little to be excited about in his going to Europe), Hemingway saw his travels—and what he imagined lay ahead—as yet another adventure. He had survived the Kansas City *Star* experience with aplomb, and he knew how much he had learned in a very short time. The likelihood was that another six months or a year in France or Italy would bring immense returns; it was hard to negate the appeal of the attraction of war, the camaraderie and bravery of young men, and— his constant, if unexpressed, theme—the legitimate escape from Oak Park. It could be that the *in our time* vignette about the naïve men aboard ship, concentrating hard on their drinking, represents the attitudes of the young Americans who were too excited to be leaving home to envision themselves in realistic battle. They were protected by their choice of service from having to learn marksmanship so they could see other men on shipboard as possible buddies rather than as fighting companions.

Hemingway saw service for slightly over a month. Sent from Paris to Italy, he drove the bulky Fiat ambulance across terrain that reminded him of hilly Michigan fields; he joked with other ambulance drivers— for a while. But his first work was transporting bodies of dead civilians killed in the explosion of a Milan munitions plant—many of the dead were women, and all their bodies were decaying in the June heat. Transferred next to the military front at Schio in the Dolomites, he saw that there would be little action, at least for a time. Impatient, he traded the ambulance for a bicycle and volunteered to man Red Cross canteen services further east, at Fossalta di Pave. There, at midnight on July 8, crawling in front of the Italian lines to reach a listening post on the Piave River, he was hit by an "ashcan," an exploding trench mortar that resembled a five-gallon can and blew "pieces of junk steel in every direction."[14] He might also have been hit by machine gun fire—either at that time or while being carried by stretcher to an aid station. At any rate, there were two machine gun bullets among the 227 metal fragments which were eventually removed from his legs.

Surviving his injuries, Hemingway was the first American to live after having been wounded in Italy; he was awarded two Italian medals,[15] and the U.S. papers—including the *Oak Park News*—made him a hero.

2
Eighteen and Fear—and Agnes

There had never been anything in Ernest Hemingway's experience at 18 that remotely resembled his wounding and the necessary serial operations, not to mention his lengthy convalescence. Hospitalized and in pain in Milan, Hemingway watched his nineteenth birthday come and go— bereft of the family that he had decided just a few months earlier was smothering him. A Michigan summer with that family, with Katy and Bill Smith and other fishing friends, now sounded idyllic to the wounded man in a hospital where nearly everyone else spoke only Italian.

In Milan, the Ospedale Croce Rossa Americana was housed at 10, Via Manzoni near the Duomo, and gave the impression of luxury. Patients lived in private rooms on the fourth floor; hospital personnel lived on the third. When Hemingway arrived, after several days of pain in a field hospital near Treviso, the American nurses—among them Agnes von Kurowsky—made much of him and his injuries. Like several of the other nurses in the Milan facility, Agnes had been trained for nursing at New York's Bellevue hospital.

Isolated in the beautiful city, the Red Cross facility was a world unto itself. Despite visitors from the ambulance group, friendships with such other patients as Henry Villard, wines and brandies smuggled in by well-tipped porters, and a great deal of U.S. mail, Ernest lived for his moments with the chestnut-haired American nurse. Ag, though seven years older than he, considered herself a rebel from social convention: she too had, after all, run away to Europe and the war just as Hemingway had. Each was comparatively sophisticated; each had grown up in households wealthy enough for music and the arts; each had little anxiety about being sexually desirable. In the States, Ag had left behind a doctor who thought she was engaged to him; and she had had the opportunity for numerous flirtations with both patients and doctors abroad.

Perhaps the young American nurse saw a great deal more behind the wounded man's bravado than he was conscious of himself. Generally considered both charming and unruly, (male observers thought him more boastful than "charming"), Hemingway was one of the more interesting patients; perhaps most of the hospitalized college-age men were too respectful of the nurses to do more than flirt benignly with them. In his memoir, Henry Villard mentioned his surprise when he saw Hemingway reach over and take Ag's hand, thinking then to himself that young Ernest had some kind of an inside track.[1] But because Hemingway had also spent his first month in Milan having surgeries and enduring his leg's being in a heavy cast, he might have seemed more sympathetic to Ag than were other more rapidly recovering patients. That she had drawn a series of night shifts had also led to her having long conversations with Ernest; in the privacy of the night, woman and boy had given confidences that would have been impossible during busy day duty.

By the middle of September, according to Ernest's letters to his sister Marcelline, he was falling in love with Ag.[2] Red Cross rules forbade her going out alone, without another Red Cross nurse as her companion, however, so whenever Ag and Ernest went anywhere—to the races, for example, once he was free of his cast—she took other nurses and patients along. Hemingway sent her notes several times a day; hospital personnel recognized that there was a kind of understanding.

On September 24, Hemingway went on a week's leave to Stresa, on Lake Maggiore, and on October 15, Ag was sent to Florence to care privately for a patient with a dangerous fever. Late in October, Hemingway was sent to the Monte Grappa front but almost immediately contracted jaundice and was brought back to the Milan hospital—Ag, unfortunately, was still gone, though she returned on Armistice Day. While she was back in the hospital with him, Hemingway wrote again to Marcelline, telling her that no one in Oak Park could compete with his new beloved (still unnamed to his sister) and that his plan was

> to stay over here till my girl goes home and then I'll go up north and get rested before I have to go to work in the fall. The doc says that I'm all shot to pieces, figuratively as well as literally you see. My internal arrangements were all battered up and he says I won't be any good for a year.

Clearly sobered by his physical debilitation, Hemingway continued, "I can't work. I'm too shot up and my nerves are all jagged." That letter closed, "you won't know me. I'm about an 100 years older and I'm not bashful and I'm all medaled up and shot up."[3]

Agnes was in Milan only nine days when she and another nurse were sent to Trevisa, where the deadly flu was raging among the troops. When Ernest visited her there unexpectedly on December 9, she laughed at his military costume, complete with the medals which (she later said) he should never have been given, since he was not even supposed to have been on the Piave at all. The casualness that some later observers report in their relationship is not borne out by the correspondence, and biographer Bernice Kert for one finds definite romantic responses in Ag's letters to Hemingway, both while they remain in Italy and after he had returned home.[4] Ag and Ernest saw each other only once more, as he sailed from Genoa to New York, January 6, 1919.

Hemingway's understanding was that Ag would follow him to the United States where they would be married. Although she sometimes signed her letters during the fall "Mrs. Kid," consistently calling her young lover "Kid," and although she talked about her love for him— which made their seemingly arbitrary separations hard to bear—there is little actual talk about marriage in Ag's letters (and Hemingway's letters to her were destroyed at the request of the man to whom she did become engaged later in the spring of 1919).[5] Ag would write, "don't forget me, nor that I love you." She called Hemingway "Dear bambino" (or sometimes "Master"), and in her letter of October 8, 1918, wrote, "I don't want you to think that I've stopped being jealous, or you'll immediately suggest that I don't care for you anymore. Don't you sometimes wish we could skip a year?"[6] Her reference to "a year" complements Hemingway's November 23, 1918, letter to Marcelline when he sounded definite about planning a wedding with his beautiful American nurse: "Oh Ivory but I love that girl" and later in the same letter, "The wife is up at the front."[7]

By the time Ernest had settled in at home, however, Ag was writing less frequently, and eventually instead of his getting letters every few days, they came every few weeks. Morose at the inevitability of the end, he read in his room mornings, listening for the mail to come and hoping for a letter from Italy. By the time Ag sent her March 7, 1919, letter, addressed to "Ernie, dear boy," he knew she was downgrading their romance to friendship—and, as it turned out, to a friendship between a woman and a younger boy. "I am now & always will be too old, and that's the truth, & I can't get away from the fact that you're just a boy— a Kid." In the last paragraph she explained that she was in love with an Italian officer and expected to be married later in the spring.[8] By the time that lieutenant had broken the engagement, at the behest of his mother, however—and Ag had written that news to Ernest in June—everything had ended: Hemingway had exorcised his love. He had written many bitter letters (and some stories) about the broken romance—and the fact that his beloved Ag had "gypped" him; and he had become a man on the loose romantically.

Giving up his plan of marriage did not send Ernest into a search for employment, however. Much to the horror of both Grace and Clarence, the convalescing older son was behaving like a wastrel. For Clarence, who believed that industry was every person's salvation, his son's social-izing in late spring—still struggling with insomnia, still reading during the mornings in his room, still taking his meals with his family, still content to be supported—was more suspect than his pining after his American nurse had been. Without rehabilitation, Ernest's leg injuries caused great pain; without therapy, his midnight wounding had left lingering, fearful traces of shell shock—conscious as his family was that he left the house lights on all night, there seemed to be no reasonable way to talk Ernest out of his fears.

As observant sister Marcelline recalled,

Morning after morning Ernie lay in his big, green-painted iron bed in his third-floor room. He rarely stayed in bed all day, but it seemed to help his aching legs if he was not up and walking for more than half a day. Usually he had his Red Cross knitted cover spread over him on top of his other bedclothes—the same one we had seen in the newsreel, with its gay green, red, black, yellow and white squares. He didn't like to be without this cover somewhere around.[9]

Even though Hemingway did take walks and visit his old high school, often dressed in his Italian uniform, his physical activity was paced and often labored. Marcelline recalled that Ernest had many "quiet, almost depressed intervals when he retired to his room."[10]

A month after Hemingway had returned to the States, because of the great amount of local publicity about his wounding and his service, the Italian patriots of the Chicago area contacted him. They planned a cele-bration on the coming Sunday—in fact, they did their celebrating on two successive Sundays—which involved their singing (three were members of the Chicago opera company), feasting (on spaghetti, chicken, fish salad, and cake), and plentiful drinking of red wine. Clarence Hemingway was polite for the first such event, but when they appeared a second time, he angrily went off to bed, fearing the neighbors' displeasure.[11]

It was with relief that the family decamped for Michigan. Calmed as he had often been by fishing and swimming, by seeing friends, by helping with the family life on Lake Walloon, Hemingway would surely find peace during the summer. But instead, the wounded young man seemed unable to settle down to work of any kind. Clarence sent lists from Oak Park of chores Ernest should be responsible for doing—both at the family cottage, at Grace's new cottage, and on the farm. Ernest ignored the lists. When Grace asked him to help with the younger children, especially with Leicester, again Ernest went off on his own. Some of the time he lived with Bill Smith at Mrs. Charles's farm, fishing and working her farm; at night, they drove Bill's Buick and found other young people to socialize with.[12] Constance Cappel Montgomery notes, accurately, that not only was Ernest a disappointment to his parents but also placed them in a quandary: "Hemingway was considered ready for a job, but too old to enter college."[13] By the time of his late July birthday, when he was turning 20, his mother was frustrated, hurt, and consistently upset with his behavior. (Few people at this point in history had heard of war trauma; the term *shell shock* had been used, but only sparingly, with men who had survived trench warfare, which had not been the case with Ernest—who had not even been a soldier during his European adventures. For a family convinced that work would solve the most serious of mental or physical problems, Ernest's behavior was inexplicable. But then few boys from Oak Park had gone to war at all.)

The family survived the summer, however, and Hemingway stayed on to live at the cottage—and to continue to try his hand at writing. Once the fireplace heat became inadequate there, he rented a room in Petoskey at the Potters' home at 602 State Street. Some afternoons he waited outside Petoskey High School to meet Marjorie Bump; again, he walked as much as his legs would allow to snowy fishing camps. Some townspeople thought his living at the Potters and typing all day was strange; they also objected to his wearing "rough" clothing—a Mackinaw over his old clothes—and appearing with several days growth of beard. He had several close friends, however—among them "Dutch" Pailthorp, George O'Neil, and Grace Quinlan (who was a friend of Marg Bump's as well)—and he sometimes took meals with their families.[14] But he was, too, a returning war veteran, and on one occasion, he was asked to speak to a community women's group about his experiences in Italy.

At that talk, he met Mrs. Harriet Connable of Toronto, in town to visit her mother. She saw Ernest as a possible paid companion for her young disabled son Ralph. Beginning in January of 1920, then, Hemingway lived in Toronto with the Connable family, and through Ralph, the head of the Canadian branch of F. W. Woolworth, met the features editor and began writing for the Toronto *Star Weekly* and its parent paper the *Daily Star*. He kept that position until late May, when he once again returned to Lake Walloon to enjoy his summer in Michigan. A replay of the summer of 1919 began, but this time Ted Brumback, his friend from both the Kansas City *Star* and the ambulance tour, had come to visit.

Worn after a spring, a year, and the summers—waiting for Ernest to find work, start college, or do something besides what they considered wasting time—both Grace and Clarence braced themselves for some disagreements. By this time in the Hemingway family history, Clarence spent only two weeks a summer in Michigan; the laborious process of settling in, therefore, fell to the older children. Grace, somewhat naturally, perhaps, expected Ernest to help a great deal—to, in effect, become his father. As Max Westbrook in his thorough study of the 1920 summer points out, Ernest would have balked at that assumption. He was already angry that Grace thought his writing was a meaningless pastime. He also did not need family interaction to be witnessed by Brumback, or by Bill Smith, who had recently arrived in the area.[15]

Hemingway and Ted did not stay long in the Hemingway cottage; because they were living in Horton Bay, they were seldom around. Grace felt bereft of her son's help; there was no way for her to get word to him when she needed him, and so even his usual duties, like getting the mail, went undone. Soon after Ernest's twenty-first birthday, for which she had prepared the usual family dinner for him and his friends, Grace took advantage of an unfortunate incident to speak her mind to her son. Written several days after his birthday on July 21, Grace's letter ambushed him. In it, she set up the metaphor of the child's drawing on the mother's bank account; then she announced abruptly that Ernest was overdrawn.

What had happened was that two of the Hemingway sisters, Ursula and Sunny, had planned a late night picnic and sing-along with some friends (according to Sunny's account, their friends and two neighboring girls were to be a part of this group picnic) and had co-opted Ernest and Ted to be companions on their adventure. They had planned carefully: hidden the food in the cove in a tin container, with the soda in the stream. "The secrecy was the most fun."[16] When the friends' mother had come to the Hemingway's house in the middle of the night looking for them, Grace was adamant that her children were in bed—but of course they were not. Embarrassed, Grace blamed Ernest and Ted for either instigating the girls' misbehavior or, their being so much older, in using bad judgment in going along with the midnight picnic.

When Ernest, Ursula, and Sunny went next morning to apologize to the neighbors' mother, the adults refused to see them. Sunny wrote that they all had a strict 10 P.M. curfew the rest of the summer, and the next season, she was sent to a girls' camp in Minnesota.[17]

In Grace's letter of rebuke, she asked Ernest to "cease your lazy loafing, and pleasure seeking." Perhaps more significant, she told him, "Stop trading on your hansome [sic] face, to fool gullable [sic] little girls, and neglecting your duties to God and your Savior Jesus Christ."[18] By mail, a few days later came a similar letter from Clarence in Oak Park, suggesting that the Hemingway parents were in league against their formerly beloved son. Clarence asked Ernest and Ted to leave Windemere so that they would no longer be a burden to Grace.

While accounts of Grace's insulting letter and her intentions differ, what is clear is Ernest's deep hurt and subsequent anger at both of his parents. From a boarding house in Boyne City, Ernest wrote to Grace Quinlan about what he called "the kicking-out business."[19] He subsequently blamed his mother for a multitude of errors, and much of his anger found its way into his mature fiction. Bracketed by Agnes's rejection letter in March of 1919 and Grace's admonitory letter (which Ernest also read as rejection) in July of 1920, Ernest viewed his months of convalescence as the crucible for his sorrowful loss of innocence.

In the fall of 1920, then, Hemingway returned briefly to Oak Park, mostly to pick up his clothes,[20] and then quickly moved to Chicago and rented a room with Y. K. and Doodles Smith (one of the Smiths, a brother to Bill and Katy) while he looked for work. It was in that October that Katy Smith read of the death in St. Louis of Hadley Richardson's mother, and feeling sorry for her old schoolmate, invited Hadley to visit Chicago.

3
"Dear Ernesto"

"You are dear, Ernesto, about missing me. I won't tell you how often I've read your letter. It is adorable like you"—[1] Hadley Richardson answered Ernest's first letter to her in St. Louis with six pages of enthusiastic and whimsical energy. The year was 1920, and she had been to Chicago for a three-week visit. She had stayed in the large apartment of Katy Smith's brother, Y. K. and his wife Doodles, a space where Hemingway and several other young men also rented rooms. It was only a few months after her mother's death and Hadley—at nearly twenty-nine—had lived a very protected life. In the sterile atmosphere of her mother's duplex, the talented but shy Hadley had had little chance for normalcy: she studied and practiced piano seriously, for many hours each day, and she went out casually with groups of carefully chosen people. Because she lived with her mother above her sister Fonnie's family (she had married historian Roland Usher and given birth to four children), Hadley's chief identity was as the popular and pretty "Auntie." *Restrictive* was a euphemism for the kind of life Hadley had known.

She had attended Bryn Mawr College for a year, but she had not done so well as she would have liked. She was depressed over the ghastly death of her older sister Dorothea from burns only a few months before classes started.[2] At Bryn Mawr, Hadley was thrilled with meeting talented women like herself, and so she had kept a kind of ongoing open house in her dormitory room: sometimes women stayed past midnight, talking, laughing, and then Hadley had homework to do and classes to get to the next day. Competitive as Bryn Mawr was, Hadley was not in the running for top grades, although her preparation at the very good St. Marys academy (her mother's school) had been thorough. She would have done better during a second year, but her mother thought college was too strenuous for her fragile daughter.

Hadley's myth was her fragility.[3] Because she had fallen from a second story window onto a brick wall when she was a child, damaging her spine, she had led a protected existence. Nobody understood how strong she had become through her study of piano, how much muscle had developed through her constant practicing. Besides, it suited both her parents to consider Hadley the weak one of the children, particularly after the death of their second child and oldest daughter. With one of the two younger sisters married as Fonnie was, Hadley was all that remained of the girls.

Docile to a fault, Hadley obeyed her mother because she did not want to lose that parent too. Her father had shot himself when she was thirteen, supposedly because of financial problems.[4] The suicide of the kindly but ineffectual James Richardson blunted the social power of the family, which had been considered "good" until his death. Then her mother retrenched, moved to a smaller house, and began her life of conserving resources. She turned even more to the Ouija board, to séances, to the other worldly than she had previously. To the family's comparative poverty, then, was added the reputation of strangeness. And while Hadley was uncomfortable in her mother's beliefs, she also was not going to church with the other St. Louis Episcopalians.

The three weeks in Chicago were Hadley's coming out adventure. Meeting Ernest on the first night she arrived, she was as smitten with him as he seemed to be with her, even though she saw at a glance that she was much older than he. Ebullient, loud, bright-eyed and seemingly fearless, "Wemedge," "Oin," "Hemingstein" as he was called made his move quickly. Because he was not then working (jobs were scarce even in Chicago; postwar employment remained at a premium), there were many hours in which he could take Hadley—here called "Hash" as she had been in school by her friends—to the Art Institute, the Chicago parks, the Field Museum and others, the avenues of posh houses where they could scuffle their feet in the leaves. At night, they could dance (something forbidden by Mrs. Richardson) and drink and smoke a little in the comfort, and penury, of Y. K. and Doodles' apartment. While the time passed, their intimacy increased.

As early as her November letters back to him in Chicago, Hadley referred shyly to intimacy. On November 5, she wrote that she was wearing Doodles' blue silk kimono, which she promised to return "when I can wrench myself apart from it," and then she asked Ernesto, "What do *you* want that I have?" She also asked him why he had replied that she knew "too much" after she had complained about knowing nothing. In a later letter, she closed by asking him to kiss her—"any way at all."

A week later she mused about how "enlightening" dancing was and said wistfully that she had always been "wild to dance."[5] Dancing, drinking, smoking—Hadley was able in Chicago to do publicly things that had to remain covert in St. Louis, and her letters to Ernest are filled with memories of the fun they had had doing scandalous things. Her November 11 letter closed with her word play, "I affectionately wish we were bumming togetheringly,/ Close/ 's ever, Hash."[6]

There are more scattered references to the things they did in Chicago—long walks, drinking contests, and in her December 11 letter, "Do you miss me still? I often think of the darling room at Kenley's—the piano, the couch, the big window, the victrola, the rugs pushed aside and two people dancing. What jolly things have happened in this world! Surely some more should."[7] And her January 2 letter closes, after seven pages, "I want you here my dear. I know just ezzactly what I would do for you—but I can't do it so I won't tell you—did do it once."[8]

The usual accounts of Ernest's correspondence with Hadley mention that he wrote her, on occasion, two or three letters a day; the Kennedy Hemingway archive, however, does not bear this out. There is a week in December, 1920, when Hadley came back to Chicago for the weekend—alone—and her next letter was late. Then she apologized, with quasi-sexual phrasing, "Anyway, I don't want your hand to go into empty boxes *any more*—such loving hands—no, they mustn't." In some remarks about their being able to be honest with each other, Hadley admitted that her own "conscience is rather strained lately—but it's not altogether my fault."[9]

As early as her November 25 letter, Hadley tried to clarify how she felt about the difference in their ages (she thought Hemingway was a year older than he was, but even so, there was a difference of eight years). She wrote that she had never "taken an attitude of olderness" to his "youngness" in anything that mattered. "Seems to me your [sic] a wise man and much beyond me in experience and understanding. Please don't call down the hoots of the crowd on me, Nesto. I can learn from you every minute of the time and then some."[10]

Hemingway could not come to St. Louis for the holidays, so Hadley dated men from her crowd and then on New Year's Day wrote to him emphatically, "You are mine, my own, do you understand?"[11] On January 9, she asked him "This isn't an infatuation is it?" And then she told him, "I love you so dearly—you are all that Kate says."[12] By January 12, Ernest was suggesting that they marry and go to live in Italy.

Whether his tone had been jocular, or whether the speed with which the idea of marriage was announced baffled Hadley, she replied by return mail, "I don't say yes because I want to think—that's right you know." Evidently, as Ernest's subsequent silence proved, her response was not "right." He was disappointed, feeling once again that he had been lured by protestations of love into a vulnerable—even a foolish—position. Luckily for Hash and the marriage plans, she had written him another letter later the same day where she said *Yes* and then continued with studied casualness, "Why, just off hand I think it would be jolly to get married in the fall (reaction here was so great it mightn't to be put down). ... I would like to give you the things I have to give as soon as soon." Her whole intent, she repeated, was that she become his help-meet, the partner of his dreams: "I really value your ambition so much— I couldn't help you to throw it aside even for a short while. ... I want to be your helper—not your hinderer."[13]

Euphoria settled in, although it was several days before she heard from Ernest. In her January 15 letter, then, she assured him, "There aren't any arms in the world I want around me as much as yours you see and there's no heart like yours, for me." She also reminded him of his telling her about Ag's rejection, angrily, and her advice,

> I remember clear as a bell telling you not to marry for a long time. That was good impersonal wisdom, wasn't it? Hmmmmmm. ... I want to go to Italy/ I want to go to Italy/ with Ernesto—you know who I mean—/Ernesto mio—the one that's mine!

Hadley concluded that letter, somewhat wryly, "I love you straight thru the silences."[14]

When she thanked him for an evening bag, she drew a rounded oval and wrote within the lines, "This is not a potato." She said that she used the bag all the time, and then placed the drawing on the page. That letter closed, "Oh Nesto, I love you very highly and very lowly and very mouthly and warmly and like a boy and like a girl—all of that—"[15]

In her January and February letters, she asks him about one of his colleagues, Krebs, who had planned to move into their business office to live. Later it seemed that Hadley and Ernest could not live in the office (to do all the kissing she wanted to do) because Krebs and his girl were there—and then they were marrying. (The character in Hemingway's story "Soldier's Home" was given the name Harold Krebs, perhaps to distinguish him from the usual Nick Adams persona of these early stories.)

The parts of Hadley's letters that mention the books she is reading and the authors she admires suggest that both she and Ernest were book people. She was a Dorothy Richardson fan, in the early years of the

1920s when most Americans hardly knew Richardson's experimental volumes. She loved Henry James and Dickens and much other British fiction. At Ernest's suggestion, she read Sinclair Lewis's *Main Street*, as well as the shocking *Trilby* and Floyd Dell's *Moon Calf*, but she had found Scott Fitzgerald on her own. Later she would find Faulkner. Both she and Ernest read Hugh Walpole and Strindberg's play *Married*. About G. K. Chesterton's book on Browning, which she recommended to Hemingway, she coyly wrote that she "just chanced to see, you know, chapters headed Marriage and B in Italy and the combination melted me—great reading. Mr. Browning sure did give that girl a whirl—yanked her right out of a tete a tete with her spinal column into Alpine climbs and such."[16] At first, when Ernest suggested she read sexologist Havelock Ellis, Hadley demurred but then she seemed to have read him and was interested in the maleness and the femaleness of his categories. She saw herself and Ernest as representative of the classic male and female. What she resisted was the over-intellectualization of sex. Instead, she and Hemingway used their own pet animal names—Hadley was a "scratch cat" or sometimes "Feather-kitty," and Ernest was her "waxen puppy."

In a late February letter, Hadley listed her and Ernest's individual strengths. On her side of the ledger, she noted her playing and mentioned Albeniz, Rachmaninoff, Chopin, and Bach. The second item was her skill when she played back court in tennis doubles. The third and fourth items on her list were her sense of humor and her "yards and yards of tolerance." Hadley's last item broke the grammatical sequence when she wrote, "I adore you." According to the complementary list, what she admired most about him was the fact that he was "intuitive" and that he grasped ideas so quickly. She also admired his many "sides"—"the loving side and virile side and the responsibility side and the flexibility side." In retrospect, Hadley was accurate. Ernest admired her musical ability, and the fact that she had once poured all her energy and will into practicing to be a pianist. He saw that she understood ambition of an artistic kind. He also saw that her sense of humor and her lack of interest in social position would make her a tranquil partner. But primary in his mind, and in some respects in Hadley's, was the fifth point, her clear adoration of him as the young and free spirit he was.[17]

That her list of his traits was incomplete may have, to her, seemed to represent their balance as a couple. She was already an adult woman; he was just in the process of maturing.

Part of Hadley's spring visit to meet the Hemingways was prompted by the news that Dr. Clarence had been diagnosed with angina pectoris. As her March 4, 1921, letter to Ernest said, she understood that while he

2. Hadley Richardson before she became the first Mrs. Hemingway.

hadn't wanted to live at home any longer, she could see how "rotten and sad and sort of torn up" he felt about his father's illness. She thought both Grace and Clarence had been "welcoming" and cordial.[18] For their parts, the demure and talented Hadley Richardson would no doubt have been high on any parental acceptance scale. But when Ernest came to visit Hadley's family and friends in St. Louis a few weeks later, some of her relatives were less than enthusiastic. Virtually unemployed, the Illinois young man not only had never attended college but he now wanted only to go abroad and write. Hadley's sister Fonnie was critical. She also was suspicious that Ernest might want only to spend Hadley's several trust funds; though comparatively small, they would be adequate for Hadley herself for a lifetime. For a while after Ernest's visit, Hadley wrote him that she was feeling "foolishly low."[19]

Money, however, was on everyone's mind. Hemingway accepted an offer from the *Toronto Sunday World* to write for it; Hadley planned to rent out her apartment, and in May, did so for $150. Any spare money either of them had was being exchanged in Chicago for lire (since their dream was to head for Italy after they were married) and entrusted to a friend.

The see-saw of confidence continued. Over Memorial Day weekend, Ernest returned to St. Louis, bringing his Chicago buddy, Bill Horne, along. He suggested they marry in the small church at Horton Bay, thereby avoiding a social St. Louis ceremony. Hadley was elated with the idea, and with this inoffensive means of keeping her sister from taking over her wedding plans. On June 14, then, George and Helen Breaker gave the engagement party (although Ernest could not be in town); Hadley sent him the clippings from two papers. In early July, Hadley wrote to Mrs. Hemingway that she was readying her "very simple"[20] trousseau for Michigan and that one of her best friends, Ruth Bradford, could not make the trip after September 5: the wedding date was set accordingly for September 3 at 4 p.m.

Several weeks later, however, Ernest had a blue mood—questioning his ability or his right to take on the responsibility of a household and probably questioning the whole issue of marriage. Hadley went to Chicago to surprise him after he had written that he thought about ending his life. The soul of reassurance for him, Hadley wrote that he was never again to think of "mortage."[21] At the height of her pre-marriage happiness, Hadley responded well, though she had to have wondered what had struck her ebullient courtier. When she returned to St. Louis, she sent Ernest the Corona typewriter she had long planned to give him for his twenty-second birthday (the birthday she thought was his twenty-third).

Little is known of Hemingway's real state of mind during that last month before his marriage. Most of his boyhood friends were still bachelors; he could hardly have shared his uneasiness with his parents. It was to Marcelline that he wrote about a month before the ceremony, asking her repeatedly to please come to the wedding. He refers to Hadley as

> she who in a temporary lapse of all good sense, is to assume the diffi-cult role of Mrs. Hemingstein. ... The enditer is to become man and wife on September the 3rd at Hortense Bay, Michigan, as yet I do not realize all the full horror of marriage ... and so if you wish to see me break down at the altar and perhaps have to be carried to the altar in a chair by the crying ushers, it were well that you made your plans to be on tap for that date.

The letter closes, "Come Ivory, for Gawd's sake, come. Be there ... Naw Ivory, seriously you know, come to this wedding. Please, please, please! You gotta come. I may call it off if you don't."[22]

This letter, along with an undated piece of prose about the way the author loved his trout streams and the partners who fished them with him, marks the ambivalence the young Hemingway experienced: he had set himself up (before both Hadley and his parents) as a mature, self-directed man. To relinquish that posture was to admit that, perhaps, Grace had been right as she drummed him out of Windemere. For Ernest, marrying his impressive bride and leaving the mundane Oak Park existence he had been expected to take up after his war injuries was a cool rebuttal to the often-voiced opinion that he was too young to do either of those things.

Before the Michigan ceremony, Hadley moved out of St. Louis. All the packing, all the careful arranging of piano music and books, all the farewells were completed by the end of July, when she visited Ernest for a week in Chicago, going to work and lunch with him, walking along Lake Michigan, and, according to one of Hadley's biographers, finally having sexual relations.[23] Then she spent most of August at a Wisconsin fishing camp with friends and came to Michigan just a few days before the wedding. Hemingway, similarly, worked as long as he could and then, after arguments with the Smiths, rented a fifth-floor walk-up for the newlyweds to live in in September. Arriving in Michigan at the end of August, he went on a three-day fishing trip with local friends and then saw Hadley the night before the wedding at a dinner Auntie Charles gave (to which she did not invite Ernest's family).

In the silence of the Hemingway marriage that followed, one can imagine the sense of relief both Ernest's parents felt—the troublesome and somewhat idle son had been taken care of. Grace and Clarence felt that Hadley would make a good, supportive wife; her dreams of a career in music had changed, yet she still had the talent to teach should she decide to do so. Grace saw in Hadley a younger version of her own capable self. Admittedly, she did not like the fact that the two would be living abroad, but she was busy with the other Hemingway children. She attended the Horton Bay wedding with all the children dressed in their Sunday best (except for Sunny, who was away at camp) and gave Ernest and Hadley the use of Windemere for their honeymoon—after an arduous cleaning and clearing out of the Hemingway family on the days before the ceremony. As Leicester remembered the turmoil,

> the confusion was something to see. Closing the cottage for the season had always been a grand hassle with so many harum-scarum kids, a calm but disorganized mother, and a haggard father who showed the strain by hurrying through everything and then fretting about it long afterward. That year the Hemingway dither involved getting each member impeccably groomed for the great event and being ready to head for Oak Park immediately afterward.[24]

But then, except for one visit for tea and an occasional letter, Grace left them to their own plans.

There were no parents to feel relief at Hadley's being married. Once she had moved from St. Louis, there seems to have been comparatively little interaction with what friends and relatives lived there. Hadley had made caring for Ernest her primary ambition: she was pouring all her resources into his life plan. Amiable and in love, Hadley Richardson Hemingway became the stable friend of the couple's acquaintances in both Chicago and Paris; it was Hadley who wrote the thank-you notes to "Miss Stien and Miss Toclis."[25] It was Hadley who tried to keep Ernest's unruly temper and his depressive tendencies under wraps. And it was Hadley who turned all the income from her trusts over to his keeping.

But at the start, married in Horton Bay, Hadley and Ernest spent the weeks of the rainy autumn honeymoon in the large, inadequately heated cottage on Lake Walloon—with marginal food. Both of them suffered from colds, and the housekeeping directions Grace had so carefully left for Hadley were lost until the couple was ready to leave the cottage. Living in Chicago was more agreeable, even in the tawdry rental walk-up, but they talked a great deal about moving to Europe. Getting to know Y. K.'s older friend Sherwood Anderson confirmed them in that ambition. Anderson, however, had recently returned from Paris; he was excited about French art and literature, and the work being done by U.S. expatriates in Paris. So they exchanged the lire they had been collecting for French francs, and on December 8, 1921, Hadley and Ernest sailed on the *Leopoldina* to France.

After a few weeks in Hotel Jacob et l'Angleterre, a cheap hotel where Anderson had stayed the year before, they located a fourth-floor walk-up at 74, rue du Cardinal Lemoine in the Fifth Arrondissement, working class Paris, where they moved on January 9. With letters of introduction from Sherwood Anderson to Ezra Pound, Gertrude Stein, and others, the Hemingways realized they had found one recipe for happiness—though they did not use the letters for several months. Instead, they found Sylvia Beach's English bookstore Shakespeare & Company and borrowed a quantity of books; they listened intently to the conversations around them as they sat at the Café du Dome (across the street, the Rotonde was closed for re-decorating), and Ernest modeled his beginner French after Hadley's more finished language skills.[26]

Appreciative of the avant garde as well as the real Parisian people, the two pooled their knowledge about music, literature, and art and submerged themselves in what all parts of Paris had to offer. But Hemingway was also writing as many columns as he could produce on his portable typewriter; everything he sent to John Bone, his editor at the Toronto *Star*, was accepted at the usual rates: he could not turn down what seemed to him to be easy money. Biographer Michael Reynolds records that during Hemingway's first 60 days in Paris, he sent Bone 30 features. Considering the size of Hadley's trust fund, the couple could probably have existed without income from Hemingway's writing. Reynolds also points out that the checking account which Ernest set up at the Guaranty Trust Bank was not joint: Hadley could not make withdrawals, nor did she ever know how much money was in the account.[27]

Later, with the friendship of both Gertrude Stein and Sylvia Beach, Ernest and Hadley felt permanently moored to this foreign city. Ernest with his deft ear picked up more and more language. They were intent on all things French—and then the ski season began. Once they found the inexpensive Chamby in Switzerland, where they loved the soft snow skiing, they realized that they could live abroad as cheaply as—probably more cheaply than—they had lived in the States.

Given the financial paranoia inherent in the Oak Park Hemingway family, the Paris couple's sense was, however, that money was tight.

When John Bone asked Hemingway to travel to Genoa, Italy, to cover the major international economic conference, he felt that he could not refuse the work. But, Hemingway wrote his father, the pay was bad and there was too much work for one man.[28] He was gone from Paris from April 6 through April 27, missing Hadley, missing his top-floor writing room at the Hotel Verlaine, missing the book stalls along with Seine, and the fishermen serious about their occupation along those banks. Even though Paul Scott Mowrer allowed Hemingway to charge his dispatches on Mowrer's *Chicago Daily News* account, he was broke. During those weeks in Genoa, he liked working with Lincoln Steffens, Bill Bird, Max Eastman, Mowrer, and others, and he found the political figures—especially the Russian George Tchitcherin—fascinating, but he was tired. He had injured his leg and hand when he first arrived and the gas water heater blew up as he tried to light it;[29] by the end of the conference, he also had one of his bad sore throats.

Back in Paris, still sick but happy with Hadley, Hemingway tried to resume his writing: what he discovered was no surprise. Absences and fatigue meant that the rhythms he had established with his fiction were completely gone: he had to begin again. Now that he had met and had conferences with Gertrude Stein about writing, he could see that she was right in advising him to give up journalism.[30]

Having found Chamby, Hemingway was eager to return; he also was interested in showing Hadley the parts of Italy that he knew from his war experiences. This time when he suggested the ski trip to Chink Dorman-Smith, his British friend from that conflict, Chink was able to get a leave and meet them in Switzerland. In mid-May, Dorman-Smith and the Hemingways became a less-than-compatible threesome. Somewhat to Ernest's surprise, Hadley did not think the British accented naming (Hemingway was *Popplethwaite*, for example) was as funny as he did; she also did not appreciate having to compete with the two hardy men on hikes, climbs to 7000 feet, or the ski slopes—or to listen to their exploits in cafes later. Their last hike was the ill-fated one into Italy. They climbed all day through knee-deep snow up to the Pass of St. Bernard. Whereas the men wore appropriate boots, Hadley had only some low-cut oxfords. The shoes split during the morning, but she had to keep climbing: she was a "human blister" before they reached the monastery.[31]

Dorman-Smith returned to base in Germany and the Hemingways hobbled on to Milan. Because Mussolini was in the city, Hemingway used his press card and got an interview with the as yet mysterious young leader. But the rains set in, and the rest of their Italian exploration was unremarkable—or worse. The settings that had seemed so exotic to the young Hemingway were either destroyed or completely rebuilt: nothing was left of his storied landscape.[32]

They spent the summer in Paris; then in mid-August, they suggested to Bill and Sally Bird and another couple that they hike and fish in Germany. Ernest and Hadley flew in a fragile biplane; the others took the train. The group was less compatible than they had hoped.

Once back in Paris, Hemingway was contacted almost immediately by the *Star*, John Bone telling him to travel to Constantinople to cover the Greco-Turkish war. Even though Hadley pleaded with him not to go. Hemingway understood the importance of this kind of work to his career as a journalist—just as he was beginning to understand the importance of European politics.

Hadley had understood the first absence but she was furious at the second stretch of nearly four weeks—she was alone in Paris once again, and the $75 a week that Ernest received paled in comparison to her loneliness. The arguments they had about his leaving may have led to what he later told a friend was his one instance of infidelity during the early years of the marriage.[33] Hadley, who blamed her unreasonable attitude on the beginnings of her own depressive malaise, recalled that they did not speak at all during the three days prior to his leaving, and that he left without saying goodbye. She remembered that she could hardly bear his absence.[34]

Despite the fact that none of Hadley's letters ever reached Hemingway and that he was miserable with a ruined typewriter, various kinds of intractable bugs, and a bout of malaria (so that quinine was a part of his daily subsistence), the newlyweds were reunited in late October— Hemingway comparatively wealthy from the *Star* payments, and Hadley grateful that their first argument had ended. She wore the amber beads Hemingway brought home for her until long after their marriage had ended.

Ernest braved Hadley's anger one more time, at Bone's request, when he covered the Lausanne Peace Conference, partly interested in seeing how the war would end and partly because he had come to consider journalism comparatively easy money. Hemingway left on November 22 and promptly had a relapse of his flu. This trip was a mistake, however, in several ways. To make Hadley more accepting of his going, Ernest had invited her to come along later, planning that they would take another ski trip to Chamby at the close of the conference. Because she knew he would want to write, Hadley packed all his fiction—stories, the starts of a novel, carbons, drafts—in a small valise. The porter put her large case up in the luggage compartment of the train, but left the smaller case on the floor. Unfortunately, Hadley left the compartment for a while and when she returned, the valise was gone. It was never found. She sobbed all the way to Lausanne.

Hemingway's dismay matched hers. In fact, he made a return trip alone to Paris to see what he could salvage.[35] Only "Up in Michigan" and "My Old Man" (which was circulating in New York) remained. Although Pound and other friends encouraged Hemingway that he would be able to reconstruct the stories, neither Ernest nor Hadley believed those assurances. In fact, Hemingway wrote about the loss of these early manuscripts in the drafts of both the later *Islands in the Stream* and *The Garden of Eden*. In the first, Hemingway described the emptiness the writer felt at the loss (his search in Paris through the shelves of the cupboard, blindly touching surfaces to find a single sheet or scrap of paper); in the latter, David Bourne—newly in love with Marita—is able to rewrite the stories which his wife, Catherine, has maliciously burned.

As Ernest and Hadley skied in Chamby with Dorman-Smith, both tried to pretend the lost stories were of little permanent consequence. But neither could forget that the very person who had pledged to support Ernest in his devotion to becoming a writer had been the person who had scuttled a great amount of his progress.

Partly because of this loss and partly because of Gertrude Stein's insistence that he give up journalism and live on his savings and on Hadley's family money, Hemingway was ready to agree.

4
The Route to *In Our Time*: The Arrival

Hemingway's concentration on his writing was unflagging. Once he and Hadley had determined that his work would be fiction writing, she took on as many of the household responsibilities as she could. Hemingway rented a small room near their apartment and set off every morning soon after breakfast—in fact, he asked Hadley that breakfast itself be silent so that his concentration from the time he awoke would be uninterrupted.[1] As he worked on the stories that would become part of his *In Our Time* manuscript, he mined sources of the valuable emotion Stein had suggested would give him momentum. The brief character sketches from his Petoskey and Chicago days were long gone; in his 1922 and 1923 stories, Hemingway was creating more complex webs of both character and theme.

One theme that surfaced was the elitism of the Oak Park, Illinois, residents toward any people who did not fit into their notions of suitability in their snobbish, middle class community. When Ernest had been welcomed back from the war by the Italian veterans, for instance, his family had thought those celebrations inappropriate. Similarly, whenever he had made friends among the Michigan Indians, his parents had warned him about "those people." Michael Reynolds described the Oak Park attitudes as "benign racism,"[2] and living as he was now among the working people of France, perhaps Ernest remembered his years of quiet frustration with the Oak Park attitudes. At least three of these early stories deal with his father's prejudice against the Indians—"Indian Camp" (with the deleted introductory "Three Shots"), "The Doctor and the Doctor's Wife," and, to come somewhat later, "Ten Indians." The younger Ernest could hardly have been offended by Anti-Semitism or racism about blacks when all parts of his life were so laced with his family's prejudice against Native Americans.

The line between studying Indian anthropology at Chicago's Field Museum and considering the Michigan Indians "heathen" seemed only arbitrary to Hemingway. Steeped in his friendships with the Michigan Indians, Ernest could not help but cringe at his overtly Christian father's patronizing behavior toward them. As his sister Sunny recalled, the Indian camp was only about half a mile from the cottage, so the Hemingway children knew the Boltons, the Gilberts, Billy Mitchell, Billy Tabeshaw and others well. Further, however, "Ernie was always particularly interested in anything Indian."[3] The children watched lumbering, basket weaving and marketing, and pageant performances. And when Ernest seemed to have become interested in one of the Indian girls, he knew that his behavior was thoroughly objectionable to his parents.

The story Ernest chose to place first in *In Our Time*, "Indian Camp," is key for a number of reasons, and especially with "Three Shots" as its opening. What he conveyed in this compound fiction was the paralyzing fear the young white boy experienced: while his father and his uncle fish on the dark lake, the boy stays by the campfire. Their instructions are that he fire the rifle if he hears anything, or if he is afraid. When he pulls the trigger (and immediately regrets having done so), they return. Then they grow angry that he has called them in; they quickly discount the fact that he was afraid, because they see no reason for that fear.

Seemingly disconnected from the story of the doctor's delivering the Indian woman's baby, this preface links with the medical story to show that the boy's fear in either circumstance was in no way assuaged by his father's behavior—or by his language. Just as his father brutalized the woman in her agony, saying that her screaming was insignificant,[4] and bragged at the effectiveness of his crude implements (why had he no suitable tools or anesthesia with him?), so the doctor-father had no explanation for the dead husband who had killed himself in the bunk above his wife. For the father to respond to his nervous young son with a platitude (as he does on the boat ride back, answering Nick's question, "Is dying hard, Daddy?" with "I think it's pretty easy, Nick") is worse than silence. The boy, who is bloodied from the experience as if he had participated in a hunting ritual because his father had asked him to hold the basin to catch the afterbirth, wants nothing more to do with medicine, with white paternalism, or with his father, the "great man" of his uncle's snide insult.

"Indian Camp," if read autobiographically and then in conjunction with "Ten Indians," shows the son's complete alienation from his proper, racially superior Oak Park family. The stories as a pair also show the meanness of the father's telling his son about what he saw in the

Michigan woods—*if* he saw Prudie in the woods at all. The works together damn the father character. Readers know that Dr. Hemingway was probably not much in Michigan during these later summers, so the fabrication of his act in "Ten Indians" (like his performance as doctor in "Indian Camp") is Hemingway's attempt to get back at the man who he thought had betrayed him in many ways—by giving him false information so as to control his behavior, by physically and emotionally punishing him, and by setting himself and his family above others. (Two more early stories include the protagonist's commentary about a father's failure—"Three Day Blow" and "Cross-Country Skiing" in particular.) It was evidently crucial to Ernest that he disassociated himself from his father now that he was leading his own life, and no longer dependent on the Oak Park Hemingways. In a letter to F. Scott Fitzgerald, Hemingway wrote, "If you take real people and write about them you cannot give them other parents than they have (*they are made by their parents and what happens to them*). ... Invention is the finest thing but you cannot invent anything that would not actually happen."[5] When Gertrude Stein advised Ernest to find the real emotional center of his life in order to write truly, she had probably not realized that Clarence Hemingway would so often come to the fore.

In many of Hemingway's stories, he does not anchor his characters in families at all. If he were to do so, however, this advice to Fitzgerald implies that he would imagine their parents and their homes entire. Part of the spareness of a Hemingway story (and one of the reasons magazine editors rejected his early stories so quickly) was, in fact, this lack of conventional description—of setting, of place, of characters, and of families. By doing away with the background information which readers early in the twentieth century still expected, Hemingway could begin with the drama of dialogue, the conflict between characters, the narrative import of an event—undiluted by explanations. And by doing away with background information, he also cut out of his and the reader's consciousness the coercion that he felt emanating from those seven Hemingways that still remained—prosperous, healthy, and quietly condemnatory—in Oak Park, Illinois.

It is somewhat ironic that Hemingway's early work is often placed in the "realist" category. Realism implies the author's use of full details about just those elements that Ernest was carefully leaving out of his fiction. Instead of the realism that Theodore Dreiser made famous to American readers, Hemingway was working toward a poetically intense prose that used the vernacular and stripped language of classically American literature to draw scenes in which only the essential lines showed, only the important characters, only the determining events. All background, and detail that belonged to the background, was weighed on the scales of essential versus non-essential: Hemingway was alone in modernist literature in taking it on himself to call the balance. Few other writers knew how to truncate the expected parts of a story so that the heart of the fiction was laid bare.

By combining Ezra Pound's superb close editing (Pound's technique visible in the manuscripts of T. S. Eliot's *The Waste Land*)[6] with Gertrude Stein's larger imperatives that usually dealt with capturing emotional states,[7] Hemingway could pare away some parts of the conventional story and leave the stark bones that comprise his best works. He later said he had always thought his work was "suggestive" rather than didactic.[8] In his choice of that word, he calls readers back to his early focus—on the poem and on the poem-like fiction, whether in the page-long vignettes or in the major stories of *In Our Time*. His months in Paris were spent making this journey to a concept of writing that was so new readers could seldom appreciate how skillfully achieved it was.

Another way in which Hemingway's writing differed from realism was that it was, for the most part, imaginary. If the impetus for a realist novel was a real event (as it was said to be in Dreiser's *An American Tragedy*, or some of Stephen Crane's fiction), Hemingway argued against that premise. Just as he seemed to have fabricated the father's role in both "Indian Camp" and "Ten Indians," for example, he wrote to his brother Leicester about the younger man's fiction writing attempts, "If you can't make up stories you shouldn't try to write. A real one remembered is always sort of flat compared to a made up one."[9] While there are often autobiographical elements in Hemingway's fiction, the uses to which the writer puts those elements are more than likely imaginary.

Critics have tended to read Hemingway's early stories as indictments of the character of the mother, given his frequent comments to friends that he disliked Grace Hall Hemingway. In each of the stories mentioned as illustration of his animosity, however, there is also an indictment of the father. In "The Doctor and the Doctor's Wife," for instance, the character of the wife is oblivious to any reality, and through her belief in Christian Science undercuts her doctor-husband's very professional life—hence the emphasis of the story's title. In "Soldier's Home" she lives again in her own fantasy world, coercive as it is, and is cloyingly religious to boot. But in "The Doctor and the Doctor's Wife," the doctor himself is wrong to steal the logs and then to become angry when the Indians accuse him of doing so. His claim of moral superiority when he answers his wife is simply a lie. Then he fabricates a story about the

Indian's not wanting to pay him for his care of the "squaw's" pneumonia during the winter (again, the Hemingways would not have been in Michigan during the winter).

Using the story to emphasize the father's easy lies, Hemingway still allows the son to go away with him into the woods instead of returning to the possessive mother. While readers have sometimes decided that the story makes a determination between the two parents in favor of the father, Hemingway's ability to draw complex characters is the real point of the fiction: the boy's choices are severely limited. The reader's attention must remain with the boy, who overhears all the lies as they are spoken in sequence. (He also sees the father's hand on the gun's trigger and even if that silent scene is ambiguous—who would the father shoot?—it darkens an already dark fiction.) In this regard, the line about the doctor's having a pile of unopened medical journals in his room, which Hemingway had added after the story was drafted,[10] becomes more negative.

"Soldier's Home" is similarly ambiguous. Even though the father is usually absent in this story, the household runs on his rules. His presence is implied; the mother works around the patriarchal rules in order to get Harold permission to use the car. The mother is, at best, aware of what her son will need; at worst, nosy and interfering. The story indicts both parents, however, because all the action occurs only so that Harold Krebs will once more be acceptable to Oak Park society. What is "normal" for the wounded man? To heal and be given therapy for his trauma? Or to have a girlfriend and find a job, to marry and give his parents a grandchild? One of the reasons Hemingway begins this story with a page which parodies a Gertrude Stein fiction (in effect, asking Stein who knew more about the returning veteran or about the trauma of wounding?)[11] is to make clear the reality of war to a person who has been injured set against the fantasy of civilians at home thinking they might understand any of that reality. When Harold's mother tries to "understand" his trauma by referring to her father's experience during the Civil War, the reader is horrified at her assumption.

The story moves swiftly through passages of dialogue which pain the reader: the gap between Harold's psyche and his mother's is so wide nothing could bridge it. But the impact of the story as a whole belies its seeming randomness. Only in the sequence of the dialogue sections does the author chart the veteran's full alienation from the very people who "love" him and are trying to care for him. In the progression through the story, Hemingway creates a doubly ironic title: at first, "Soldier's Home" misleads the reader to believe that the man has been institutionalized in some impersonal veterans' "home." But the awful realization that, had he been somewhere else besides his own home, he might have made some real recovery, gives the reader a second turn—the initial positive reading of "home" is changed to one of sadness. As the bacon fat hardens on Harold Krebs' plate, and the reader envisions his finding somebody who knows nothing about his experiences to take out in that prestigious family car, the sorrow the story has created leaves a miasma of gloom in its wake. The sustained tone of frustration is a real part of that miasma.

By implication, "Soldier's Home" is a story about a man returning from the war—a man damaged and yet inarticulate about his experiences. By conventional social rules, he would be most comforted by his father, not his mother. If gender means anything, a man should understand what this young man has gone through. In his later fiction, Hemingway is to create an older mentor, always male—until Pilar in *For Whom the Bell Tolls*—so that the young man has, if not a guide, then someone to test his ideas and his emotions against. That male mentor is never a father; it more often is a complete stranger.

Months later, Hemingway returned to the theme of the soldier's return. As he wrote the extremely long "Big Two-Hearted River," he was careful to remove his unnamed protagonist entirely from any mention of home, family, or culture. There is no father in "Big Two-Hearted River," nor is there a mother. The balance between Hemingway's having given "Soldier's Home" the central position within *In Our Time* and ending the book with the story he knew was his most Cézanne-like work,[12] all import resting on the physical description of a place and the man's actions within that place, was perfect, and as the artist he had become, Ernest knew that. He did not need to show the manuscript to either Gertrude Stein or Ezra Pound: his apprentice days were over.

When Gregory Sojka presents Hemingway's primary theme as the establishment of what he calls the "aesthetic of contest," he emphasizes the role of individual will against seemingly overwhelming odds (using both Santiago and the earlier Nick Adams); he also says of this story,

> Hemingway describes the trout and their movements with all the accuracy of both an intelligent ichthyologist and observant reporter. The description of Nick's reaction, however, has more purpose than a mere subjective background for the objective descriptions. For the trouts' struggle to hold themselves steady in the current externalizes the inner conflicts in Nick's mind ... [and] the real battleground of this story ... is an inner terrain.[13]

There are other stories about fathers in *In Our Time*, although they are often unconnected with "The Doctor and the Doctor's Wife" and "Indian Camp." One of the earliest stories to vent Ernest's disappointment with his father, though somewhat obliquely, is "My Old Man." Not that the proper Hemingways would have used that slangy locution, but by choosing to voice the story of the jockey's dishonesty in the childlike speech of his young son, Hemingway disguised the class and occupation of the father as protagonist. In a family without women, creating the same narrative situation as "Indian Camp" in that the boy has only male mentors, the son here has no choice but to admire his father, the successful (or at least successful enough) jockey. Disillusioned as the boy becomes, his closing sentence ("Seems like ... they don't leave a guy nothing")[14] reinforces the earlier markers of class and lack of education. (Years later, Robert McAlmon criticized the pose of the child that Hemingway used in this story saying that such language creates a "falsely naïve manner ... the hurt-child-being-brave tone."[15] McAlmon might have thought, however, of the protection such a pose gave the author, especially when he was writing pretty close to autobiographically.)

In this story as in "The Doctor and the Doctor's Wife," the father's real character flaw is his lying. Fathers do not tell lies to sons, no matter how moral their motivation for doing so. Just as the logs do not belong to the doctor and the young Indian woman had not betrayed Hemingway with another boy, neither had the Indian husband killed himself out of weakness but rather because he was tortured by the screams—and then by her violation by the white man—of his wife in childbirth, the litany of his father's lies seemed to be inscribed indelibly on Hemingway's consciousness. In a great many of his stories and novels to come, after 1928, the year of Clarence Hemingway's suicide, there is continued reference to the honor between men—often, between a father and his son, but increasingly between men who are together fighting (in his military fiction) or working (in the fishing, hunting, or artist stories).

When he organized *In Our Time* for submission to American publishers, Hemingway created a kind of obfuscating distance by inserting the prose vignettes about both war and bullfighting between the longer stories. Borrowing these page-long prose poems from his earlier *in our time*, he carefully alternated Michigan stories with expatriate ones, as if to keep readers off balance.[16] It was true that the overall form of the collection received much attention, and there was hardly any commentary about the reality of the fiction: there was certainly no commentary about autobiography, since for all the literary world knew, Ernest Hemingway was a "young Chicago poet" (as he was described in the Contributors Notes to *Poetry* magazine) who had turned to this sensationally new prose. None of the reviews from the 1920s mentioned Oak Park, or his being a doctor's son, or his mother's early singing career, or his first wife—and second wife—being from St. Louis. A few reviewers had learned that he was wounded in the war, though most assumed he had been fighting there (and so the title of the returning veteran story, "Soldier's Home"). A few others assumed that his life in Paris was funded by his journalism for Toronto papers, not by his wife's trust fund. Caught up in the innovation of modernism, and hoping to forget the devastation of World War I, critics wanted to see post-war art, literature, and music as springing from adventurous and brilliantly talented people cut loose from their points of origin.

That Hemingway drew from the surrounding aesthetics of Paris and modernism was only another mark of his sensitivity to his contexts: not for nothing did he call himself Sylvia Beach's "best customer" at Shakespeare & Company.[17] There he could read O'Neill, Millay, Dos Passos, Hughes, Fitzgerald, Anderson, Stein, Cummings, Eliot, Williams, H. D., Du Bois, Lewis, Pound, Glasgow, Aiken, Cather, Hurston, Wharton, and Toomer, and many other American writers—even before he met them in the cafés. Part of the impetus for *In Our Time* may, in fact, have come from the aesthetic success of Jean Toomer's mixed form *Cane*, published in 1923; there poems, long stories and short ones, and a play appeared in one slender book.

Diligent in his reading, Hemingway was writing—and rewriting—his Michigan stories so that they were less provincial: beautiful descriptions of ice and snow on Traverse Bay, for example, melted into taut scenes of urban life. These were the years of escaping the village to find the urbanity of city life—not only Paris but New York, San Francisco, Milan, and London. Hemingway would keep the Chicago connection, but he would erase nearly all tranquil farmlands, lakes and rivers, and forests. He would keep the exotic Indians but he would erase the propriety of church-going middle-class families. And increasingly, he would erase the four sisters who had shaped much of his life before his marriage to Hadley, when he was barely twenty-two.

Seldom commented upon, Ernest's role as older brother to three younger sisters (and of younger brother to Marcelline, to whom he wrote letters which seemed more truthful than those he sent his parents) was an important shaping influence as he matured. When in "Soldier's Home," the young sister asks the returned veteran to come to school and watch her play indoor baseball, Hemingway knew the pleasure Harold's going would give the girl. Yet in the Hemingway stories, there are surprisingly few references to sisters, or to a family with daughters: all attention instead falls on the son of the family, and he is often an only son. The siblings' memoirs all make clear that in real life, Ernest as the tall, active brother added energy and even joy to the children's existence in the orderly and somewhat staid Oak Park household: even though he was seldom at home after he had finished high school, except for his convalescence, Ernest was a presence they remembered and admired.[18] No matter how critical his parents were of his writings, the siblings read his books with interest—partly because they were somewhat shocking, partly because their friends read them, but mostly because they loved their brother.

For a house built in the early twentieth century, the Hemingway home on Kenilworth Avenue had too few bathrooms for the family's four daughters. Someone was always in the bathroom too long; someone else was always waiting, and waiting, and the someone waiting was likely to be Ernest. Fear of interrupting one of the sisters was part of his mannerly life: fear of seeming to be curious about girls' affairs—or girls' bodies—was an even worse situation. In the unfinished story "Summer People," the brother of the family leaves the house (here, the Michigan house, not that in Oak Park) in order to escape from a deputy (he has killed an animal out of season) and as the younger sister, Littlest, follows him, bringing food and supplies, he creates a wilderness idyll that allows them to leave behind house, family, and convention. While they hike through the intractable wild, he is a comfort to her—but she, in her calm demeanor and her confidence in him, is also a comfort to him. In fact, one of the reasons the story went unfinished was probably the harmony between adoring sister and fearful brother: it smacked of a romance plot rather than that of an adventure story. Autobiographically, it also recalled the devotion of Ursula as she sat by his bedside when he tried to sleep during the weeks of his convalescence from his shrapnel injuries, as well as the consistent near-adoration of Sunny, nicknamed by her big brother Nunbones.

If the stories of *In Our Time* are read in the context of Hemingway's personal life, they cluster into works about the young man—now named Nick Adams in most of the works—as a child and as a returning veteran, often beset with parents he would rather escape from than spend time with. They also valorize the young man's friendships with other men. What they do not emphasize is a positive sexual relationship, the kind of romance plot that had made F. Scott Fitzgerald's stories and novels the best-selling works of the early 1920s. In 1925, for example, Hemingway wrote to Fitzgerald from Spain,

> I wonder what your idea of heaven would be—A beautiful vacuum filled with wealthy monogamists, all powerful and members of the best families all drinking themselves to death ... To me heaven would be a big bull ring with me holding two barrera seats and a trout stream outside that no one else would be allowed to fish in.[19]

Perhaps all Hemingway's writing was more autobiographical than reviewers wanted to see it as being: just as Hemingway himself was happiest in the company of good friends with whom he had a great deal in common—his fishing friends, his partners in a hunt, his military buddies—so the young writer may have seen the sexual alliance between a man and a woman, the conventional heterosexual marriage plot, as less interesting—or perhaps more predictable—than other configurations of intimacy.

One of the strongest of the *In Our Time* stories, Hemingway thought, even though he had claimed to friends that it took only half an hour to write, was "Three-Day Blow," the dialogue-based narrative between Bill and Wemedge, the frequent Hemingway character. As they drink together from one of the parent's liquor cabinets, the boys discuss what impacts their late-adolescent lives most: sports, the state of world politics, the severe storm, their fathers' lives, and, finally, their friendship. They also make lame jokes and talk of past experiences that they find comforting, and they finish each other's sentences—particularly as they become more and more drunk. Structurally, this dialogue fiction must be appended to a story placed earlier in the book, "The End of Something," where after the protagonist Nick has broken up with Marge, his girlfriend from the summer who is said to "know everything"[20]—how to fish and row, to predict the weather, and engage in some sex play—the character Bill appears, jaunty in his conviction that his friend has ended the romance with the local girl (who is, Bill thinks, beneath him socially). As he picks up one of the left-over sandwiches, Bill asks, "Did she go all right?" To the bereft Nick, lying face down on the blanket, Bill's question is harsh; to the reader, Bill's question is revealing. Because of the way Hemingway wrote the story, the reader had not known that the boys together had worked out the plan that led to the break up—Marge's rowing off and leaving Nick to find his own way home.

A later story that also privileges boys' friendships is "Cross-Country Snow," and while the young men are differently named, they are even more nostalgic about their important friendship. Lamenting that there will not be many more ski trips, they flirt innocently with the pregnant Austrian waitress: they are young, they are seemingly unencumbered, they are healthy American males out for a few days of exercise in the snowy beauty of Germany. What their conversation reveals, in a mode something like the revelation of "The End of Something," is that Nick's wife is pregnant. She, therefore, is not with them, nor is she likely to be skiing in the future; more significant is the prospect that Nick won't be skiing either, and that the boys' ski trip too may be "The End of Something." Although never published, there is a note in the Hemingway archive written about the time of his marriage to Hadley, where the speaker expresses a similar kind of lament—will he ever fish the streams with his friends again? Will there ever be that kind of friendship and that kind of joy in each other's company? Relinquishing his male friends seems to be the only downside to his marrying Hadley.

The only effective *In Our Time* stories that are about marriage relationships rather than men's friendships are "Out of Season" and "Cat in the Rain." (There is also the thoroughly nasty "Mr. and Mrs. Elliott," the vignette in which Hemingway insults both heteronormal relationships and lesbian ones, emphasizing particularly the inadequacy of the male sex partner.) "Out of Season" works like "The End of Something"—widening the literal meaning metaphorically to suggest that the husband and wife who hire the fishing guide, only to become angry with each other over the guide's lying and ineptitude, are at an impasse about all parts of their life. To use the title "Out of Season" for the ill-fated fishing trip makes sense, but to categorize the marriage as somehow out of its season is bleaker. Why is it that the wife cannot develop a sense of humor about the chicanery of the cheating guide? Despite sparse dialogue between husband and wife, the story casts the wife as wrong—even though the reader can see that is not the case. It is in the camaraderie between the non-English speaking guide and the young husband that the story draws its moral lines. In the sympathy between men, the fishing trip seems somehow productive, a worthy endeavor for them. In "Out of Season," Hemingway succeeded in writing a story whose action was largely dependent on body language, surely an accomplishment for any verbal construct.

Many of his *In Our Time* stories show the power of the suggestive title, one that seems to be literal but then spins outward through the story to connect elements of characterization as well as plot to the whole. Just as

3. Hadley and Ernest soon after their marriage, probably in Austria.

the reader was sympathetic with the character of Marge in "The End of Something" because she had created the original metaphor to describe the old mill as they rowed past it (and Nick didn't identify with her poetic language), so "Out of Season" worked to align reader sympathy with the male characters, moving ironically past the literal language. One story from this period of writing that failed for a time (and was then finished and published in a later collection) was one of the best of Hemingway's early fictions, the much-anthologized "Hills Like White Elephants." Structured in its final stage to replicate the metaphoric impact of the American girl's comment which gave the story its title, the draft story began with the couple's traveling to Spain by train. They are on the train, observing the hills in the distance but not commenting on them.

What Hemingway achieved by changing the organization of the story so as to begin with the woman's metaphor, exactly as he had used Marge's comment to open "The End of Something," was to create sympathy for her rather than for her irritated companion, the man who was responsible for the pregnancy which was their reason for disagreement: to abort (a "perfectly simple" procedure,[21] in his words) or to have the child (her desire) was the unspoken conflict between them. An extremely short story, hardly longer than some of the vignettes from *In Our Time*, "Hills Like White Elephants" was a concentrated description of a key emotional event in the couple's life as a couple.

Lines are less clearly drawn in "Cat in the Rain." Here the young wife is described bluntly—she wants to go home and she wants to have a home, with candles and silver and a stylish hair-do and clothes that have not been packed and unpacked until they are as frayed as her nerves. In Spain, living the rootless expatriate life, she has become jaundiced—or at least sorrowful and hungering for a different kind of life. Her husband, who could be drawn with some empathy as he listens to her list of complaints, is instead depicted as crass: buried in his book as he lies on the bed, he just wants her to keep still. As Hemingway wrote the story, the husband's behavior suggests that her complaints have no validity. Yet the intricacy of the story shifts the blame to that husband when the courtly Spanish hotel keeper sends a maid out into the storm to retrieve the cat huddled under a table, the cat the woman has seen from her window. As the story ends, she holds the bedraggled animal in her arms, and the reader is as happy as she is at the small victory. Here, with only a suggestion of the battle marriage can become, Hemingway manages to equate the less powerful partner (here, the woman) with the equally powerless animal. By choosing to title the story without an article (the title is not "*The* Cat in the Rain" or "*A* Cat in the Rain"), the author gave the nameless woman character the nickname Hadley had chosen for herself, "Cat" or "Kitten" or "Feather Kitty," which she sometimes in letters changed to the woman's name "Catherine." His title, then, is synonymous with his first wife's name.

When in 1927 Hemingway titled his second collection of short stories *Men Without Women*, he had found appropriate language for his aesthetic. As the stories and vignettes of *In Our Time* had already suggested, his writing about men without women—or, more accurately—of men with other men, had become one of the stock narrative situations that he drew on in his work. Not that any writer's fiction need be read as a personal statement about emotional alliances or disruptions, but even as the young Hemingway rationally understood that marrying Hadley had enabled him to leave the States and become a writer in Paris and other parts of Europe, he still longed for his boyhood freedoms and his boyhood friendships.

Perhaps that kind of nostalgia explained Hemingway's writing a letter to Agnes von Kurowsky in the autumn of 1922. If she had not answered, so that her letter was forwarded with their other mail to Chamby, Hadley would have known nothing about her husband's act. Ernest had evidently told Ag not only that he was married but that he was a published writer living in Paris. Her reply was warm: she was glad to be in touch with him, after their bitter parting. For Hadley, however, the fact of Ernest's reaching out—or reaching back—to his first great love, and doing so secretly, was difficult to accept. The strangely inappropriate letter suggests the psychiatric profile put forth by noted psychiatrist Irvin D. Yalom and his partner Marilyn Yalom, that Hemingway never grew past his early rejections—first, that from Agnes, which was followed a year later by the "kicking-out" letter from his mother. Because of what Hemingway saw as his lack of acceptance by these loved ones, he built an idealized image around his mastery of his art. Accordingly, he would never be able to accept criticism, nor would he ever feel secure, able to love or to be loved.[22]

The letter from Agnes, coupled with the loss of the manuscripts, shadowed the excitement and beauty of the ski trip, and when Chink left and the snow softened, the Hemingways moved on to the beautiful seaside town of Rapallo, Italy, where Ezra and Dorothy Pound now lived. Playing tennis, reading in the sun beside the Mediterranean Sea, getting ready to take a walking tour with the Pounds, Hadley was exuberant when she learned that she was pregnant. Hemingway, who was sure Hadley and he had always had protected sex, found himself stunned and, accordingly, unable to write at all. And when he resumed his fiction writing, weeks later back in Paris, he felt much older than his twenty-three years.

5
Of Babies and Books

A pregnant Hadley was a thoroughly fulfilled, and an even more loving, Hadley. As was the custom during the 1920s, pregnant women ate well, and they also smoked and drank in moderation. With a life that was unrestricted physically, Hadley also continued to ski, hike, dance, practice piano, and bicycle: hers was a rare pregnancy.

For Ernest, however, there was less reason to enjoy such pastimes. All he could think about was earning money; other than going back to being a stringer for the Toronto papers, he knew he had to publish fiction. In 1923, Bill Bird would bring out *Three Stories and Ten Poems*, but the slim pamphlet would never make any money. Toward the end of that year, the equally slim booklet of prose vignettes, some of which had appeared in *Little Review*, was scheduled to appear in Paris as *in our time*. The Hemingways would see almost no money from the issue of 170 copies.

Hemingway was, however, writing good prose. Under the tutelage of Stein's acerbic reading, as she demanded more and more often that he write directly from his emotional center, Hemingway's prose was taking on more significant themes: his fiction managed to lay bare the complications of the Oak Park Hemingway household, to describe the weaknesses in the characters of both his father and his mother, and to recognize the relatively minor place he had held in their relationship. Such writing was a bold step into his own psyche. Several of these stories had appeared in print, but most of them had been rejected by journals and magazines. These stories would comprise the heart of his next book, the story collection he called *In Our Time* and hoped to have published in the States. Sandwiched throughout the stories were the short prose vignettes (from *in our time*) that Ezra Pound so admired.[1]

Meanwhile, Hadley's thoughts were largely of the child she carried. For Hemingway, however, the anxiety of not only fatherhood (with the model in his mind of his Oak Park family) but what he knew was his financial responsibility for the child shadowed his mood. Hadley's tiredness began to subdue the tennis games they had been playing with Robert McAlmon, and with Mike Strater and his wife Maggie.

Then in mid-March of 1923, John Bone in Toronto took Hemingway up on his earlier proposal to write a series of front-page feature articles about the French occupation of the German Ruhr Valley. Although Hemingway tried to refuse, Bone persisted. So Ernest returned to Paris to await his visa, writing a few articles there so the time was not wasted. Visa secured, he went to Germany; by April 12 he was back in Italy with Hadley and a few weeks later they returned to Paris.[2] In France, however, the city they both loved seemed less magical. They had a bothersome new puppy; Hadley was feeling ill. In the Hemingway manuscripts appears a sketch written in an unusual stream-of-consciousness style, the author complaining that the housework takes all his time.[3]

Sensing that the bullfights which Gertrude Stein and Alice Toklas described so excitedly would be useful to his fiction, Hemingway traveled to Spain with Bill Bird and McAlmon. Immersed in not only the fights themselves, the three also learned about raising bulls (taking in Ronda and other sites), the religious dimensions of the ritual, and the Spanish people's reverence for the sacred bullfight. Then in early July, Hemingway took Hadley to Pamplona for the Fiesta de San Fermin. Despite uncomfortable lodgings, Hadley loved the graceful ritual as much as her husband did; they arose at five to see the parades and the running of the bulls, and took in the bullfight each day at two.[4]

When they returned to Paris, they went to an exhibit of Andre Masson's work at the Gallerie Simon, and bought some of his drawings.[5] Admonished by both Pound and Stein to invest in the European art that surrounded them, the Hemingways carefully monitored their spending so they could acquire at least modest art objects.

It happened during the late spring that Hadley became nervous about having her child born in Europe. Although they both were restive about returning to the States, Hadley insisted that they leave for America in late summer. What struck Ernest about this attitude was that Hadley was beginning to change the pattern of unconditional support she had originally offered him. That had, from the start, been Hadley's tacit agreement: she had the financial resources, she had the calm understanding, she had the intellect to be his bulwark against both his tendency to depression and his fear of failure. For Hadley to want something for herself—as she had wanted the child, despite Hemingway's belief that they should wait longer to start a family—was at odds with what her husband considered her character. And then, to complicate his push to become a known writer in the heady atmosphere of Paris, that Hadley wanted to give birth to their child on the other side of the Atlantic was another unexpected demand.

What Hemingway feared was that once they returned to the States (or, as it turned out, to Toronto where he would write for the papers there), they would relinquish their chance to return to France. He did not let that happen; he insisted they leave for only a year (it turned out to be only a few months because of the hostility of his current editor, a man who disliked John Bone's protégés). Because of the editor's sending Hemingway far away on assignments, he missed the birth of John Hadley Nicanor Hemingway on October 10, 1923.

Mother and child were healthy. Hadley's breastfeeding the baby went reasonably well. What Hemingway had not expected was the amount of time and attention the large, eager baby demanded. Coupled with the often unreasonable demands of his work for the Toronto papers, the baby's care left little time for Hemingway's own writing: by January, 1924, the family had returned to Paris.

Before their return, however, Ernest spent Christmas in Oak Park. Although the Hemingway family was disappointed that Hadley and the baby would not make the trip (Hadley said she needed to rest to maintain her milk supply for the Atlantic crossing, a time during which mother's milk was the safest food for the infant), they welcomed Ernest fondly. They had sent a substantial check when the baby was born, large enough to cover the birthing costs. They had wanted to have the new family with them for the holiday.[6] One of the ironies of Ernest's visit was that it would be nearly five years before his next visit, and that would occur late in 1928.

Ernest, Hadley and Bumby arrived back in Paris after an extremely long and unpleasant crossing. They rented an apartment above a sawmill at 113, rue Notre-Dame-des-Champs, in Montparnasse rather than in working-class Paris. Settling in happily despite no electricity, showing off Bumby at every opportunity, Hadley and Ernest thought they had arranged their lives capably. When Chink Dorman-Smith came for a visit, he urged them to have the christening (he was to be Bumby's godfather; Gertrude Stein, his godmother). So on March 16, 1924, dressed in his father's christening gown, the baby was baptized at St. Luke's Episcopal Church (despite the fact that Dorman-Smith was Catholic and Stein, Jewish).[7]

In April, 1924, Ford Madox Ford published Hemingway's story "Indian Camp" in his *transatlantic review*, the same issue to feature the first installment of Stein's *The Making of Americans*, which Ernest as (unpaid) assistant editor was typing and editing. But that spring as well, Hadley got the unexpected news from her friend and financial advisor, George Breaker, that because of earlier changes in bond investments, her trust had lost a good bit of its value. Hadley wired frantically, trying to understand what had happened; Hemingway also wired, suspecting some malfeasance. The replies were the same:[8] money was gone and their lifestyle, which had never been luxurious, would need to be further curtailed.

The Hemingways saved enough from their daily expenditures to make two trips during 1924. That is, depressed by the change in their financial circumstances, Ernest made three. He had immersed himself in van Gogh's letters, and because he was considering studying painting himself, the magic of the artist's aesthetic transformed his own existence.[9] In late spring, he made a kind of pilgrimage by himself to Arles, traveling through the surrounding area and ending with St. Remy, the asylum where van Gogh had been institutionalized. Hadley had encouraged his going: he had written hard since they arrived back in Paris, and the disruptions of living with Bumby and the new cat—and their ever-widening circle of friends—were telling on Ernest's humor.

The first of the couple's trips was their July return to Pamplona. Marie Cocotte (Rohrbach) cared reliably for Bumby, so that Hadley and Ernest did not only attend all parts of the Pamplona festival (with Sally and Bill Bird, Donald Ogden Stewart, George O'Neil, John Dos Passos, Chink Dorman-Smith, and Robert McAlmon) but they also fished the Irati River. They rode the bus with Basque farmers, sharing wine from the wineskins. Even though Hadley missed her child, she knew that staying close to Ernest was her primary role in life.

In the awful July heat, Hemingway found his depression hard to escape. Even while at Pamplona, he worried about money—much to Hadley's surprise. When she asked him why their funds were so low, he admitted that he had loaned money to all their friends, so that they could also stay on and see other parts of Spain. Always the generous friend, Ernest considered that any restriction on his finances was a double hardship.[10]

In December, Hadley and Ernest went to Schruns (an Austrian ski area rumored to be as cheap as the Swiss places they loved). It was while they were skiing that telegrams came from both Harold Loeb and Donald Ogden Stewart announcing that Boni and Liveright would publish *In Our Time* in the fall of 1925. The collection of Hemingway vignettes and stories had been carried to the States by Stewart, who was acting as on-site agent; the book had also been touted to his publisher, Liveright, by

Harold Loeb—and of course Hemingway benefited from the fact that Sherwood Anderson was a Liveright author. Back home in Paris, Ernest found the letter from the publishing house. It was a good way to end their year of near-poverty.

The prospect of a real book, published and distributed by a legitimate American publisher, made Ernest even more convivial. The Hemingways were already being sought out by the expatriate literati. *New Yorker* correspondent Janet Flanner recalled that the Hemingways' hospitality was, somehow, "magnificent. ... They usually had an egg at lunch, so if you were invited to lunch, you had an egg, too. There was always a glass of wine, usually some boiled potatoes."[11] Evening meals were taken out, often at the Negre de Toulouse, where the proprietor kept personal cloth napkins for Hadley and Ernest.[12] As their social circle widened (by late spring, to include F. Scott and Zelda Fitzgerald and their American friends, the Murphys), their evenings ran longer—and cost them more.

In the turmoil of living in Paris with an increasingly active child, Hadley and Ernest could feel their closeness begin to loosen. Still his "feather cat," Hadley thought their diminished sexual activity was probably normal for the circumstances; Bumby, after all, was often in their bed—and was often breastfeeding there. Ernest, however, turning twenty-six, was restive.

When he began planning the 1925 summer trip to Pamplona for the San Fermin festival and its many bullfights, Hemingway felt as if he were entering a new phase of life. He had loved the glimpse of the festival that he and Hadley had experienced in 1923, after his quick tour of Ronda and other bull-raising locations with Bill Bird and McAlmon. Hadley and he, with good friends, had returned to Pamplona in 1924. Now, in 1925, not only was the beautiful and sophisticated Duff Twysden on board for the trip, but the group of men who made Ernest happiest were also coming—Donald Odgen Stewart, Harold Loeb, Pat Guthrie, and his Michigan friend Bill Smith among them. (Duff did not fit into the party as a "wife," as Hadley did, but was in some ways an icon for the men's adoration—engaged to Pat Guthrie, she was far from off limits to the other men of the party, as her recent liaison with Loeb suggested.)

As Hemingway came into his own as an avant garde writer, which he had done with the limited publication of *in our time* and several of what he considered his good, recent short stories, he felt confident; and the fall publication of *In Our Time* by Liveright should bring him both stature and income. Helping out at *transatlantic review* as a sub-editor for Ford Madox Ford had showed him how quickly he and his contemporaries had absorbed the principles which Ford and his collaborator Joseph Conrad had worked for decades to establish. Of course, he—the comparatively young American—understood the new modernist aims; of course, with practice, he would make himself into a skillful and imaginative prose writer. In some stories—"My Old Man," "Indian Camp," "Out of Season"—he was already writing better than his contemporaries.

To become a writer of note, however, Hemingway knew he had to write a novel. He was admittedly nervous about that prospect—partly because he had had trouble writing and selling stores and partly because he had read enough reviews to know how stern, even carping, U.S. critics were about the novel as form. Heavily immersed in the New York edition of the fiction of Henry James, American and British critics overlooked what was really happening in modern writing and lamented that there were not enough complex, and involving, prose texts being published. Fiction was caught in contradictory aims, the fact that—according to Pound and others—prose needed to resemble poetry, to be deft and direct and short, and the existing critical premium that the novel must be so elaborate, its sentences so complete, that it would run to 400 or 500 pages: Ernest as the reader he was could see that he was faced with a challenge. After all, he had prevailed upon Ford to publish parts of Gertrude Stein's long novel, *The Making of Americans*. As he had typed out her handwritten texts, he felt the rhythms that were more or less dependent on the work of Henry James. He knew that his writing in any novel would be nothing like Stein's.[13]

Intuiting that the Spanish setting and religious scaffolding which dominated the Pamplona festival could give him an exotic novel, Ernest was more eager than ever to spend the whole of the celebration there. Leaving Bumby in Paris with Marie Cocotte solved the child care problem, but Hadley was also resistant to being away for so long because she had watched Ernest increase the amount he drank over the months since their return to Paris; she knew it was only their financial situation that kept his drinking in check. She dreaded the kind of partying that Pamplona would foster. She dreaded the presence of the beautiful Duff. (Hemingway's tendencies to flirt innocently with beautiful women had increased along with his drinking.) During the winter and spring of 1925, in fact, Hadley used the excuse during evenings out that she needed to stay home to care for Bumby; when she did accompany Hemingway, she often left early. She also knew that once Hemingway had submitted the manuscript for *In Our Time*, he had written little: his anticipation of the book's being published seemed to have fulfilled his ambition. While Hemingway studied the new novels and tried to find the right niche for his characteristically spare fiction, Hadley studied their social milieu and wondered how long she would remain happily married.

In 1925, Hemingway had begun his serious study of the conventional novel. As both Gertrude Stein and her brother Leo advised him, Jane Austen's dialogue could not be improved upon.[14] That Edith Wharton's novels, like those of Willa Cather, were best-sellers also influenced him: their books had strong characters, good dialogue, accessible plots. Hemingway read widely; he tended to keep the sources he found most helpful somewhat secret. He might have been devouring Wharton's *The Age of Innocence*, but he would talk about the latest Sinclair Lewis book. Hemingway knew he had a choice subject in focusing on the Pamplona fiesta—an occasion few Americans even knew existed.

It is a matter of literary history that Hemingway took notes all through the 1925 fiesta itself, and that he was writing away on the novel even while the roman a clef was occurring. Then in the late summer and autumn, he took seriously the need to rewrite and reassess what he had drafted. Using his understanding of Cézanne's foundational principles of art, which Stein had pointed him toward and for which he had thanked her the year before, as he was writing the two parts of "Big Two-Hearted River,"[15] Hemingway came up with an organization which—though it is straightforward chronologically—makes some use of flashback and manages to include characterization for each of the lead figures. One of the most interesting points about the book that was to become *The Sun Also Rises* (originally and in England titled *Fiesta*) was the absence of the Hadley character.

Even though the Hemingways were at Pamplona as a couple (as they had been the previous two years), even though there seemed to be no question of Ernest's love for his wife, Hemingway in the novel chose to omit any wife character. Sure of the appeal of the sexual Lady Brett, he emphasized that woman so that she was the only woman in a gallery of competing men—and she was far from being tainted with boring Oak Park domesticity. But as he obliterated his own Hadley, who was one of the best-liked women in the group, a person necessary for the harmony of the travelers wherever they were, he may have telegraphed a decision that was more than literary.

The Sun Also Rises is a more traditional novel than it might seem. It works through a number of conventions regarding male characters. Because of his war injury, the writer protagonist Jake Barnes is separated from sexual fulfillment. So isolated, Hemingway's protagonist takes on qualities of the Everyman survivor of war, damaged as was Harold Krebs in the story "Soldier's Home" but forced, relentlessly, by his culture to keep up a pretense of wholeness.

In the novel, Brett's love for Jake is a part of that often bothersome force—with an ironic modernist reversal of what "love" ought to mean to the parties involved. Unable to physically consummate their attraction fully, Brett and Jake substitute other panaceas for their frustrated sexuality: drink and hilarity, religion, knowledge, alternate partners, philosophy, friendship. Hemingway owned the galley proof of T. S. Eliot's *The Waste Land*, and in *The Sun Also Rises*, that great poem of 1922 came to different and more titillating life. In the novel, there are many sexual liaisons; there is anger over existing love affairs and wistfulness about those which do not exist. There is a Count who knows his values and lives in his scarred and yet undefeated body. There is the burden of friendship to allow men to survive, even prosper, in the midst of sexual competition. There is omnipresent sport—not only the bullfight but fishing and bicycle racing—and there is the aura of vacation, holiday, festival set against the daily work of the journalist. There is the beauty of the natural Spanish world and the sometimes unacknowledged stability of religious belief. But when Jake Barnes commented to Brett Ashley at the end of the work, "Isn't it pretty to think so?" he underscored the same wrenching waste land atmosphere—in fact, he ironized that atmosphere to drain away the pity Eliot had managed to express at the end of his long poem.

Never simply a novel about drinking and sex, as it was sometimes reviewed as being,[16] *The Sun Also Rises* was structured like a modernist painting, juxtaposed scenes working like part of a collage; its impact somehow went beyond its author's intention. In the gaps between the segments, readers found connections they could interpret in light of their own experiences. It was the readers who made the fishing scenes, and the fly-tying episode, so central to the book: they capitalized on the fact that random sections were sometimes left to float in the midst of the more compelling romance narrative, and they found ways to integrate those separate passages into the full work. Jake Barnes, in their readings, was a man who knew the value of going off to fish, to have rapport with the native people of the town and country, to share adult intimacies with his childhood friends. Such a perspective deepened the character of the American reporter who seemed bent exhaustively on only the fiesta and its roi roi dancing, its drinking and its expected—or unexpected—sexual alignments. Without the fishing scenes, Jake is less of a complex character. Without the bedtime scenes and the sorrow of his looking in the mirror, Jake is less of a man. And without the scenes with Brett at the church, Jake is less wise, less a real survivor. For a writer who had never before used any apparent religious motif, the interplay with churches, locations germane to church history, and characters' abilities to both worship and pray came as a surprise: readers wondered where in Hemingway's experience he had absorbed the tenets of Catholic belief.

As Hemingway worked and re-worked the novel, he began to see a way to bridge that chasm between the traditional novel which established critics so admired and the new novel that modernism demanded. In Hemingway's version of the new novel, vestiges of the conventional form lay, nearly hidden, just beneath the surface. The way this structure played out in the revisions of *The Sun Also Rises* was Hemingway's reliance—for both characters and narrative—on Henry James's late novel, *The Ambassadors*. What James created in his study of male lives in Paris was an almost surreal prolegomena of instructions for masculine behavior.[17] Seeming the antithesis of true masculinity, the American Lambert Strether comes as an emissary to Paris to rescue a young male friend and instead grows to understand true masculine sexuality through his observations of Marie de Vionnet. Taking the unaware though mature Strether as a starting point, Hemingway created the Jake Barnes who was himself removed from sexual action because of his injury—but there was never any question that he needed sexual tutoring. Instead, Barnes became the tutor, the center of knowledge for not only the other men in the novel, but also for Brett Ashley, the foreign woman like Marie who here played the Circe role.

The Sun Also Rises became something of an amalgam of Hemingway's readings. I have written elsewhere about the use Hemingway made of Ford Madox Ford's *The Good Soldier*, one of the most acclaimed treatments of war injury to be published during the 1920s.[18] Whereas in Ford's fiction, suicide is the answer for the veteran who loses his great love upon his return home, Hemingway's answer—based in part on his personal experience and in part on the caveats of modernism—is Jake's cynicism. That Hemingway drew on these works (and probably others) to create a successful pastiche of narrative elements is plausible because mid-way through his revisions of *The Sun Also Rises*, he detoured into writing his parody novel *The Torrents of Spring*. While he had at that time to immerse himself in Sherwood Anderson's *Dark Laughter*, as well perhaps as the Turgenev that gave him the title, he learned to some extent how valuable such immersion might be—especially if the writer were experiencing writer's block (or in his case, was ignorant about the process of writing a novel). It seems likely that Hemingway, with his astute critical eye, learned a great deal during the brief process of his writing *The Torrents of Spring*.

Capturing key elements of a number of texts was not difficult for a person of Hemingway's background. Not only was he a fast and comprehensive reader, training for excellence in his own writing, but he also had many years of musical study to draw on: when Hemingway later used terms like *counterpoint* or *harmony*, he did so with authority. His secrecy about his practice in and knowledge of music paralleled his reticence about literary works that had influenced him.[19] Whereas he was much more forthcoming about painting and graphic art, so that critics assumed those were his areas of expertise, Hemingway's wide reading gave him information about a quantity of fields.

Convincing in its use of modernist fictional techniques, *The Sun Also Rises* was appropriately marketed as a glimpse of expatriate life. Heavily sexual, its publicity campaign, such as it was for a first novel, was meant to draw in those readers in search of the new. In this regard, Hemingway's book benefited to some extent from the earlier success of F. Scott Fitzgerald's three novels—all published, as was *Sun*, by Scribner's. Even though Hadley had appreciated the innovation of Fitzgerald's college novels, she did not think of them in comparison with Hemingway's work. Neither, as it turned out, did the American reading public. In the case of Fitzgerald's third, and best, novel, *The Great Gatsby*, in fact, sales were lower than those of his first two "college" novels. Just as Fitzgerald had written the most expert, and most modernist, of his 1920 fictions, his fame began to diminish. Hemingway, in contrast, broke upon the literary horizon with the *In Our Time* collection and followed that 1925 book with *The Sun Also Rises* in 1926. Critics could write of little else.

6
Pauline Pfeiffer and Hadley Richardson Hemingway

In spring, 1925, when Hemingway and Fitzgerald met, the famous Scott found himself enthusiastically talking to Ernest about his becoming a Scribner author.[1] Once that idea embedded itself in Hemingway's mind, his exuberance about *In Our Time's* being published by Liveright began to fade. Although he did not mention breaking his three-book contract with the latter company, Ernest knew that Liveright had the option on his second novel only if they bought it; if they didn't want that manuscript, the contract would be invalid. Hemingway was sure the manuscript he was now calling *The Sun Also Rises* would be a big novel (at least on the comparatively modest scale he was imagining); he knew that he did not want that book to be the second one Liveright would see. For their advance of $200 for *In Our Time*, the company hardly deserved his first serious novel.

So Hemingway devised a plan that would keep Liveright from taking *The Sun Also Rises*: the book he would offer them would be a different work. It would be a parody of their best-selling writer, Sherwood Anderson. Disappointed in Anderson's recent novel *Dark Laughter*, Hemingway found it easy to write a satire. Like Anderson's, his novel was comprised of loosely connected episodes and used both white and black characters, as well as an impotent male protagonist. Returning from Pamplona, restless as he waited for Liveright to bring out *In Our Time*, Hemingway began seriously planning the project he titled, with double irony, from Turgenev's *Sportsman Sketches*. *The Torrents of Spring* would be a jejune and sprawling text, supposedly reminiscent of the worse of Anderson's prose.

Even though Hemingway made most of his decisions on the grounds of what would benefit Ernest Hemingway the writer, his personal strategy was to be relatively subtle about his behavior. When he and Hadley returned from Spain, they once more became a part of the Fitzgeralds' social crowd, although Hadley was never comfortable there. She knew they could not spend money the way Scott and Zelda, and their friends Gerald and Sarah Murphy and Ada and Archie MacLeish, did. Still heavy with the "baby weight" she had never lost, Hadley was dowdy in unfashionable clothes; her beautiful hair and eyes could not counteract the sturdy body her pregnancy had left her with. When Hadley Hemingway stood beside the slim Zelda Fitzgerald, it was as if Hadley were the younger woman's mother—even though Zelda too had borne a child.[2]

There were as well other American women in the social mix of Paris that included the Hemingways. Jinny and Pauline Pfeiffer of Arkansas (originally from St. Louis) were slim, sleek-haired sisters, one of whom— Pauline—worked for Paris *Vogue*. Comfortable with the Murphys and the Fitzgeralds as Hadley was not, the Pfeiffers did not take in the Pamplona festival, but they were increasingly visible socially. As the autumn went on, Pauline became one of Ernest's only supporters in his plan to break his contract with Boni & Liveright.[3]

So Hemingway in only a few weeks during the autumn wrote a take-off on Anderson's recent novel. Both Gertrude Stein and John Dos Passos thought the work nasty and demeaning; Hadley could not believe that her husband would turn against the friend who had brought them to Paris. Only Pauline Pfeiffer thought *The Torrents of Spring* brilliantly comic. In this first encounter between a non-supportive wife and a chic woman who, though an outsider, was herself part of the literary world, Hemingway succumbed to Pauline's flattery. Everything played out as he had hoped: he sent *The Torrents of Spring* to Liveright, who rejected it; then Scribner's took it so that they might have *The Sun Also Rises* to publish later in the season. Max Perkins arranged a $1500 advance for the purchase of the two books. In a personal sense, everything played out as Pauline Pfeiffer had hoped: by the next autumn, Hadley and Ernest were divorcing.

Fitzgerald, as it turned out, was of even greater help to Hemingway as he polished his first serious novel. The beginning of *The Sun Also Rises* had originally given readers more than a chapter about Lady Brett Ashley, a section that chronicled her battering by her shell shocked husband, her various liaisons, and the admission by Jake Barnes the narrator that he was terribly in love with her. Seeing that Brett was not the actual center of the book, Fitzgerald advised Hemingway to prune and reduce the opening sections.[4] He also noted that there was a lot of loose description, less careful writing than Hemingway was capable of doing, especially at the start. Probably hurt by Fitzgerald's cavalier and harshly blunt treatment, but recognizing the truth in what his new friend said, Hemingway did Fitzgerald one better and cut completely the first sections about Brett. The novel then began with Robert Cohn and boxing, an emphasis which itself earned Hemingway the anger of Gertrude Stein: after he had questioned her about Judaism and the problems of being Jewish, he had used her information to create an objectionable character.[5] Stein did not forgive the insult.

Keeping himself available to the Fitzgerald-Murphy crowd, Hemingway was moving further away from Hadley and his family responsibilities. With work nearly done on both his novels, Hemingway planned to set off for several months of skiing with his family in Austria. With the establishment of what seemed to be genuine friendship between Hadley and Pauline Pfeiffer, the latter woman was included in the plans. From December of 1925 through early January, Pauline struggled with her skiis and her energy level while Hadley managed to cope with not only skiing but with their active child as well. [6]

The first letters from Pauline, now back in Paris, were addressed to the two Hemingways. Her January 14, 1926, letter opened "My dears, my very dears," and two days later she wrote, "I miss you two men. How I miss you two men."[7] With the gender switching that Hadley and Ernest had used in their courtship letters, Pauline's correspondence eased in to genuine familiarity. But then her letters were going only to Hadley, because Ernest had also returned to Paris and would soon be going to New York to meet with Max Perkins. In the intervening several weeks— with Hadley and Bumby in Schruns and Ernest with Pauline doing the Paris fashion events she needed to cover for *Vogue*—the inevitable occurred. Ernest Hemingway fell in love. Or it might be said that the still naïve Hemingway succumbed to the carefully planned intimacies that Pauline had engineered. In the words of Hemingway biographer Michael Reynolds,

> There was plenty of blame to go round: blame Ernest for being a romantic fool; Pauline for taking advantage of Hadley's friendship; Hadley for her passivity, for pretending it was not happening. Hemingway would say Pauline took him away from Hadley as if he were a prized toy to be struggled over. No one believed that fiction but himself, and then only sometimes.[8]

In New York, Hemingway met with both Liveright and Scribner's, spending time with Max Perkins at the latter site. He partied with Mike Strater, Robert Benchley, Marc Connally, Eleanor Wylie, Paul Rosenfeld,

Ernest Boyd, Dorothy Parker, and others. On February 20, Parker, Benchley, and Hemingway sailed for France on the *Roosevelt*. Staying over in Paris, Hemingway delayed his return to Schruns, but finally he traveled to Austria and soon the entire Hemingway family returned to Paris.

When she let herself think about it, Hadley saw the situation as entrapment. Even as Pauline was sending her gifts and, more importantly, telling the Hemingways that Bumby would become one of her heirs (she having received word of yet another family trust), Hadley watched cautiously. In the later spring, when Bumby came down with the whooping cough at Cap d'Antibes, quarantining Hadley and himself away from the Murphys and Fitzgeralds, Hadley could not leave him: irate that his wife wouldn't come to Madrid to be with him, Ernest gave her an ultimatum—which she naturally ignored. Hadley wrote him on May 21, 1926, that Bumby was still doing a lot of vomiting. Even if she could have traveled herself, the child could not be left.[9] Luckily, the Fitzgeralds rented a larger villa for themselves and offered their smaller one to Hadley and Bumby, along with Marie Cocotte who had come to help.

For the first time in the Hadley-Ernest correspondence, Hadley complained. She felt abandoned. She told Ernest that she was down to 440 francs and that Gerald Murphy had already saved them much money by paying their doctor's bills and their hotel bills. She said with clear anger that she was spending nothing ("I'm living the cheapest possible way")—and she was certainly having no fun. Nor was that the least of it. Because nothing about Ernest's relationship with Pauline had ever been admitted, Hadley was living in an atmosphere of suspicion and hurt: she wrote,

> I've got a headache and a heartache and I work for the common good and am sorrier than I can say I haven't been able to expend myself more on you and not so much on the smaller shad. I probably have just written shit letters and that's the truth. My hand shakes writing most of them.[10]

This appeared on page seven of what was, as usual, one of her comprehensive, stylish, and writerly letters. Aside from the vernacular joke about the "common good," Hadley was again defining herself as helpmeet to Hemingway, guilty that she had not been able to leave *their* son to be with Ernest, and just as guilty that her correspondence had probably been "shit letters."

When Ernest finally arrived from Spain, he lived with Hadley, Bumby, and Marie Cocotte for several weeks. And then Pauline Pfeiffer came to join the party, explaining that she had had whooping cough as a child, so she was immune. The villa was, indeed, smallish, so Hemingway and Pauline spent time outdoors. Every evening the Murphys, the MacLeishes, and the Fitzgeralds would come to a spot outside the villa grounds, replete with cocktail shakers and snacks.

When the lease ran out on the villa, the Hemingways, with Pauline, moved to the small hotel at Juan-les-Pins; Bumby and Marie Cocotte lived in the summer house. The long, difficult month dragged itself out, with Hadley, Hemingway, and Pauline becoming a threesome. Hadley, however, did not like the diving at which Pauline excelled; she did not like learning to play bridge; she did not like getting advice from Pauline about how to dress; and she especially did not like the fact that her husband would subject her to what she finally had realized was a grave indignity—his pretending that Pauline was *her* friend rather than *his* lover.

After they all went to Pamplona for the festival bullfights, Pauline left to return to work in Paris; Ernest and Hadley continued on with their summer, sending Bumby to vacation with Marie Cocotte in Brittany. But after their weeks in both Madrid and Valencia, seeing even more bullfights, they returned to Antibes to tell their friends they were separating. Gerald Murphy, always more sympathetic toward Pauline than Hadley, offered to let Ernest live in his studio in Paris; others who knew them were shocked at the news. In early August, back in Paris, Hadley and Bumby moved to Hotel Beauvoir.

It seemed inexplicable to everyone who sensed the real situation. Why did Hadley stand for it? What kind of game was Hemingway playing? Did he really think he could house his wife and his mistress under one roof? The psychology of the great love that had swept over the naïve young Ernest, and the equally inexperienced Hadley, during their year of courtship made the betrayal possible: neither could believe that their marriage would end this way. Yet Hadley knew if she gave Ernest an ultimatum, he would leave her—even as much as he loved both her and Bumby. Whenever they were cruel to each other, each apologized: Hadley wrote in an August 20, 1926 letter about "our bitterness in that damned taxi," but followed that segment with, "Tell me when I'm to come housekeeping at your studio" and signing the letter "Kat, Your loving mummy."[11]

Even after Pauline had left Hadley and Ernest in Spain, her letters marked their days. Urging Hadley to write to her, Pauline insisted on

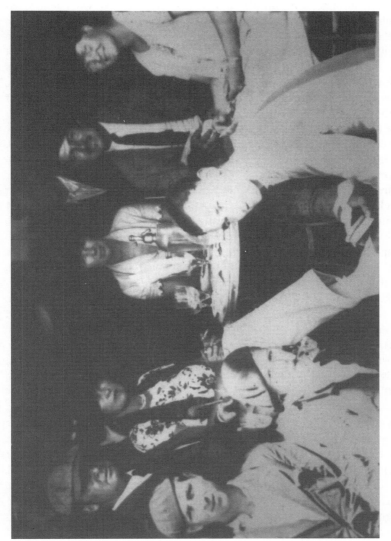

4. Pamplona (San Fermin fiesta) during the tense summer of 1926; Hemingway sits between Pauline Pfeiffer on his right and Hadley on his left.

playing the game she had begun so many months earlier at Schruns. It may have been the continuous irritation of that insistence that forced Hadley to call it quits. After she had moved into the small hotel near the Closerie des Lilas with Bumby and F. Puss, their beloved cat, she devised a plan she termed the hundred days arrangement.

Hadley's mandate was, simply, that Ernest and Pauline were not to see each other for a hundred days. If, at the end of that time, they still wanted to be together, Hadley would consent to a divorce. Perhaps showing more spunk than Pauline had expected, Hadley was being assisted by Donald Ogden Stewart (with whom, according to one of Pauline's letters,[12] Hadley had been in love—as he had been with Hadley—during the 1925 Pamplona summer), as well as Paul Scott Mowrer and John Dos Passos. She was getting her possessions in order, telling Hemingway she wanted her family silver and china, her Joan Miro painting (*The Farm*) which had been her birthday gift in 1925, and other items from their early years in Paris. But Hadley's letters to Ernest in August and September of 1926 are still love letters; they are still from "Your loving mummy" or "Catherine." On September 17, Hadley wrote, "It's true we have to make a very clean break for we don't know how long."[13] She told him that thinking of him with Pauline was too hard for her, yet if he thinks he cannot literally live through the hundred days (with Pauline in the States), she might reconsider her conditions.

Pauline's letters to Ernest from shipboard, and then from Arkansas, are vigorous protestations of her love for him. There is nothing sad about any of them, until October, when she is at home facing her parents' disapproval; then she laments how badly they have treated Hadley. Most of Pauline's attention even then is on her campaign to gain weight: she's eating and drinking milk, she's exercising, she plans to add ten pounds to her weight of 107 pounds. Ludicrous as her representation of her life at home is, consoled by her mother who has asked her to remain silent (i.e., *not* to scandalize friends, family, or her father by explaining why she is in Arkansas), Pauline leaves no question that she is a survivor—and that she will come out of this conflict with Ernest at her side.

One of the conundrums of the Pauline Pfeiffer take-over of the Hemingway marriage was her devout Catholicism. She made clear to Hemingway early on that she was interested only in marrying him—in a ceremony performed in the Catholic church. Given that Hadley and he had already been married in a Methodist church, Pauline's demands seemed unreasonable. But as John Dos Passos recalled, "Ernest had become a Catholic in order to marry Pauline, and by some hocus-pocus had managed to have his marriage to Hadley annulled."[14] Even before the liaison with Pauline, Hemingway spoke often about the fact that he had received the last rites after his wounding in Italy: clearly, that he had been bound for death, and then bound for resurrection, had impacted his imagination. Friends knew that neither he nor Hadley were practicing believers—few expatriates were. So his visible conversion to Catholicism provoked comment. It could also be noted that once Pauline assumed the religious high ground in the affair, she gained some moral support that helped to erase the scandal of behavior that otherwise seemed to be unambiguously wrong.

Pauline's letters in early fall showed her somewhat cavalier openness. Rather than disguising the real calendar of their sexual relationship, on October 1, she wrote Hemingway that he could go ahead and "say to Hadley that we were living together in Paris. ... You tell anybody anything you want. Oh precious!"[15] Assuming that "living together" means that they had had sex soon after they left Schruns, before Ernest traveled to New York and then after he returned (his considerable delay in returning to Hadley therefore explained), Pauline's outspoken letter made a worse mockery out of their summer vacation as a threesome.

Her October 2 letter was an equally bold statement: "if at the end of 3 months Hadley says 3 months more, we will go 3 months more. Because we can ... . As for me, I get surer and surer that I am in love with you all the time." This letter also suggested that Hadley was considering asking Pauline and Hemingway to stop communicating with each other; again, Pauline said, that would be possible. All things are possible if the final result is their being together—"remember, especially, that we're the same guy."[16]

Later in October, Pauline confessed that her mother was very unhappy with their situation, and very much on Hadley's side. Pauline urged Hemingway to pray hard, as she is praying, to decide how to bring Hadley back into their lives. She also told him that she was collecting reviews of *The Sun Also Rises*, which had been officially released on October 22. Early reviews were mixed, so Pauline reminded him "no matter what the critics say, we know about that book, and so far as we are concerned, it is out of our lives."[17]

Pauline's statement invalidates the usual reading of the novel as a roman a clef account of the 1925 trip to Pamplona. Readers then and now have assumed that Jake Barnes's passion was devoted entirely to the unattainable Lady Brett Ashley. By the time Ernest was rewriting his early version of the novel, however, in the fall and winter of 1925, he had become involved with Pauline. The sexual tension he was able to convey in the book was frustration of a different sort—not the impossibility of intercourse because Jake's penis had been injured during the war, but the impossibility of Ernest's (and Pauline's) hurting Hadley if they were to consummate their passion. The rapport Hemingway felt with Pauline began only weeks after the Pamplona fiesta, in the early fall of 1925, and was probably occasioned at the start by her praise of *The Torrents of Spring*. It was only a few weeks after Hemingway had mailed the parody to Liveright that he and Hadley had left for Schruns, with Pauline joining them somewhat later.

As correspondence between Hemingway and Max Perkins shows, most of the rewriting on The *Sun Also Rises* manuscript occurred that winter, once Liveright no long had any claims to the novel. After he signed the contract with Scribner's for the two novels (*The Torrents of Spring* and what would be *The Sun Also Rises*), Hemingway worked quickly on what revision remained; by early March, he had only five chapters left to rework.

Overlaying the chronology of his writing with the autobiographical chronology of his affair with Pauline shows that their intimacy had already begun. He spent early April correcting page proofs for *The Torrents of Spring*, but on April 24, 1926, mailed the typescript of *The Sun Also Rises* to Perkins. *The Torrents of Spring* was published on May 28. The cutting and revising of *The Sun Also Rises* that Fitzgerald suggested occurred in May: it was in June 5, 1926, that Hemingway removed much of the Lady Brett material, and even though at a later point Perkins suggested that he add some of that back in, Hemingway chose not to.[18]

During October, 1926, Hadley's letters showed her anger. She missed her husband; she could see that living alone with a small child, no matter how much loved, was and would continue to be tedious. In her October 16 letter, she asked Hemingway never to mention to Pauline that she had once said that Ernest's affair had just about killed her love for Bumby. Thinking that Pauline might use her comment to try to get custody of the child for Ernest and herself, Hadley said that of course she had not meant her remark. But she also pointed out to Ernest that "Pauline is so clever and quick and she might maybe think of a way to gyp me or is it teach me a lesson."[19]

Hadley had the last word, however. On November 16, she wrote to Hemingway that the three months separation was officially over. She had been gone from Paris for ten days and was therefore able to see more clearly; she also absolved herself of any guilt. "The entire problem belongs to you two—I am *not* responsible for your future welfare."[20]

Hadley may have been responding in part to a letter Pauline had privately sent her the month before, in which Pauline said that she believed Hadley was the most trustworthy person she had ever known, and that she knew she would do the right thing in every instance: "you know what I always said about you—that you not only couldn't do a low thing, you didn't even think one."[21]

After Hadley filed for divorce, Hemingway wrote to her that she was brave and unselfish and generous. He explained that she would have all the royalties from *The Sun Also Rises*, at least partly because she had supported him in all kinds of ways, and he would never have written "any of them [his books] ... if I had not married you and had your loyal and self-sacrificing and always stimulating and loving and actual cash support backing." He closed this November 18 letter that he would always remember her mind and her heart and her lovely hands.[22]

One stage of the divorce was final in January, 1927. In a letter written that month, Hadley asked for the money Ernest owed her and their lawyer for the divorce settlement, and in another, cajoled him (when he was in her home) not to read her letters or bills, kidding him that he needed to be a "reformed puppy!"[23] Final at the end of March, the settlement specified that Hemingway was not free to remarry until between the 20th and the 30th of April. Meanwhile, Hadley had been on vacation with the Mowrers and then in April, she was planning to take Bumby to the States.

The way was clear for Hemingway and Pauline Pfeiffer to marry. In the States, Clarence and Grace Hemingway were shocked into silence. Marcelline wrote to her younger brother in February of 1927 that "We were surprised at the latest news dispatches about you and the family, but life is so perplexing to all of us that one should never feel surprised."[24] According to younger sister Sunny's memoir, however, "Dad and Mother got so upset" that she had to serve as intermediary. As she explained, "Divorce was unheard of in our family." It is in Sunny's account that she tells about Hadley's later admitting to her that she should have fought harder for Ernest, and about Pauline's later role as Mrs. Ernest Hemingway, encouraging Sunny to go after the married man she was in love with; after all, said Pauline, other women have done it.[25]

7
Marriage in the Midst of *Men Without Women*

Any merely factual account of Hemingway's marrying Pauline Pfeiffer omits the emotional nuances of the pair's relationship once Hadley had bowed out. Just as Hemingway had considered suicide before his wedding to Hadley, so he wrote to Pauline in November of 1926 that he was feeling very low, depressed, guilty, and he was not sure that he had the right to marry again. Part of his angst seemed to come from Pauline's assertion that she was returning to New York (from Arkansas) to resume her work for *Vogue*: in his mind, the only reason she would leave Arkansas would be to join him.[1]

In an unpublished fragment of fiction about "James Allen," Hemingway describes the loneliness of the man's sleeping and living by himself. In one segment of the text, he has endured this living arrangement for three months; in another, for four. Desolate as he is now, he considers that while he might not have been "happily" married, he had been "comfortably married."[2] But then he had fallen in love with "a girl," and there had been many scenes at home. As a result, James Allen as a writer was "ruined" because "his delicacy [had been] cauterized away by too much emotion."[3]

It is in this handwritten piece that the protagonist takes up painting, since his writing has been so disturbed. Unable to sleep or eat, however, James Allen also failed as a painter. There is also the suggestion that sexual frustration is to blame for his misery.[4]

Hemingway's emotional rockiness passed once Hadley removed the hundred days caveat and he went skiing with friends while he waited for Pauline to arrive in France. She came with her younger sister Jinny, recruited to help with setting up housekeeping, and backed by Uncle Gus Pfeiffer's checkbook. In early spring, Pauline and Jinny cleared out Ernest's apartment and looked for a larger suitable one for them to live in as a couple. In March, Pauline wrote to Hemingway in Italy, where he had gone to work on his fiction, "I find you have a lot of splendid sweaters" as well as an "Awful lot of papers … I may just develop a firm platform about papers. And then, of course, I may not. But you got a LOT of papers."[5] Jocular as she tried to be, Pauline was an orderly person, and the eventual result of her disapproval of Hemingway's writing process (and all those papers) was that he did his writing in space which was separate from their living quarters. Even though Pauline had majored in journalism at the University of Missouri, she was less empathetic about the reality of fiction writers' lives than Ernest had expected.

Pauline wanted Hemingway as a husband rather than as a writer. While it was comforting to have his picture in *Vanity Fair* and other glossy magazines, and to know that some part of the literary world was talking about *The Sun Also Rises*, Pauline—like her parents—was a conservative Midwesterner, steeped in the virtues of family living and adventuring (but adventuring as a family endeavor). She had watched Jinny try out more radical lifestyles (her sister purported to be lesbian), but Pauline knew she was inherently monogamous. Ernest was all she wanted.

Younger than Hadley by four years, Pauline was still more than four years older than Hemingway. Accordingly, she wanted to become pregnant as soon as it seemed feasible, but first, she was intent on making a home for her comfort-loving partner. She signed a lease for a large, two-bathroom apartment at 6, Rue Ferou, a much roomier place than anywhere Hemingway had lived before. (Hadley was then living at 98, August de Blanqui, in a more modest setting, and she and Bumby sailed for the States on April 16.) On May 10, 1927, at L'Eglise de St. Honore d'Eylan, Pauline and Ernest were married, with Jinny in attendance; afterward the MacLeishes gave a luncheon for friends. Even though the Murphys and MacLeishes had championed Hemingway's leaving Hadley for Pauline, thinking the latter a more suitable wife for a successful novelist, most of the Hemingways' expatriate friends were bewildered about his divorce and remarriage.

Lack of money was no longer a reason to curb expenses: Pauline knew she could count on Uncle Gus, as she had with the apartment lease, for whatever funds they needed. So for their extended honeymoon, the new Hemingways went to Grau-du-Roi near the mouth of the Rhone estuary, an isolated but stunningly beautiful location Hemingway was to make famous in his posthumously published novel, *The Garden of Eden*.

Except for some unpublished fragments (and chapters toward a novel which was never finished), Hemingway's writing during the period when he and Hadley had separated and he and Pauline had married was

5. The newly married Hemingways, with the chic Pauline as the second Mrs. Hemingway.

working toward what he planned as his next book of short stories. That collection from early on was titled *Men Without Women*. Given his focus on male friendships and male allegiances, to the exclusion of women's involvement, the book may have conveyed more than Hemingway intended about his state of mind during those eight or nine months.

The acceptance of several of these new stories by *Scribner's Magazine* might have ameliorated Hemingway's depression in this interval between wives. In early November, 1926, *Scribner's Magazine* accepted the poignantly understated "A Canary for One," paying him $150. The story described a seemingly happy American couple who were returning to Paris to set up separate residences. (It was one of his only surprise-ending stories.) In early December, *Scribner's* accepted the even stronger story, "In Another Country," where the older wounded Italian continued his physical therapy although his beautiful young wife had recently, suddenly, died and he was inconsolable.

Both of these stories were published in the April, 1927 issue of the magazine. More importantly for Hemingway's reception in the States, in the March issue *Scribner's* ran his "The Killers," one of the stories that was to become the epitome of classic Hemingway style. Stripped of most description, the stark minuet of Ole Andreson's fear dominates the prose poem. Observed by the young yet highly perceptive boy, both the scenes of the crass Chicago killers talking in the diner and the prizefighter huddled in bed, awaiting his execution, resonate with unexpected nuances of emotion. The intaglios of drama are etched more deeply in the reader's mind because of the aimless chatter of the landlady and the boy: the woman who runs the boarding house has no conception of the brutal world of boxers and hired killers.

The development of "The Killers" shows Hemingway coming to a finesse he had seldom previously reached. "The Killers" in draft was an Upper Michigan story. It began with the stark beauty of the iced over Little Traverse Bay; the boy observer was another Nick Adams. But in this writing attempt, Hemingway realized that the natural surroundings of the tranquil Midwest were working against the inevitable terror that should suffuse the story. So, as he had cut the opening of *The Sun Also Rises*, in "The Killers" Hemingway cut out the beginning description of the Michigan bay. He was already self-conscious about what he feared critics might see as his provincialism. As he had written several times in the "James Allen" segment, what he wrote was "rather delicate, and un-read. ... It was very believing, very delicate and very un-read."[6] Acceptance by a leading United States magazine marked the point of his work being read by intellectual and important readers.

Hovering over what little remains of Hemingway's correspondence to Pauline is the sense that writing these stories is the way he invests his lonely hours. In what remains of Pauline's letters, only rarely does she mention his writing (she does like "In Another Country").[7] It is rather in Hemingway's correspondence with his Scribner editor, Max Perkins, who also seemed to be the conduit for the stories Hemingway submitted to *Scribner's Magazine*, that Hemingway's absorption in his writing becomes clear.

At the start of the relationship with Perkins, Hemingway is somewhat distant, trying to show off his taste and his wide reading; as the correspondence progresses, however, Hemingway becomes the marketing expert. When Perkins pushes him for the completed short story collection, for instance, Hemingway reminds him,

> do you think it would be wise to have another book out so soon as Spring—rather than wait until early fall? In Our Time came out last November—Torrents in the early summer—The Sun in Oct. Don't you think we might give them a rest? Or isn't that how it's done?[8]

The young writer went on to describe how much of what he called "the bull fight book" was finished: he talked about the illustrations and photographs, some of which should be in color. Because *Death in the Afternoon* did not appear until 1932, the fact that he was working on it, and collecting materials toward its publication, as early as 1926 is somewhat surprising. Hemingway's primary aim, he noted then, was to complete a very strong collection of stories and then, another novel "when things get straightened out and my head gets tranquil."[9] Beyond this kind of oblique reference to his state of mind and his unsettled life, Hemingway's letters to Perkins seldom divulge the personal.

There was much conversation between the two about the reviews of *The Sun Also Rises*. In his letter of November 16, 1926, Hemingway denied even having read Michael Arlen's *The Green* Hat (the novel that popularized the flamboyant New Woman), and made some comic fodder out of misspelling the British novelist's name. Hemingway was surprised at many of the reviews of the novel—especially the criticism of the character of Brett Ashley—and at the critics' apparent inability to understand the post-war malaise that fed into the manic fiesta atmosphere. Perhaps the most unexpected reviews were those that criticized the lack of a happy ending for the romance between Brett and Jake Barnes. It would be many years before Hemingway would write any fiction that resembled a traditional romance with a happy ending.

That he was somewhat bewildered by the range of the reviews—and the points various critics thought worth emphasizing—seemed clear in his April 14, 1927 letter of thanks to novelist Hugh Walpole:

> I have not felt so damned cheerful about it—it not seeming such a bloody masterpiece but really a failure. ... You work very hard and then afterwards (after the thrill is gone) it seems so very awful and the thrill all comes back to have someone that you respect really like it.[10]

Besides the somewhat awkward comedy in Hemingway's letters to Perkins, there is his submission of the macabre "An Alpine Idyll" (which *Scribner's Magazine* did not buy), a story in which the dead wife's frozen jaw serves through the long winter to support her husband's lantern. Upset because the story did not sell, Hemingway may have been laboring under the belief that he wrote good satire. He had also sent Perkins the essay titled "My Own Life," which appeared that spring in *New Yorker* (but which *Scribner's* had again rejected). "My Own Life" is clearly aimed at extending his reputation as a satirist from *The Torrents of Spring*; it describes his breaking off friendships with Donald Ogden Stewart, Robert Benchley, "My Wife," and Gertrude Stein (both Stewart and Benchley were themselves humorists). Then he promised his readers that there would be a sequel in which he told about ending his relationships with Dos Passos, Coolidge, Lincoln, Mencken and Shakespeare.[11]

There is little comedy in *Men Without Women*, though the story collection which Scribner's published October 14, 1927 did include "An Alpine Idyll." Nearly all the stories were about men's business, men's lives, men's sorrows. As if continuing the themes of the *In Our Time* vignettes, which gave cryptic glimpses of both bullfighting and war, many of the *Men Without Women* stories extend those subjects into regular-length fictions: the tone of the book is much like that of the earlier *In Our Time* and so too is its structure.

Hopeless in the face of war, no matter which side the characters were on, men in battle (or planning battles) knew only the most elemental truths—soldiers were executed as if for sport; animals that belonged to one side were killed by the other; women giving birth during battle were not aided but only covered over. To contrast his treatments of war, his Spanish bullfighting stories were less ironic. The nobility of the bloody ritual of bullfighting accrued from the belief of the Spanish people, although it was often misunderstood by the observers who were tourists and watched the slaughter of the bulls with little realization of the ritual. In some respects, with these stories, Hemingway was still defiantly challenging women readers, such as his mother[12] and perhaps even Hadley, to make accurate sense of the elliptical narratives. In "The Undefeated," the story which opens *Men Without Women*, for instance, men's trust in each other is the pervasive theme. When Retana agrees to put the aging matador into the bullring, even if for only a nocturnal, he briefly shows his respect for the man's career. But when Manuel asks for money to hire one good picador, Retana refuses him that. Hiring Zurito, the best (and oldest) picador, shows Manual's dependence on another strong and talented man: Zurito agrees to pic for him, virtually for free. In the breathlessly detailed description of Manuel against the heavy, bloody bull, Hemingway evokes the reader's sympathy for the inevitable: Manuel will lose, despite all Zurito can do to help him. Yet he does not die, nor is his pigtail cut off, which would have signaled the end of his career as matador.

With typical irony, Hemingway rather chose to end the life of matador Manual Garcia Maera in a one-paragraph ending to "Banal Story" which comes near the end of the story collection. Ruined by the hostility of the bullfight critics, the aged matador finally drowns from pneumonia in his lungs. The honor given to him then by his profession is shown by the funeral processional, in which 147 matadors marched. His greatness known only to those of his skill level, Manuel's story appeared to be quite different than it was.

The stories of *Men Without Women*, like the texts of *In Our Time*, work through implication and suggestion. That the hired killers were going to kill the prize fighter in "The Killers," just as they endanger the punch-drunk fighter in "The Battler," even though he was protected by his black friend, provided a realistic base for many of these stories. Heightened by the possibility of brutality, the suspense Hemingway seemed to be avoiding (by making the characters' dialogue, rather than the action, carry the weight of the plot) was in the end visible.

Hemingway's best boxing story, "Fifty Grand," appears midway through *Men Without Women*. A story *Scribner's* had felt was too long, the text was readily accepted by *Atlantic Monthly*, and published in their July, 1927 issue. Stringently terse, the story of the aging welterweight is told almost entirely through dialogue among the fighter, his trainer, and his friend. The title points to the crookedness of the boxing culture, as Jack Brennan is talked into throwing the championship fight (and allowed to bet against himself at 2-to-1 odds). The quiet narrative takes place as Jack trains at Hogan's training farm; beset by insomnia, missing his wife, worried about his future in the ring, Jack is morose, lifeless, monosyllabic. Interchanges among the men are similarly disappointing: the fight crowd uses "broad," "Kike," and other offensive words. There is little nuance to their dialogue.

Once the story moves to the ring, however, Hemingway's physical description is superb. And the story is another ironic one, because though the critics had considered Jack's career over, he could have won this fight. But the set-up turned into a double cross: the fighter who was picked to win fouled Brennan and so he would have lost the match. Jack would not let the referee call the foul and stumbled through the remaining minutes. He was going to win the damned fight—until he realized he could foul his opponent in the same vicious way. So Jack lost the bout, but won his bet, after doing great harm to his body and effectively ending his career. The layers of chicanery the story reveals unfold in the seemingly endless boring dialogue.

Men Without Women closed with another great story, "Now I Lay Me." Combining the effects of war with the possibility of a romance plot, Hemingway again drew two men in conversation. It didn't matter that their nationalities were different, or their life experiences. One man's belief that marriage would salve all post-traumatic horrors is set ironically against the American's understanding that traditional romance provides no such benefits. The frame of the story emphasizes these two belief systems, yet—despite the differences—the men's friendship endures. One of the most striking scenes in the flashback segments of the story is the searingly bitter account of the placid way the young boy's mother has burned her husband's treasured Indian artifacts when the family moves from one house to another. Worse than her action is the aplomb with which she greets the devastated man as he comes home and sees the fire and the remnants of his treasures in the yard. His frantic scrambling to retrieve those remnants marks Nick's memory forever. As with many of Hemingway's Nick Adams stories, Nick is here the distraught observer to the heart-breaking scene. Given this episode of completely willful destruction, the boy has learned never to trust another person, even one who proclaims to love him.

True to the title of the collection, women here figure minimally in men's thinking, and if they impact their lives, that effect is negative. That Hemingway had managed to complete one earlier story ("Hills Like White Elephants") and so included it in *Men Without Women* breaks into the pervasive tone somewhat: in this story, it is the man's hardened response to his pregnant partner's pain that alienates the reader. Despite being a fiction about abortion, "Hills Like White Elephants" is no romance.

The collection's title confirms that as long as Hemingway stayed with American characters and narratives, his imagination privileged the esprit de corps among men: he remembered that the good part of his own past had been spent with male friends, young men who were as excited by a good catch, a quiet evening row on the lake, a new kind of beer, a glimpse of a girl's nubile body, as he was. But Hemingway was also a reader. He had learned that his own somewhat protected experiences and emotions were not the stuff of commercial fiction, no matter how technically adept he had become at conveying those experiences. The writing was not the entire meaning of the work: the form had to encompass the meaning, but there had to be a relevant experience to share, a strong character to either understand or like.

After he had written "Soldier's Home," for instance, the story he had placed at the center of *In Our Time*, he had reached the nadir of his representation of middle class America. As Harold Krebs insulted his mother, particularly in the matter of her religious belief, Hemingway showed the chasm that existed between men who had been to war and the people at home in the stultifying country that had so joyously, piously, sent them to Europe, to their possible deaths. No attempt at normalcy could reach the boy home from a war that was nothing like his culture had taught him it would be: his experiences were, instead, those of the bloody vignettes in the collection. He could make neither sense nor language from his experiential knowledge. And his family saw his behavior as only hostile rather than the result of learning how wrong American patriotic ideals were.

So Hemingway turned for the sources of his fiction to other cultures, partly out of being stymied by what he saw as the fallacy of people in the States who created their American dream based on material goods and shoddy principles. For a time, he refused to write again about the parent figures he had so thoroughly scrutinized in "The Doctor and the Doctor's Wife." When he did turn once again to the American dream, as he did in "Big Two-Hearted River," he cast the returning veteran in a wilderness where he could escape the misleading influences of that Oak Park home, and then he chose to change the name of the Michigan river to suggest the presence of Native American culture. When Hemingway's nameless veteran took his cans of beans on his lonely fishing trip, he was also taking leave of the society that had baptized him, taught him, and then led him into the frightening conflict that so few civilians in the States understood.

Escaping with his own life and most of his sanity, but with no thanks to any of the social forces he had earlier been told would protect him—family, religion, education, community—Hemingway's protagonist depends only on himself. He trusts nature, he reserves his limited strength, he lives hour to hour, day to day. Contrary to what Harold Krebs's mother told him in "Soldier's Home," the protagonist of "Big Two-Hearted River" does not need a girlfriend, a job, his father's car, or his mother's religious belief: none of these elements enters his mind. His mind, in fact, is tranquil, stripped of the memory of people and things—and certainly distant from his Illinois community. His mind in the later story is taking him back to a nearly primeval condition, one in which he eats, fishes, sleeps, makes coffee, washes in the river, and survives. It is the condition he learned to know—so unexpectedly and so abruptly—in wartime. It is the condition he hopes will continue and not be shattered by the explosions that nearly took his legs, and his life. The peace of the natural world, an unpeopled natural world, is all that Hemingway's protagonist in "Big Two-Hearted River" wants.

Just as in his first collection "Soldier's Home" is answered by "Big Two-Hearted River," with the latter story—much longer and more controlled in its emphasis—coming at the end of the book, so does Hemingway arrange *Men Without Women*. In that book, "The Undefeated" is in some ways answered by "Now I Lay Me." The resilient if unrealistic dreams of the aging Manual, the "undefeated" matador, balance with the battle-scared younger man's refusal to believe in any dream—and certainly not to attach any possibility of happiness to the dream of marriage. For him, all that remains in his present life is insomnia, sorrow, guilt, and frustration. Whether "Now I Lay Me" is set within the context of war, or within that of separation, divorce, and remarriage, the irony of its simple prayer-like title resonates through the fiction. Hemingway's fiction suggests that there is no simple story.

Lest the reader miss the animosity toward the role of women in the story, the protagonist as the story ends counts over the objects of his life that bring him pleasure. Chief among these are the trout streams: "I could remember all the streams and there was always something new about them, while the girls, after I had thought about them a few times, blurred and I could not call them into my mind and finally they all blurred and all became rather the same."[13]

Decades after Hemingway's death, at the height of feminist and gender criticism, Robert Scholes and Nancy Comley drew on passages such as this to support their contention that Hemingway had never recovered from the deep hurt of rejection—by his mother, by Agnes von Kurowsky, and perhaps by Hadley Richardson, who relinquished him to Pauline with scarcely a struggle. In the critics' assessment,

This experience of being jilted continued to haunt his imagination … demanding to be written yet one more time. If the first version was a farce ["A Very Short Story"], the next would be closer to tragedy; but it too would take its motivation from a man's desire to be loved by a kind, beautiful nurse-mother. In *A Farewell to Arms* young Ernest's role is played by an older and more sophisticated soldier, and the object of his affections, Catherine Barkley, is also provided with a past that serves to make her more interesting.[14]

Part of the motivation for Hemingway's continued writing may well have been his need to quiet his own torments.

8
A Farewell to Arms

As Ernest waited for the publication of *Men Without Women*, he worked hard toward what would be his next novel. Realizing as he wrote so well the story "Now I Lay Me" that the war and its aftermath was still his real subject, he was planning a novel about the innocence of the common soldier in war, a young man something like the two figures he had created for "Now I Lay Me." Regardless of nationality, regardless of their country's beliefs in the conflict, the single soldier carried the brunt of the responsibility for the outcome, and he also experienced the sorrow over that outcome. Creating such a character would be an effective way to get all the abstract platitudes out of any discussion about war. In fact, Hemingway made that comment explicitly in *A Farewell to Arms*.

Some of the reviews of *Men Without Women*, however, gave him pause. When Virginia Woolf wrote about the story collection and *The Sun Also Rises* together, he paid attention to her critique. He knew Woolf's writing, and he pretended to think that her war novel (*Jacob's Room*) like Willa Cather's Pulitzer-Prize-winning *One of Ours* were insults to the genre. He learned from both, however. Woolf was a force to be considered and when she undercut the usual positive reception of his spare writing, saying that it was "a little dry and sterile"[1] perhaps because there was too much dialogue in it, he worried that others would echo her views. (Gertrude Stein was thrilled, for example, that Leonard and Virginia Woolf's Hogarth Press was going to publish the lectures which she had given in London and Oxford the year before.) Hemingway knew he could not be disdainful of the prestigious Bloomsbury clique.

His knowledge base was completely different from Cather's and Woolf's. Whereas Woolf could pretend she understood the trauma that affected Septimus Smith in her novel *Mrs. Dalloway* (or her Jacob Flanders, a character Hemingway had drawn on in *The Sun Also Rises* for his own

Jacob Barnes, he of the "Flemish" name), Hemingway knew that he was still living through that kind of post-traumatic malaise. In 1927, he still attributed his mood swings and insomnia to his injuries in Italy; he seemed not to have considered the possibility of his having inherited his father's nervous instability.

Luxuriating on the Grau-du-Roi with Pauline gave him time for writing. Largely uninterrupted by friends, he and the new Mrs. Hemingway constructed their days and nights to privilege Ernest's writing. After the often exuberant praise for *The Sun Also Rises*, capped by Edmund Wilson's writing him that the book was "a knockout—perhaps the best piece of fiction that any American of the new crop has done," Ernest took his work even more seriously. He started his day writing; what remained afterward was Pauline's time. A deep cut on his foot shortened their stay, however, and once back in Paris, Hemingway was bedfast for ten days while the infected wound healed. Well enough to go to the bullfight fiesta in Pamplona, they once again enjoyed the time (somewhat relieved that Hadley was in the States, so they and their friends were not reminded of Hemingway's earlier trips there with her).

Although Hemingway missed Bumby, he was happy to know that Hadley was having time in the States to show off their son. Before spending the summer in St. Louis and New York, she had taken Bumby to Oak Park to meet his Hemingway grandparents and relatives. The pride of his grandfather's heart, Bumby made the rounds with Dr. Clarence in his Ford touring car—although the child could speak only French and Clarence only English.[2] Hadley and the boy then lived for some weeks near friends in Carmel, California. When Hadley returned to New York before going back to Paris with her strapping son, Paul Mowrer—who had been such a help to her throughout the breakup with Ernest—met her and told her that he and Winifred, his wife of many years, were setting up separate households: he wanted Hadley's friendship.

When Hadley wrote Ernest that she and their son were returning to Paris, she did not mention Mowrer. Instead she referred to Bumby as "the football hero type" they had "produced in one of Mummy's careless moments." She told Hemingway that she appreciated the income from *The Sun Also Rises*, and she was looking forward to resuming her life in Paris.

In their new apartment, Hemingway and Pauline were enjoying all the opportunities and comforts of Paris. In the fall, they went to Berlin for the six-day bicycle races and in winter, with Pauline delighted that she had become pregnant, they returned to Gstaad to ski, with Bumby along for most of the trip. Experiencing some nausea and discomfort in her pregnancy, Pauline was less the effervescent young wife than she was the woman insistent on order. Back in Paris after skiing, Hemingway went to bed with a bad chest cold, muttering about what a year this had been for strange health episodes (his stronger eye had been injured inadvertently when Bumby had stuck a fingernail into it). The strangest episode was yet to occur: in early March of 1928, at 2 a.m., Hemingway pulled on a cord that was attached to a broken skylight, and the glass crashed down on his forehead. The two-inch gash bled profusely, so Pauline called Archie MacLeish to take him to the emergency ward. Partly as evidence of the young writer's comparative fame, national papers carried the story. Upon reading the news of his young friend, Ezra Pound wrote to Hemingway from Italy, "Haow the hellsufferin tomcats did you git drunk enough to fall upwards thru the blithering skylight!!!!"[3]

When Dos Passos visited Paris later that spring, he raved about the beauties of an island off the southern coast of Florida. Key West as Dos described it was free from tourists. Some of the roads through the village were not yet paved and flowering shrubs and luxuriant trees were everywhere. People were friendly. Best of all, living was cheap. Feeling sorry for himself and concerned about his health, Hemingway had been thinking of returning to the States. Now this report on an intriguing place added to his resolve. They made the arrangements for their Paris apartment and moved within weeks.

Although Pauline did not like Key West's humid heat, she liked being in the States for the birth of their child. She liked the fact that the fiction Ernest had been trying to write once they were back in Paris was, in the quiet Florida mornings, going well. After they had spent several months in Key West, Pauline went on to Arkansas to prepare for the baby's birth toward the end of June. Hemingway stayed on in Key West, writing well, as he told Max Perkins, on what had become *A Farewell to Arms*.[4]

The novel seemed to be the fruition of all the months and years Hemingway had spent trying to capture war in his writing. The work was going so quickly, and needed so little revision, that he could scarcely believe his progress. No longer aiming to achieve effects entirely modernist, Hemingway was here allowing himself to use more conventional narrative techniques. The novel was retrospective: the deserting soldier, Frederic Henry, told his own mournful story to the reader. As if in competition with Ford Madox Ford's veteran narrator, Henry was challenging *The Good Soldier* as to who had lived through the saddest story.

Frederick Henry volunteered to fight in the Italian campaign of the First World War. Innocent of any real political or religious knowledge, he quickly came to see that the cynicism of Rinaldi and the other Italian officers was self-protective. He began a dalliance with one of the British nurses, but because Catherine's fiance had been killed in the war, she tried to replace him with Frederic. The war trauma in this case was hers. Caught up in a romance that surprised him, Henry realized some of the random brutality of war when he saw friendly officers being executed during the Caporetto retreat. To save himself, he deserted. The rest of the novel is the story of the hegira of escape he and Catherine take together, moving from place to place. A *Farewell to Arms* is a story about the victims of war—by implication, any war—and the victims as Hemingway draws them are both female and male.

He took the novel as far as he could in Key West, but in late May, he drove to Arkansas for the baby's birth, which would take place at Kansas City's Research Hospital. The birth, so difficult and frightening that it recurred in this novel and in Hemingway's later fiction, entailed many hours of labor and finally a Caesarian delivery. Born on June 28, 1928, Patrick weighed over nine pounds. Pauline was warned not to attempt another pregnancy for at least three years. Frightened as he had been during his wife's labor and delivery, Hemingway was restless to get to Wyoming for some fishing, and once Jinny Pfeiffer arrived from Paris to manage the baby and his care, Ernest picked up Bill Horne in Kansas City and started driving west. Pauline joined them soon after Patrick's baptism in Piggott on August 14.[5] She and Ernest stayed in Wyoming for several months, and when *A Farewell to Arms* was completely drafted, they toured over 1000 miles of the country before returning to Piggott. In the Arkansas heat, Pauline yearned for Paris. Ernest, however, had decided that he might want to live in Key West. He had written so well there that the milieu was obviously conducive to work. Pauline, accordingly, looked for houses to rent.

Then Ernest traveled to Oak Park to see his family. Shocked at his father's visible deterioration, he talked seriously with his sisters about the fact that Clarence was unable to sleep, sometimes incoherent, usually fearful. They told him about their father's alarming secrecy—that he locked drawers and burned papers, and told Grace nothing. He made Leicester, then only 13, his confidant. Ernest could make no headway into his father's secrecy either, but the situation in Oak Park added to his feeling that his father's distraught state was Grace's fault. One of the problems Clarence Hemingway faced was that his family was entirely dependent on his earnings because Grace, who had taken up painting, was no longer giving music lessons. Another was that the Florida real estate investments he had made with all their savings had depreciated so much that they were in danger of losing even their original money.[6]

Indecisive as Dr. Hemingway had become in this last stage of his mental illness, he could not sell off the land, but he worried continuously about those investments.

Concerned that his sister Sunny was wasting her life working in a dental office, Hemingway invited her to drive to Piggott with him in his Model A Ford. He convinced her that she could help with the baby, as well as typing the final version of *A Farewell to Arms*, once they had all moved to Key West. Unfortunately, Sunny recalled, "I really felt unwanted by Pauline from the moment I entered her life. ... I felt immediately that she had put me on the servant level."[7] None of it was simple: traveling by train and car from Arkansas to Key West, settling into a rental house, caring for a baby who was barely five months old, and working to get hundreds of pages of manuscript in perfect shape. Sunny found that the typewriter, as well as much of the baby's paraphernalia, had been located in her small room.

The Key West household was tense. After a time, Hemingway left Key West to go to New York to pick up the five-year-old Bumby and bring him back to Florida by train. During that interval, his sisters wired him that Clarence, in his bedroom before lunch, had killed himself with his father's old Smith & Wesson revolver. Leaving Bumby in the care of the Pullman porter, Ernest wired friends for money and turned west to Illinois. (Bumby did arrive safely in Key West.) After the funeral, Hemingway told his mother that he would help educate the two younger children and would send monthly checks for her support. Then he returned to Key West to continue work on *A Farewell to Arms*. On the outer leaf of the folded manuscript in the Kennedy archive, Hemingway wrote that his father had killed himself.[8] Given that years later he told George Plimpton that he had remained unsure how the novel would end— thinking that the child might live and the mother die, or the reverse; or that both child and mother would live, or that neither would live—it seems likely that the outcome of the novel was more dependent on his sorrow at the loss of his father than has been recognized.[9] *A Farewell to Arms* was always conceived as being a deeply sorrowful novel, but the war itself—and the young men's loss of innocence—would have made it that. The coup de grace to Hemingway's own emotional existence was his father's careful choice of a way to commit a sure suicide.

While Sunny was typing the finished manuscript, Max Perkins traveled to Florida to pick up the book—and do some fishing as well. When he had finished reading through *A Farewell to Arms*, the enthusiastic Perkins arranged that the novel would be serialized in *Scribner's Magazine*, for which privilege Ernest would receive the highest payment the company had ever made—$16,000. There was no question that Scribner's would promote this important war novel. Hemingway was even more convinced he had made the right decision in leaving Liveright for Scribner's.

Perkins was not the only visitor to Key West. Dos Passos arrived for some fishing, as did Mike Strater and Katy Smith; six months after they met at the Hemingways', Dos Passos and Katy married. With Ernest's usual pattern of finishing a long work and then needing release, he had invited many people to Key West; but then he decided what he really wanted to do was return to Paris, where their beautifully furnished apartment—and friends that might be envious of the *Scribner's Magazine* serialization of *A Farewell to Arms*—waited.

Financially afloat, despite what he felt were going to be continuing unreasonable obligations to his Oak Park family, Ernest with Pauline, Sunny, Bumby and Patrick sailed to France on the *S. S. York* in April, 1929. Again, Sunny found herself on the 16-day trip bunking with not only Bumby but also with Patrick.[10] The *York* put into Vigo, Spain, and docked at Le Havre; the Hemingway party then went by train to Paris. Sunny stayed several months, both helping and learning a great deal on her first trip abroad.[11]

Although Pauline never loved Paris as Hadley did, she was enjoying the return—though she insisted that they avoid the Fitzgeralds, who had rented a flat on the next street. As Hemingway had warned Perkins, they didn't want unruly middle-of-the-night visits by Scott and Zelda to cost them their lease.[12] Even before installments of the novel began appearing in *Scribner's*, Fitzgerald—hurt by being so often excluded from the Hemingways' social life—read the manuscript and conscientiously gave Ernest suggestions that amounted to a full critique. He found Catherine's dialogue and demeanor unbelievable (and long; if Hemingway were to cut anything, he said, he should cut her speeches and not Frederic's). He then advised Ernest to listen to women, as he had done in "Hills like White Elephants" and "Cat in the Rain." He thought the novel should stay with the war, instead of drifting off into what he called the old story of the unmarried and pregnant woman. He admired the retreat from Caporetto and called it "marvelous." Fitzgerald's commentary was long: he thought there were a number of extraneous scenes, which he pointed out. And he wondered whether all the prose about courage and honor was going to stay in the book. When he appended to his lengthy criticisms his note "A beautiful book it is!," the manuscripts show that Hemingway wrote his own marginal comment, "Kiss my ass."[13]

The eventual separation between Fitzgerald and Hemingway probably dated back to 1929, when Scott still assumed that his younger friend

6. A domestic scene: Pauline cutting Ernest's hair in the yard, probably in Bimini.

would take advantage of his own seasoned criticisms of this novel. Distanced from the literary world as Fitzgerald had become, unable to produce the novel he had promised Perkins several years earlier (the novel, *Tender Is the Night*, which Scribner's would not publish until 1934), Scott took pride in the fact that he had discovered Ernest, and that his commentary on *The Sun Also Rises* had improved that book. But Hemingway was never a writer to accept being patronized, and he had already polished his manuscript of *A Farewell to Arms* thoroughly before it began serialization in the magazine. Admittedly, the subtle continuing rhythms of *A Farewell to Arms* were unlike anything in his earlier novels: Hemingway was employing a kind of poetic "organ base" of tone—a technique Ezra Pound would appreciate—to unite the seemingly disparate sections of war and romance. With his own bleak philosophical vision, Hemingway knew that those fields of action were not so different after all. Just as he had introduced the crimes of marriage into the reader's consciousness of the damage of war in the story "Now I Lay Me," so in this novel he was showing the way both war and love trampled a young man's belief in honor, sacrifice, truth, and romance. What Frederic Henry realized at the end of *A Farewell to Arms* was that happiness was evanescent, dependent only on luck—and that most people in the modern world were not going to be lucky.

What Hemingway knew *A Farewell to Arms* deserved was the kind of praise Archie MacLeish wrote him. His poet friend began by saying he had worried that Hemingway would eventually be limited by his technique, "the restrained and tense understatement" that he had perfected in the stories. But *A Farewell to Arms* has erased MacLeish's doubts: "Now no one can wonder about that. The world of the book is a complete world, a world of emotion as well as of feeling. ... You became in one book the great novelist of our time."[14]

If critics were to connect Hemingway's stories about war with his great war novel, they would find the stream of affect, and influence, clearly delineated. They could watch Hemingway's own developing consciousness as he wrote about war, starting with the bitter bewilderment of the harsh *in our time* vignettes, from the young soldier's innocence to the wounding that demands a "separate peace"; to the numbing anger of a Harold Krebs who cannot figure out what his culture now wants of him; and the simple escape patterns of the unnamed protagonist out there on the Fox ("Big Two-Hearted") River.

Hemingway's own life, however, did not end with his wounding and his convalescence. His other deep wounding occurred with the end of his fantasy relationship with the beautiful American nurse in the Milan hospital—or, rather, with her letter in which she ended her love affair with "Kid" Hemingway. It was compounded with the end of his relationship with his mother, one that had been largely loving and supportive—until Grace Hall Hemingway wrote that his convalescence was over and he had overdrawn his emotional account with her. When Clarence asked him to leave the Michigan cottage so that he would not be a burden to his mother any longer, Hemingway felt orphaned. Writing the stories about mothers and fathers who were themselves seriously disappointing people was one way to diminish those figures, but it wasn't until "Now I Lay Me" that Hemingway found a means of bringing all those losses into one text, of seeing how they related: the personal emotional losses covered over, hidden inside, the scarifying losses of war.

When he conceived of *A Farewell to Arms*, drawing in some part on the repeated motif from Hadley's months of love letters—that she wanted his arms around her, and she wanted to put her arms around him—he saw the way to combine those separate genres, the love story and the war story. What would connect them would be the sounds of lament, achieved through a combination of word choice, pace, and simultaneity. Hemingway's word choice as he wrote about war paralleled his word choice as he created the love story. The deft prose poem which opened the novel established that rhythm, and at key points during the narrative he consciously returned the reader to it. Even in the raucous sections of the men at base, Rinaldi's laughing at Henry's innocence, there was no ribaldry in the language itself. For readers who picked up the novel, its somber tone was its main impression and that sobriety stayed with them. *A Farewell to Arms* was a piece of writing that resonated in the reader's mind. And it turned out to be another fiction about Hemingway's long-beloved Catherine, the idealized woman character who in herself embodied both the fulfillment and the myth of perfect love.

9
The Bullfight as Center

Proud of the way *A Farewell to Arms* had come through revisions, serialization, and the necessary changes in language before its publication, Hemingway returned to Pamplona in the summer of 1929. Whether the fiesta served to ground him in a belief system other, and older, than any he knew, or whether the gathering of his male friends comforted him no matter what else was happening in his life, or whether by imagining himself a matador (or at least an aficionado), Hemingway could keep his sometimes dejected imagination fresh, he saw the San Fermin festival as the center of his annual calendar.

The skirmishes Ernest had had with Scribner's over which of the soldiers' words should be censured had been resolved. The more objectionable issue, of Catherine's pregnancy out of wedlock, ironically may have led to even greater book sales.[1] When the second of the six installments of the serial in *Scribner's Magazine* was banned in Boston on June 20, 1929, *A Farewell to Arms* became notorious. Boston bookstores and newsstands were not allowed to distribute the magazine for the coming four issues. Consequently, when the hardback novel appeared in mid-September, people rushed to buy it.

Buoyed with what Ernest felt would be the financial success of the novel, the Hemingways headed for Spain once again—Hemingway driving Jinny Pfeiffer and Guy Hickok to Pamplona in the new Ford which Uncle Gus had provided. (In return, to the generous G. A. Pfeiffer, Hemingway dedicated *A Farewell to Arms* and also gave him the manuscript, as he had earlier given him drafts of several short stories.) Pauline came to Pamplona somewhat later after the baby Patrick had gone to France with his nurse; then in late August, they all went to Madrid for the bullfights there. It was September 20 before the party returned to Paris, and the reviews of *A Farewell to Arms* began.

Filled as he was with information about the bullfight, and keenly interested in writing a history—as he put it, an *accurate* history—of the sport and its great matadors, Hemingway thought that would be his next major book. During the fall, however, he took on some smaller projects. One of these was writing an introduction to *"Kiki's"* (Alice Prin's) *Memoir*—and translating several of its chapters from French to English. Considered one of the most beautiful American women in Paris, along with Zelda Fitzgerald and the actress Flossie Martin, Kiki, a small town woman from the Midwest, had become a model, a singer, and a starlet.[2] With the introduction copyrighted in Hemingway's name, he gave E. E. Cummings' *The Enormous Room* a plug, carped about the general state of literary criticism, and played the know-nothing reader. He also took a swipe at Virginia Woolf, complimenting Kiki's writing as the product of "a woman who, as far as I know, never had a Room of Her Own." He went on to admit that Kiki was never a "lady," but for a decade, she had come close to being a queen of the Parisian scene.[3] To show the power of Kiki's writing, Hemingway translated the twelfth chapter "Grandmere," a comic tableau of an old woman of chary innocence. Assembled from discrete sections, each one dedicated to a single character or experience, Kiki's slim book of memoirs may have given Hemingway the idea for his own Paris reminiscences, *A Moveable Feast*.

Aside from working on new short stories, Hemingway was excited to have a commission from *Fortune*, the prestigious United States business magazine, for a 2500-word article on bullfighting. For the brief essay, *Fortune* would pay $1000. Most of his financial worries disappeared that fall, however, because of the phenomenal sales of *A Farewell to Arms*. By mid-October, Scribner's had sold 33,000 copies; by November 12, sales stood at 45,000. Less than a year from the time of his father's suicide, Hemingway's writing was proving his talent—and his appeal to world readers. In the midst of his celebration, he mourned the irony of Clarence's never knowing of this success.

While Sunny had lived with Ernest and Pauline in both Key West and Paris, she could not ignore the fact that her brother's life was increasingly built around drinking. As a social rite, as a masculine pastime, and as a means of quelling the doubts and depression that recurred at unexpected times (what Hemingway called "black ass"), drinking had become integral to the writer's life. Sunny described his introducing her to imbibing (which was forbidden not only in her Oak Park home but everywhere in the States during Prohibition) by urging her to try sweet vermouth. In Europe she had learned to like apricot brandy and champagne.

But Ernest drank a range of alcohol: she had seen him even filter the poisonous absinthe which he warned her away from through a paper cone into water and then nurse the drink as he wrote.[4]

Drinking was the pastime in Paris; Hemingway and the friends that had caught up with him and Pauline during the celebratory autumn of *A Farewell to Arms*—Donald Ogden Stewart, the Fitzgeralds, Allen Tate and Caroline Gordon, Harry and Caresse Crosby, Dorothy Parker, John Dos Passos and his new wife, Katy Smith—were happily immersed in partying. Hemingway conducted new friends to the salons at Gertrude Stein and Alice B. Toklas's, and in October, he went to Berlin for the six-day bicycle races. Pauline did not accompany him on this trip, just as she had missed most of the Pamplona festival. Friends noticed Pauline's patterns of absence: she had left Paris on July 2, once the baby had left town with his care-giver, and did not return until September 20. Patrick's care-giver was often his Aunt Jinny; she had taken care of him immediately after his baptism when Pauline and Hemingway traveled out west. The Pfeiffer family noted that the two sisters, together, made up one good mother. Pauline and Jinny's reciprocal mothering of Patrick (and later, Gregory) seemed to satisfy them both. In the words of biographer Bernice Kert, "Jinny liked mothering … if the final responsibility lay elsewhere." Coupled with the fact that "Pauline's maternal instinct did not run as deep as Hadley's,"[5] this convenient alternation allowed Pauline the freedom to travel and hunt with her husband in both the States and abroad.

On January 10, 1930, Hemingway, Pauline, and Patrick—accompanied now by the French nursemaid Henriette—sailed to New York. It was also Kert's observation that the Hemingways lived and traveled best with an entourage—on the crossing, Sunny had traveled with them; now her spot was filled by Henriette. Pauline's need for assistance was costly, and she spent a great deal of her money and her family's money to meet that need.[6] From New York the Hemingway party made their way to Key West, this time renting a house on Pearl Street. Friends gathered even though Hemingway began serious work on his bullfighting study, writing the text as well as collecting pictures and newspapers from Spain. The year in the States was pleasant although Hemingway continued to suffer physical injuries. He cut open his right index finger working out with a punching bag; he injured his arms and legs, and received a deep cut to his chin, in a fall from a horse.[7] Bumby crossed the Atlantic under Jinny's care and Ernest went to New York to meet him and drive him to Piggott, where the family had traveled to spend the summer. Ernest, Bumby and Pauline then left Arkansas and headed for Wyoming to fish, hunt and ride, leaving Patrick with Pauline's family. Hemingway caught trout by the hundreds, hunted bear, and shot bull elk and mountain sheep.

In late October, Bumby headed back to Paris, and Pauline was in New York to see him off when word came that Ernest had been in a serious auto accident leaving Yellowstone National Park and had broken his upper right arm in several places. It was an oblique spiral fracture.[8] With John Dos Passos and some local friends, Hemingway had been hunting near Crandall and Timber Creeks and around Crazy Lakes; he had planned to have *Death in the Afternoon* finished before Christmas. But he was hospitalized for six or seven weeks in Billings, Montana—caught in the pain of both the surgery and his resulting immobility, and then various infections and recoveries. Pauline's letter to the Oak Park Hemingways gave information about the state of medical treatment in the early 1930s. Her information is even more sobering when one realizes that Hemingway's usual process of composition was to write in longhand and only later to type. Pauline wrote that Ernest was having

> a very tough time of it, with pain practically all the time, and sleep-less nights. It's been more than four weeks now since he changed his position. He sat up this morning for the first time. ... The numbness in the elbow and the paralysis of the wrist still persist.[9]

By the time he was released to go to Piggott for Christmas, he was nearly wild with frustration and pain—and he had grown a full beard.

Although Pauline did her best to travel with Hemingway when she could make arrangements for others to care for Patrick, she and he were often separate. Friends speculated that the Catholic method of birth control (or, rather, the prohibition of the use of birth control) made sexual compatibility difficult for Hemingway and his second wife—particularly once Pauline had been warned not to become pregnant for at least three years after Patrick's difficult birth.

Over Christmas, Ernest and Pauline decided to rent another house in Key West; Hemingway was confident the climate would help him heal. They moved back to Key West in January and then, a month later when Pauline found that she was pregnant, she began serious house hunting there. The somewhat derelict house at 907 Whitehead had all the space they would need, though it was in serious disrepair. With help from Uncle Gus, they bought the house on April 29, 1931, for $8000; the costly renovations were still ahead. Because the summer of 1930 had been spent in the western United States and not in Spain, in 1931,

Hemingway was hungry for a return to the bullfights. Perhaps it was just as well, not to have written for months on *Death in the Afternoon*, because now their travels could feed into that project. Pauline and he, accordingly, made plans to return to Spain.

Although Ernest objected to the continuous generosity of Pauline's family, she wanted adequate space for her growing family and her writer spouse. She had long ago discovered that her seemingly independent husband was really quite dependent: one of the bleakest of his memories was being asked to leave the Michigan cottage a few days after his twenty-first birthday—by both his parents. Whenever Hemingway told the story, embedding it deeper into his consciousness with each telling, his having to leave the family came soon after his rejection by the first woman he had loved, the beautiful American nurse. That more than a year separated the events was negligible: he remembered only that Ag had left him, and then his family had abandoned him. In his nostalgia, it was his beloved Hadley who had rescued him from his desolation. Hadley, however, as Pauline had witnessed, had done little to give him a secure home.

Pauline believed with Gaston Bachelard, that "the most powerful psychospatial image is the house in which we were raised, which is 'physically inscribed in us' and 'imbued with dream values which remain after the house is gone.'"[10] While she did not want to return to Oak Park (and she seldom did, knowing how objectionable her Catholicism was to the Hemingways), she wanted to give Ernest a space somewhat like his Oak Park homes—but with the added advantages of the exotic, the tropical, and the healthful. She planned to furnish the Whitehead house with the antiques from their Paris apartment. True to Pauline's projections, Hemingway loved the Key West house. He loved the writing station built out back, and he filled the house with friends, sons, and cats. He left it frequently but he always returned; emotionally, too, he left Pauline frequently, but he always appeared to return.

Pauline had judged Hemingway correctly. She did not need the benefit of the short stories he was currently writing to see where his true emotional center lay. That center, however, came across clearly in one of his best stories, "A Clean, Well-Lighted Place." The narrative recounts the story of the old man, eager to remain in the bright bar as long as he can so that he does not have to face returning home, alone, to the darkness of both the physical space and his own imagination. He has already tried to commit suicide, the waiters who observe him say—perhaps a nod to the desolation Hemingway felt when he had heard of Harry Crosby's suicide in December, a loss that recalled that of his father the year before.[11] The active story line belongs to the waiters, one a young man, the other older, but both empathetic enough to stay at the café so that the old man can continue to sit there. In mood and tone, this perfect story reflects some of the beauty of the limited choice the protagonist of "Big Two-Hearted River" has accepted. Both stories puncture the false report that life offers many choices, just as both stories derive much of their strength from the accurate detail of the surroundings. In each, the title signals the importance of that context. If being alone in the natural world is ideal for the young man, battered physically by war, then being alone but in the company of understanding people is the ideal state for the old man. As Hemingway aged, he understood the importance of human contact.

In "A Clean, Well-Lighted Place," however, the ending of the story, in which the perspective shifted to that of the older waiter, a person not yet despairing but apparently as lonely as the old man, gives the reader the parody of "The Lord's Prayer" as a coda to the waiter's realization that "it was all a nothing and a man was nothing too." In the chain of "nada's" that brings the story to its bleak close, Hemingway created an apt pronouncement for the state of the national mind, and for the international mind soon to occur. As his readers knew, he could not have written the story unless he identified with the angst of both the protagonist and the older waiter.

Another key story, this one placed at the close of his 1933 *Winner Take Nothing*, was an explicit description of the sorrow Hemingway felt at his father's suicide. As the narrator tells his son about his grandfather, in the story titled "Fathers and Sons," he lists the wonderful things about the grandfather and also his weaknesses, primarily his misuse of sexual information to frighten his child (the narrator) into behaving. Hemingway draws the grandson, obviously young and saddened by the loss of his grandparent, to parallel the early sensitive character of Nick Adams in stories like "Indian Camp" and "The Doctor and the Doctor's Wife." That Hemingway did not often return to the child as character in his later short fiction may suggest his sense of completion as he turned away from his own family experiences to find different, less nostalgic themes.

By closing the collection with "Fathers and Sons," Hemingway may also have intended to emphasize the undercurrent of sexual difference that the grandfather had forbidden his son to recognize. Hemingway had a good radar for the kinds of things readers would find objectionable. He may have hoped to help those readers understand such stories as "A Sea Change," "The Mother of a Queen," "God Rest You Merry,

Gentlemen," "The Light of the World," and "Homage to Switzerland," all of which dealt with more overtly sexual themes—sexual preferences, prostitution, lesbianism—than polite conversation in the early 1930s allowed.

Many of the stories Hemingway wrote then challenged prospective readers. His descriptions of sexual practices, as if he were testing what the commercial market would bear, seemed in line with his two recently-completed war stories, "A Way You'll Never Be" and "A Natural History of the Dead," which were among his most grim. The former narrative gave the fullest description to date of the trauma Nick Adams had experienced after his war wounding. "A Natural History of the Dead" was also slated to appear in the midst of *Death in the Afternoon*. It was clearly a story that jarred a reader's sometimes passive reactions to any bitter drawing of the inhuman conflict of war. For Hemingway, the bullfight was ritualized and in some ways comforting, whereas the practices and casualties of war were ultimately meaningless.

The story he chose to open *Winner Take Nothing* was representative of his stripped down mood and style. "After the Storm" is a thoroughly male story, from its narrative voice to the scavenger's mode that becomes the entire story. Angry that he has been gypped of looting the sunken three-mast schooner, the narrator supplies meticulous, arduous, and dangerous detail; in a manner almost Londonesque, the Hemingway style here echoes the devices he is to use in "A Natural History of the Dead." There is no subjective or reflective consciousness. The flat speaking voice is the grid for the reader's reaction; even though what the story is about is exotic and rare, the manner Hemingway chooses to convey his information is almost colorless. There are two episodes within the text that break into the rapid-fire delivery. The first is the appearance of a woman's naked body floating, hair spread behind her, on the other side of the porthole. The second is the attention to the boat's being trapped in quicksand as the observer reconstructs the tragedy; it is in this section that the reader is told that 450 passengers died in that mired vessel. Another story that could well have been included in the earlier *Men Without Women*, "After the Storm" continues the somber atmosphere of the earlier collection—but in *Winner Take Nothing*, that sobriety intensifies.

Neither of Hemingway's story collections, *Men Without Women* in 1927 or *Winner Take Nothing* in 1933, was received well, even though Scribner's promoted both. Compared with the excitement of his novels, books everyone could read and talk about and—in the case of *A Farewell to Arms*—could then see on stage or in film, the collections of separate stories had much less appeal. Their darkness was unrelieved, and most readers were not so interested in craft and effect as they were in characters and plot. As Clifton Fadiman cajoled the author in "A Letter to Mr. Hemingway,"

> Well, here are these short stories, as honest and as uncompromising as anything you've done. But that's not enough. Somehow, they are unsatisfactory. They contain strong echoes of earlier work. ... It is true enough that the face of life is grotesque, but surely you are fit for something more than merely showing us its grotesquerie.[12]

What surprised Scribner's most, however, was the pallid, if not hostile, reception of *Death in the Afternoon*, the bullfight book published in 1932. It also received negative reviews; in fact, during the 1930s, Hemingway's writing would collect a number of uncharitable comments. At odds with the cultural mood now dominating the States, Hemingway's interests as a writer—intent on finding the new and the exotic as subject matter—seemed to disregard the poverty and fear most Americans were living through as a result of the economic depression. Clarence Hemingway had not been the only upstanding citizen to take his own life in the late 1920s; by 1929, hundreds of disappointed investors and over-committed businessmen had committed suicide. Families everywhere were forced to re-trench; wives who had never been employed looked for work; book clubs and book stores disappeared, as did restaurants and beauty salons. People began to think of barter rather than money as a viable means of exchange.

World-wide financial chaos made even the least sophisticated people conscious that things were not good. For the celebrated author to so purposefully separate himself from the real life of the United States seemed perverse. Let the great expatriate stay out of the country, then, readers seemed to say. Let the great writer keep his precious, accurate information about bullfights, and about the Catholic beliefs which had never played significant roles in American culture. After all, look what had happened to Al Smith when he ran for the presidency in 1928. As the first Roman Catholic politician to enter that elite arena, Smith was whipped soundly by Herbert Hoover. The book buyers of America were as impoverished as the rest of its citizens; nobody had money to buy what seemed to be a bullfighting manual, fully illustrated with over a hundred photographs. Judging from the current financial circumstances of most Americans, nobody would be traveling to Spain—or any other part of Europe—in the foreseeable future.

After the huge success of Hemingway's *A Farewell to Arms*, complete with its dramatic version and its movie, Scribner's had been sure that the magic name *Ernest Hemingway* would retain its charisma. But sales figures for his books were disappointing, and Hemingway was worried. With Hadley receiving the U.S. income from *The Sun Also Rises*, his only steady royalty stream was from *A Farewell to Arms*. Eager for a way to make some ready cash Hemingway accepted Arnold Gingrich's offer to write for his new monthly men's magazine. *Esquire* could pay only $250 an essay, but the magazine would buy something from him for each issue. (Early issues of the magazine also included essays by F. Scott Fitzgerald, who was even hungrier for that monthly check than was Hemingway.)

For anyone who did read *Death in the Afternoon*, Hemingway's prose was likely to have been problematic. Was he writing in his own voice to lead the reader, or to confuse him? What was the purpose of the strange digressive scenes between the narrator and the old woman at the back of the lecture hall (scenes Hemingway had added only in galley proofs, sections never intended to be a part of the bullfighting exposition at all)? Was he writing satire again, and if so, why? What reason did he have for casting the ignorant old lady as an adversary in this book, unless it was to answer Gertrude Stein's comments about him (as a "Rotarian" rather than a truly innovative writer, as someone who had disappointed both her and Sherwood Anderson) made in her *The Autobiography of Alice B. Toklas* and worse, excerpted and published in *The Atlantic Monthly*.[13]

His inclusion of the short story "A Natural History of the Dead" at the center of *Death in the Afternoon* was another inexplicable choice. Brutally grim, phrased with what Hemingway intended (given the title) to be realistic and non-sentimental detail about those dead men of his reference, the story is another answer to the squeamish reader who may in principle object to the bullfights: rather than dead bulls, perhaps dead men are more aesthetically acceptable? In any case, Ernest Hemingway, writer, knows about both subjects and will here give the reader a fair assessment of each "sport."

Most of the book, as might be expected, is a compendium of accounts of the splendor—even glory—of Hemingway's favorite matadors, conveyed with a wistful elegance that is often undermined by the more acerbic sections. *Death in the Afternoon* might be considered the first of Hemingway's desperation books. In it, he tried to do a great many things. It was a history of the sport and its beliefs, as well as a storehouse of maxims about writing. It was a kind of answer to people Hemingway believed were his critics. It was a new kind of prose that showed its innovation when compared with the formal story that centered it.

Innovation in form and style had always saved Hemingway from being just another writer; he could not believe that same innovation would not save him in 1932.

Death in the Afternoon did not save him at all, in fact. It rather seemed to start him on a downward spiral that continued through the decade. That book was followed by *Green Hills of Africa*, about his safari with Pauline; by *To Have and Have Not*, the novel he constructed from short stories; and by *Across the River and Into the Trees*, the novel of the World War II veteran—ill but still eagerly in love—returning to Venice at the end of his life. Taken collectively, these books did not satisfy Hemingway the writer. They had not been composed as *A Farewell to Arms* had been, written through cogently and directly—and always surprisingly—from the author's deepest understanding of what the characters knew from their experience and what the historical circumstances of their lives made plausible as they chose their courses of action. But Hemingway was hounded by the belief that he was a visible commercial author; therefore, he needed to keep Scribner's house supplied with full-length books, or else he could no longer claim to be an active writer. Without a steady stream of publications, he would appear to be a rummy like Scott, or a political hack like Dos Passos, or a failure like Harry Crosby or Hart Crane. Caught in his own successful image, Hemingway continued to write with bravado and complacency—but at heart he knew he was not writing as well as he previously had.

When he did write well, it was in the short stories about his father's suicide or the war veteran's mental state—or, somewhat later, the account of his own life as a writer ("The Snows of Kilimanjaro"). That was the emotional wellspring for Hemingway in the 1930s. Calmed by the steadiness of his life in Key West with Pauline and the boys, working off his inevitable frustrations with the fishing and the good companionship with the men who came to fish with him, Hemingway, however, found the solace of writing well only occasionally. As his letters to Max Perkins showed, during these years he talked about the subject matter of his work, but he seldom expressed real satisfaction with either the process or its result.

10
Hemingway as the Man in Charge

It may have been the combination of the brutal physical pain that Hemingway had been enduring and what he saw as the brutal financial pain he had, martyrlike, inflicted on himself after the death of his father—whatever the reasons, Hemingway, in 1931 and 1932, was an irascible man, even in his correspondence with the long-beloved Max Perkins. The weight of having to provide for his own pleasure, his own family, and that of Grace Hall Hemingway and the two youngest children, Carol and Leicester, kept Hemingway off-balance.

During 1929, he had sent Grace $100 each month and had paid her property taxes (she had taken in boarders, was once again teaching—this time some art pupils, and was trying to run her household economically).[1] But with the visible success of *A Farewell to Arms* during the winter of 1929–30, Hemingway followed through on the suggestions of people who knew about establishing stable financial streams to set up a trust for Grace's use. He contributed $30,000 (nearly all the royalties from *A Farewell to Arms*); Pauline and her uncle Gus Pfeiffer supplied another $20,000. The Grace Hemingway Trust, then, was funded at $50,000, a more generous sum than it might seem, considering the economic realities of 1930.[2]

According to Sunny Hemingway's version of the Oak Park finances, Grace had later asked her to contribute money to the household budget. Sunny worked as a doctor's assistant and had helped with grocery shopping, errands, and keeping the car running, but her mother's need for money in the fall of 1931 surprised her. When she wrote Hemingway about Grace's request, he advised her to comply, saying that the way the trust was set up, there would eventually be money for everyone. Supposedly, Grace was running short because the trust officer at the bank had invested in European bonds, which had been hurt by the United States market.[3]

Hemingway also wrote to Sunny that he had paid out more than 88 percent of what he made in 1930 and that the stage version of *A Farewell to Arms* had not made any money. He was counting on the income from the film rights, but had washed his hands of the movie itself. He joked with Sunny that the Hollywood types would probably "have Catherine give birth to the American flag and rename the movie 'The Star Spangled Banner.' "[4]

Despite his confident tone to Sunny, however, it became clear that once he had established the trust, Hemingway seemed resentful. Working hard at his writing, impatient at the needs of his young family, still struggling to feel healthy, Hemingway could see how much his giving Hadley the United States income from *The Sun Also Rises* was costing him. Besides those royalties, he was responsible for a monthly payment for Bumby's care—and for the child himself several months of each year (or sometimes longer). Hemingway seemed restless to take control of Bumby's life in this period: Hadley wrote to him in January, 1930, that she did not want Bumby to become a Catholic (evidently, this was Hemingway's desire). She wanted him to remain as he was baptized, an Episcopalian. When he turned eighteen, she said, he could make up his mind for himself.[5]

To go from being Hadley's husband, cared for and funded by her and her income, to being Pauline's spouse, a man expected to assume traditional male roles within the family, was a definite lifestyle change. And although it seemed to Hemingway—and to his friends—that his writing was earning him a great deal of money, he had little to show for that earning power. Unfortunately, when Paramount bought *A Farewell to Arms* as a film, the fee was $80,000; after agent fees, taxes, and publisher's costs, however, Hemingway was left with only $24,000.[6]

A great deal of his bitterness came through in his correspondence with Max Perkins. As he said at the close of one letter, apologizing for his rudeness, "please remember that when I am loud mouthed, bitter, rude, son of a bitching and mistrustful I am really very reasonable and have great confidence and absolute trust in you."[7] Later, he argued that *Death in the Afternoon* when published should have more than the proposed dozen illustrations—that he has 100 prepared and ready, but he does not want the book priced out of readers' reach. In that letter, he writes to Perkins about all the "real troubles" that Perkins, Fitzgerald, and he have had but, Hemingway boasted, "I get my work done in spite of all troubles. ... The first and final thing you have to do in this world is last in it and not be smashed by it and your work the same way."[8] In February, 1933, Hemingway referred again to their many troubles, telling Perkins that his own are "bad" now and asking for an advance of $6000 on the new story collection, *Winner Take Nothing* (or an early royalty payment on *Death in the Afternoon*).[9]

Until the publication of *Death in the Afternoon*, Hemingway's track record as an author who made substantial profits from every book was unbroken. The successes of *In Our Time* in 1925, *The Torrents of Spring* and *The Sun Also Rises* in 1926, *Men Without Women* in 1927, and *A Farewell to Arms* in 1929 had been unexpected for a writer so new to the commercial publishing scene. Accordingly, even before many figures were in from *A Farewell to Arms*, Scribner's had re-negotiated his earlier standard contract, so that he received 20 percent after 25,000 copies had been sold. Perkins noted, "I think I told you once that if you asked for 20% from the very first copy, we would give it ... because we think the value of publishing you is a great one in itself."[10]

Pauline and he were spending some of their money on acquiring art. Tutored well by Gertrude Stein and already owning works by Masson, Miro, and others, Hemingway in November, 1929, bought a Paul Klee (*Construction of a Monument*). Doing business with Alfred Flechtheim at his Galerie Simon was a pleasure for Ernest, since Flechtheim had earlier founded and run the German little magazine *Der Querschnitt* where Hemingway's early work had appeared. The Klee cost him 30,000 francs.[11] In September of 1931, he and Pauline bought two paintings by Juan Gris—*The Guitar Player* and *The Torero*, the latter to be used in *Death in the Afternoon*. Along the way they had acquired Georges Braque's *Still-life with Wine Jug* and sketches by Goya—the latter probably for use in the bullfighting book.[12] Again, true to Stein's instruction to spend money on paintings and not on clothing, Hemingway had by the early 1930s begun his practice of dressing either very informally—as if he were a laborer—or wearing safari-type clothing (the long-awaited African safari, promised in 1930 by Uncle Gus, would occur in 1933).[13] One of his annoyances with Pauline's spending (even though much of "their" money was "her" money) was her love of fashionable outfits.

The real frustration in Hemingway's life, however, early in the 1930s, was probably not financial. As he had with Duff Twysden (the apparent model for Lady Brett Ashley in *The Sun Also Rises*) in 1925 and with Pauline Pfeiffer in 1926, Hemingway was playing the dangerous game of extramarital flirtation. This time, five years after his first divorce, he was playing it even more seriously.

Hemingway had met the beautiful, young Jane Mason in September of 1931 on the *Ile de France* as he and the seven-months pregnant Pauline, accompanied by Donald Ogden Stewart and his pregnant wife, were returning to the States so that Pauline could have the baby in Kansas City. Both Stewart and Hemingway were smitten with the blonde, twenty-two year old wife of the wealthy Pan American airlines executive, Grant Mason; the Masons made their home at the palatial estate they had helped to design, in Jaimanitas, just outside Havana. Perhaps best of all Jane Mason's qualities was the fact that she was an avid sportswoman— and she loved to fish the ocean waters.[14]

Hemingway was consistently attracted to beautiful and charming women, but the single element in his psychology that made a woman genuinely attractive was her physical readiness to be his companion: Hadley, for example, had become a willing hiker, skier, and dancer. Pauline was less willing to put herself out for Hemingway's wishes but she loved the adventure of traveling with him, and she became a good marksman (deep sea fishing from either their Key West location or Havana, however, was not something she enjoyed). To find all the physical skills he so admired in Jane Mason was thrilling for Hemingway; and to find those in the person of Jane at the time of Pauline's second difficult birth and convalescence, when the Hemingways both were faced with the care of yet another baby in a household that already seemed disorderly, made her impossible to resist.

Hemingway's younger brother Leicester recalled that Jane Mason seemed to be "another kid brother" to Ernest whenever there was a summer marlin fishing expedition (at first on the rented *Anita* and eventually on Hemingway's new boat *Pilar*). Lasting at least two weeks, each fishing jaunt was taken on a boat with a full crew, with everyone on board cooking. In the child Patrick's later memory, Jane was "the Jean Harlow, the Grace Kelly of her day—perfect features, hair sleek and blonde, married to an insignificant husband, which was characteristic of other women my father became fond of. When he asked Marlene Dietrich what her husband was good at, she replied, 'very good at getting theater tickets.'"[15]

Hemingway's tendency to philander may have been encouraged by events with both Hadley and Pauline during 1931 and 1932. In May of 1931, Hadley wrote to him that she wanted his "advice and opinion as a friend on Paul's and my situation, particularly apropos of Bumby. We have been up hill and down dale since last I saw you."[16] On June 15 she thanked him for his visit.[17] (It was this season that Hemingway took Bumby rather than Pauline with him to Pamplona for the bullfights; father and son were gone from July 5 through the 15th.)[18] Hadley's seriousness in her relationship with Paul Mowrer, a journalist Hemingway admired, meant that Hemingway had lost her for the rest of his life—and the nostalgic mourning for this idealized first wife that appears in *A Moveable Feast, Islands in the Stream,* and other later writing began.

In the case of Pauline, pregnant through much of 1931, the birth of another nine-pound son, Gregory, on November 12 meant both another Caesarean delivery and the warning that she could never become pregnant again. While she was pregnant, Pauline was sexually available; otherwise, she and Hemingway practiced coitus interruptus.[19]

After weeks of her convalescence, moving from the Kansas City hospital back to Piggott, Arkansas, and then to Key West (to the home that was still in the process of being renovated), Pauline found suitable nursemaids and in early spring, went to Cuba with Hemingway. From their hotel, she phoned Jane Mason at her estate, and the threesome renewed their friendship from the autumn crossing. For the next week, the three fished for marlin. (Most of the letters Jane wrote to the Hemingways were directed to Pauline, whom she thought witty, funny, and tastefully devoted to her husband.) When Pauline returned to Key West, Hemingway and Jane fished on. Bernice Kert describes a note jotted in the ship's log during that time period—"Ernest loves Jane"— not in Hemingway's writing.[20] Pauline, however, analyzed the situation and was not alarmed.

On May 10, 1932, Pauline and Ernest were separated for their fifth anniversary—Pauline in Key West and Hemingway in Cuba. Jane was enroute to New York for a surgery, but wired Pauline that two flamingoes were awaiting her in Cuba as the Masons' anniversary present. On June 6, Pauline went to Cuba to retrieve the birds and wait for Jane's return; on June 11, Jane was back in Cuba. When Pauline returned to Key West with the flamingoes, Hemingway stayed on another few weeks to fish with Jane. Pauline still seemed unworried, but she changed her hairstyle back to the becoming bangs she had worn when they first met. (It is Pauline's correspondence that describes her hair color and style, with frequent comparisons to the color and style of Hemingway's hair.)[21]

Pauline prided herself on knowing her husband. She knew when not to push him to be attentive (or even to be present); she knew she was the wife who was in control of the household and the family. But she also knew Hemingway was feeling sorry for himself—about their sexual situation, about his recent lack of income from his writing. Ernest had told Waldo Pierce that he was responsible for his wife and three sons, an ex-wife, a mother, two sisters, a brother, and three servants.[22] With his newfound passion for fishing, he envied the Masons their 46-foot Matthews cruiser, the *Pelican II.* (He admired any fishing boat that could travel the Cuban waters safely.) He was feeling the pressure of maintaining the Key West house and the care of his three sons. (Pauline had at least one nanny working at all times; occasionally, that woman would take one or the other of the little boys back to her home on the mainland to separate them from each other. Both Patrick and Gregory, especially the younger, grew up fearing that Pauline might permanently leave them). The staff and the grounds keepers, as well as the continuing repairs on 907 Whitehead, cost what seemed to Hemingway to be large sums. And there were the clothes—for the boys and for Pauline—and her gifts for her family and for him. There was the Paris apartment; there were the trips abroad and the hotels. And there was the fishing.

Hemingway had found marlin fishing, without benefit of either Pauline or Jane, in the early spring of 1932. Soon after Gregory's birth and their return to Key West, he had resumed his trips to the Dry Tortugas; but then in April, Joe Russell (who owned Sloppy Joe's Bar) offered Hemingway a trip to Cuban waters on the *Anita*, his 32-foot cabin cruiser. Often used to run rum, Russell's *Anita* this time was only a fishing boat. He charged Hemingway just $10 a day and for another $2, Hemingway stayed at the Ambos Mundos Hotel in Havana.[23]

The planned two weeks stretched into more than two months. Hemingway found that he could read proof for *Death in the Afternoon* in his hotel room, so he did not fall behind with work. But the more important passion became marlin fishing with rod and reel. With Carlos Gutierrez as his guide, Hemingway became an expert marlin fisherman; he loved the fast, strong fish with the tenacious mouths. As became clear from the superb new story he finished, "A Way You'll Never Be," about Nick Adams' hallucinatory nightmares after his wounding (and his disorientation, being unable to read or write, fearful that he was indeed mad—a story referencing the fears of Jane Mason), he was equally passionate about his growing friendship with the loving, talented, but fragile young woman.

Even as Hemingway thought of himself as the rough sportsman, living and fishing cheaply in the Cuban spring, he continued to worry about money. It had seldom surfaced during their affair and then marriage, Pauline's aim to live an upper middle class life. It was not one of the urgent considerations during Hemingway's divorce and remarriage. But for the older daughter of the Pfeiffer family, living in any other way was unsuitable—even during the depression. Yet as the years passed, in Ernest's imagination, he, the young writer, had been much put upon in his married life, and he had succeeded as a writer only through diligence and financial deprivation. He wrote in a 1935 autobiographical profile that he had made his own way since he was 16; and since 1926, had supported himself and his family from his writing. In this sketch, Hemingway conveniently forgot the income from Hadley's trust funds, his friends' lending him money and apartments, and the wealth the Pfeiffers had contributed, and were continuing to contribute, to their present household. In short, Hemingway was pretending to have a financial success he had never, at any time, experienced. He clearly wanted the world to see that he was what his burgeoning celebrity status suggested that he was—self-made, rugged, resourceful, common, talented, able, hard working, handsome, intelligent (though not college educated, since he had supported himself from the age of 16), virile (with at least two wives to his credit, not to mention three *sons*—rather than three *children*, which would have been another way of phrasing that fact), and above all, an objective journalist, who called things as he saw them. Even if those things were sometimes fantasy.

Despite Hemingway's fantasies, he was driven to return to the home Pauline had created for him in Key West. As Patrick recalled decades after his father's death, Key West "was the one place in his own country where he lived and was happy."[24] And in Leicester's *My Brother, Ernest Hemingway*, he too had tried to convey the tranquility of the remote island:

> The Key West in which Ernest and Pauline were doing their pioneering had not had any resident writers or artists since John James Audubon stopped by half a century earlier. When Audubon was there, the quiet, gray town had been a booming seaport, full of affluent wreckers and salvage merchants, their families and retainers. But in the late 1920s, it was an almost-forgotten place. ... a wonderfully quiet place to work in, an inexpensive place to live in, and an easy place to relax and raise children.[25]

In a Lacanian sense, as critic Ben Stoltzfus reminded Hemingway readers a decade ago, the position of power (in this case, Hemingway's taking financial control) is one way of usurping the dominance of the father; it also locates the male child as a competitor for the mother's affection. Just as Hemingway had become the source of Grace Hall Hemingway's income, so he had become the head of household for his second wife and his three sons.[26]

His great currency lay not in the dollars he could earn but in his writing itself: in Stoltzfus's assessment, "The act of writing is a triumph over symbolic impotence."[27] That Hemingway wrote both fiction and memoir to prove his value—and his superiority—was a continuous battle against his feelings of inadequacy and loss (the loss of his mother's love). Several decades later, Hemingway would finally write his way to the power he had coveted his whole life as he created David Bourne, the consummate artist, whose writing enabled him to find—and secure—the mysteriously dark-skinned Marita, the (m)other character of *The Garden of Eden* who brought his writing powers to full fruition.[28]

11
Esquire and Africa

It was getting to Hemingway, the reviewers' chary and catty commentary, even before excerpts from Stein's *The Autobiography of Alice B. Toklas* appeared in the *Atlantic Monthly*. Writing candidly, as he claimed he always did, to Max Perkins (who by now had become not only his editor at Scribner's but his fishing friend in Key West), Hemingway ridiculed the kind of personal attacks his critics (including Stein) had been making. In July 26, 1933, he wrote about the Stein excerpt and then segued into his own third-person defense:

> Poor old Hem the fragile one. 99 days in the sun on the gulf stream. 54 swordfish. Seven in one day. A 468 pounder in 65 minutes, alone, no help except them holding me around the waist and pouring buckets of water on my head. Two hours and twenty minutes of straight hell with another. A 343 pounder that jumped 44 times, hooked in the bill. I killed him in an hour and forty five minutes. Poor fragile old Hem posing as a fisherman again. Weigh 187 lbs. Down from 211—//I'm going to write damned good memoirs when I write them because I'm jealous of no one, have a rat trap memory and the documents.[1]

Tired as he had become of the literary world, Hemingway liked thinking of the columns he would write for *Esquire*. His steady production of books and stories, each one requiring a complete investment of his abilities and his concentration, had worn him down. Although he spent more hours of his days on non-writing activities than on writing, his focus from day to day remained on his work. At first, his *Esquire* essays were about deep-sea fishing and other Key West, Cuban, or Bimini events. Then he turned to writing about writing and other more retrospective themes; at times he published fiction. Later, his *Esquire* pieces became much more socio-political.[2]

With the negative reception of *Death in the Afternoon*, however, Hemingway's energy seemed to wane. He felt that he had explored most of the themes he then thought were interesting in his short stories; he didn't have the next novel in mind. Pauline, always an astute observer, could see that her husband was drifting. Without his work to tether him to their life, he was more aimless than she had ever known him to be. While her accompanying him to the west for their summer of hunting, fishing, and riding cheered him, the lackluster reception of *Death in the Afternoon* had erased that equilibrium. She had decided that Uncle Gus's offer to send Hemingway on safari to Africa might be the only thing that would save her husband's psyche.

When early spring of 1933 brought the excitement of marlin fishing to the fore again, she knew that planning the safari was the answer. Ernest's friendship with Jane Mason had continued to not only exist but to expand: they were writing to each other about their writing, now, and Hemingway had given her the manuscript for at least one story, "A Way You'll Never Be." The focus for their relationship still seemed to be marlin fishing, so Pauline tried to accompany Ernest as often as she could. At heart, she disliked the whole business of fishing: the deep waters troubled her, the baits and rods were unpleasant, and she was not naturally athletic. When Bumby came for visits, he liked the adventure; sometimes Pauline stayed in Key West with the smaller boys and let Ernest's oldest son do the surveillance she was attempting for herself. In the spring of 1933, she took Bumby and Patrick to Cuba for the fishing and then returned to Key West; she also reassured Ernest in a letter that she had received an unexpected interest check and so would pay the house bills, and keep those accounts separate.[3]

By this time, the affair between Jane Mason and Ernest may have been sexual. There is a story of Jane's entering Hemingway's Havana hotel room by crawling through the transom;[4] there is the acknowledged privilege of the extremely wealthy woman who can do much as she likes. But life often takes unexpected turns. The same May in 1933 that Bumby arrived, when Jane was driving him, Patrick, and her adopted son Tony back from Havana to Jaimanitas, she had an accident and rolled her large Packard: the four barely escaped injury. According to Alane Salierno Mason, Jane's car (a Chevrolet) was forced off the road by a bus and "tumbled 40 feet into a ravine, turning over 3 times."[5] Several days later, Jane "fell or jumped"[6] from the second-story balcony of her home and broke her back. Alarmed at her erratic behavior, her husband

7. Hemingway poses proudly with his sons Patrick, Bumby, and Gregory—and a wall of the large fish—marlin—he loved to catch.

finally insisted she get help. Accompanied by a nurse, she was sent by ship, in a stateroom with barred windows, to a New York facility where she underwent psychotherapy for months with Dr. Lawrence Kubie, a well-known Freudian therapist. She had to wear a back brace for more than a year, and she was instructed to curtail her drinking.[7]

Never attracted to unstable women—as his unsympathetic attitude toward Zelda Fitzgerald indicated—Hemingway seemed to have made little change in his fishing life, except that he was content to go alone or with male friends. Only the story "A Way You'll Never Be," which appeared later that year in *Winner Take Nothing*, bears any suggestion of his involvement with Jane Mason. Later, there would be "The Short Happy Life of Francis Macomber," but before that time, Ernest's life continued to change.

There was some fallout from the Mason relationship back in Key West, however. Two events occurred that seemed intended to keep Ernest in his marriage. One was that Ernest and Pauline decided to buy a fishing boat. Borrowing a large advance from Arnold Gingrich's *Esquire* funds,

Hemingway was able to pay over $3000 toward his order for the 38-foot $7500 *Pilar* when they were next in New York, which, as it turned out, was upon their return from safari. The other was that safari: Uncle Gus Pfeiffer had come up with $25,000 to fund an East African adventure for Ernest: given the recent events of Hemingway's life, Pauline decided to go along. The safari, then, was for Pauline and Ernest, not Ernest and another male friend.[8] With the help of Jinny and the Pfeiffer parents, the Key West household staff, extra nannies, and this largesse, Pauline and Ernest left their children and their home for more than seven months between late summer of 1933 and the spring of 1934.

As he did with all his projects, Hemingway had already made a study of all elements of the safari—Africa (climate, terrain, people, culture), big game hunting, trophy preservation, supplies, clothing, health precautions, hunting guides. He was absorbing everything he could, partly because he knew he would write about the experience, partly to rid his mind of any guilt he might have about Jane Mason's breakdown.

Leaving little Gregory in Key West with one of the nannies, the family sailed from Havana in early August. Pauline, Jinny, and Ernest then left Bumby and Patrick in Bordeaux with their former French nanny in order to spend weeks in both Madrid and Paris. Hadley visited Pauline during her Paris stay, telling her that she and Paul Mowrer had married on July 3. As Hemingway wrote his mother-in-law on October 16, 1933, saying nothing about Hadley's marriage, everyone is excited about the safari, and Pauline is "in fine spirits and very good health and looking splendid."[9]

Their Key West friend Charlie Thompson arrived in November to accompany Ernest and Pauline on the trip to East Africa and on the safari proper. The three sailed from Marseilles on the *General Metzinger*, November 22, 1933, arriving in Mombasa after both Pauline and Charles survived food poisoning en route. After a few days rest, they took the train 300 miles west to Nairobi.

As organized by Tanganyika Guides, Inc., their party was assigned to the care of British white hunter Philip Percival. The experienced hunter and his wife operated a large farm at Potha Hill 20 miles south of Nairobi. While the final safari arrangements were being made, Pauline, Charlie, and Ernest hunted impala and guinea fowl at the farm. Also in residence there was Jane Mason's friend, the young Alfred Vanderbilt, who wanted to become a writer. In fact, it was probably Jane's new friendship with Richard Cooper, a British army major whom she had met on the *S. S. Europe* crossing from New York to London that got Percival to take on the Hemingway party, since his fees were usually higher than he charged them. Cooper owned a coffee plantation in Tanganyika, and was friends with the best-known and best guides, Percival and Bror von Blixen.[10]

The safari party left the farm on December 20; there were two lorries for gear, and the open-sided overland vehicle for the hunters. As the caravan traveled from dusty camp to dustier camp, they could intermittently see Kilimanjaro, the majestic mountain above them. In Arusha they had hotel rooms; otherwise it was the ritual of the camp. Porters prepared warm baths in a canvas tub; then the party drank good whiskey by the fire and Percival and Hemingway exchanged stories.

On Christmas day, they came to the immense game preserve, the Serengeti plain, complete with hundreds of birds, zebras, and gazelles. Percival had decided that the first big kill would be Pauline's shooting a lion: he and the hunters planned for this and finally maneuvered what he thought was exactly the right lion into Pauline's area. She shot and missed, but Ernest then killed the animal. M'Cola, Pauline's loyal bearer, pretended Pauline had indeed shot the lion and a large celebration was had. Pauline's diary recorded that she accepted the acclaim, gave everyone a shilling, but wished she had shot the beast. When Hemingway wrote the book based on the safari, *Green Hills of Africa*, he created excited context and dialogue for scenes like this, key moments in the trip. As he had written in the opening of this book, his aim here was to tell a story truly.[11]

As the safari continued, however, Ernest was less often a triumphal character. Charlie Thompson had better luck shooting and so the larger trophies were his. Percival sometimes had to bail Hemingway out. Then Hemingway came down with dysentery and a prolapse of the lower intestine that nearly hospitalized him. Weaker by the day, he finally stayed in his cot at camp. Alarmed, Pauline and Percival had the driver go to the nearest town over 100 miles away and wire for a plane to take Hemingway back to Arusha. Waiting for the plane in the darkened camp, watching Hemingway dehydrate, Pauline thought she might be losing her husband. Once he had been lifted off, Hemingway made it to Nairobi where he took a series of emetine shots which cleared up his diarrhea. When Percival (who had himself become ill) and Pauline made it to Arusha and Hemingway was not there, they had to wire in order to find him and re-connect. Returning to the safari, they were all somewhat sobered. The killing of kudu, topi, oryx, buffalo, zebra, sable, and rhino completed their hunt schedule—again, Thompson shot a rhino first but Ernest would not give up. Finally, a few days from the end of that part of the safari, Hemingway shot a very large rhino from such a great distance that Percival admitted he was amazed and said that it was Ernest's best shooting of the trip.[12]

When Pauline wrote to the Oak Park Hemingways, a month into the safari, she told no alarming stories. Writing to Sunny, she asked after Grace's health (after breaking her leg, Grace had contracted pneumonia). Pauline reported simply that African life was "enchanting" and that both she and Ernest had shot lions. (Ernest, she said, had also killed buck, leopard, buffalo, and a variety of birds.) About his dysentery, she reported that he was cured, though the weeks of illness had "thinned him considerably." He was now "as hard as nails."[13]

The competition between Thompson and Hemingway continued. The only pause in the hunting was when the group stayed at the estate of Richard Cooper, on Lake Manyara.[14] Vanderbilt and his white hunter, Baron von Blixen, who had once been married to fiction writer Isak Dinesen, were also a part of the Cooper party; on board the luxurious *Gripsholm* for the return trip to the Mediterranean, the Hemingways and Thompson again traveled with Vanderbilt and von Blixen. Hemingway enjoyed this early version of the international jet set and decided he could adapt his enthusiasm to mimic the bored wealthy. When they docked at Haifa on March 16, 1934, Lorine Thompson, Charlie's wife, joined them, carrying recent photos of Gregory and Patrick.[15]

Sailing for New York on the *Ile de France* nine days later, Hemingway met film star Marlene Dietrich, who became a good friend. Again, Hemingway's opportunism led to his acquaintance with the internationally known movie actress: never shy in social situations, in this case, Hemingway saw that as Dietrich moved toward a table of seated people, she realized she would be the thirteenth person seated. As she turned away, he stepped to her side and told her he would be happy to make the fourteenth guest.[16]

In New York, before starting home to Key West, Hemingway placed the official order for the large cabin cruiser, proud that it would be paid for—at least in part—with his earnings; in May, 1934, he sailed the *Pilar* from Miami into Key West harbor himself.

It was a busy summer of writing the safari book and the *Esquire* columns, and fishing. Because Paul and Hadley Mowrer had moved back to Chicago where Paul had become managing editor of the *Chicago Daily News*, Bumby was with the other Hemingway sons for the entire summer (although the nanny took Gregory to the States for part of the time). Back into Ernest's fishing life had come a recovered Jane Mason, who was now seriously interested in Richard Cooper. Reticent to spend the kind of time with Hemingway that she had once enjoyed, Jane still liked seeing the boys—and she liked fishing on the *Pilar*. Pauline came and went, in a process that resembled checking in rather than partnering. In fact, from July 18, when Hemingway arrived in Cuban waters on the *Pilar* until October 26, when he and the boat returned to Key West, Pauline saw little of him.[17]

Shortly before Thanksgiving the safari trophies—mounted heads, rugs, other skins—started arriving. On November 16, 1934, Hemingway announced to Pauline and to Dos and Katy, who rented an apartment nearby but were often with the Hemingways, that he had finished *Green Hills of Africa*. When he gave the polished typescript to Perkins who had come to Key West briefly, he was disappointed that his editor's response was comparatively mild: although Perkins arranged for the book to be serialized in *Scribner's Magazine*, the offer for the serialization was only $5000—five years after *A Farewell to Arms* had brought $16,000 for its serialization. For Hemingway, the comparatively small fee meant that he had disappointed his publishers, although the size of the fee was more than likely mandated by the increasingly depressed economy.

It had probably been hard for Hemingway to write honestly about his competition with Thompson. Ernest had always been a good shot; it was difficult to acknowledge that Charlie Thompson, his friend of many years, was a better one, and that his own debilitating illness had caused changes in the safari plans. Through his convalescence, Hemingway had had to watch everyone accommodate him and his health. Writing about his dysentery was, in fact, somewhat shaming. Whereas in December, he and Pauline had been excited to see their photo in the *New York Herald Tribune*, with the announcement of their leaving on safari, now *Green Hills of Africa* would show the more human side of Hemingway. And much of that human side might be read as weakness.

Perhaps partly for that reason, Ernest added in a number of comments about aesthetics, comments that implicitly linked writing well with shooting and hunting well. He waxed enthusiastic about what he was achieving in prose, creating the concept of a fourth and fifth dimension. Attaining this level "is much more difficult than poetry," he claimed, and such prose must be written "without tricks and without cheating."[18] He discussed the state of contemporary fiction, and of American letters, privileging Mark Twain above most other United States writers. He no longer criticized Stein as he had in *Death in the Afternoon*, but his generally positive inclusion of Pauline in the safari story was marred somewhat by his referring to her as P. O. M. (Poor Old Mama). Several reviewers commented on Hemingway's inappropriate word choice, and Fitzgerald told Perkins he thought such naming was in poor taste.[19]

Insignificant as Hemingway's choice of name for his partner (and for the woman whose family had yet again made possible such a rare experience) may seem, recent criticism of Hemingway's work from the perspective of gender studies employs contemporary readings of both the fiction and the prose to suggest a case for the writer's damaged psyche. When Comley and Scholes depicted Hemingway as a distressed boy and young man, they linked the treatment he received from not only his mother but also Agnes von Kurowsky; then they applied the writer's wounding from those rejections to the way he characterized women in his fiction. Titling one section of their book "Mothers, Nurses, Whores," they found pervasive links in men's writings between mothers, sisters, and nurse figures—and thereby read Hemingway's caring women such as Catherine Barkley in *A Farewell to Arms* to be a prototype of both mother and nurse, which Catherine literally is. (They also imply that his attraction to older women—Agnes, Hadley, and even Pauline—stemmed from his rejection by his mother.) They then hypothesize that when the mother-nurse figure became the male's sexual partner, he felt guilty (after all, he would never have had sex with his mother or sister).[20]

The reader might speculate that so long as Hemingway remained in control of the woman character, creating her and her performance, he felt no animosity. But in his non-fiction writing, when he was the male protagonist-writer who promised to write truly, some of his anti-female attitudes surfaced. Just as he had satirized Gertrude Stein in *Death in the Afternoon*, so in *Green Hills of Africa* he needed to defame Pauline, the source of the money that made possible their safari (and his somewhat less-than-heroic behavior on it). Whereas Hemingway himself, and some readers, thought he was expressing affection for his wife, others took offense at his labeling his wife and the mother of his family "Poor Old Mama." Perhaps Hemingway himself didn't understand what his choice of names meant.

12
Hemingway in the World

If it had not been for the early stirrings of the Spanish Civil War, it seems likely that Hemingway would have learned what it was to reach bottom in 1935 and 1936. He had discovered tuna fishing, and he had found the almost unpopulated islands of Bimini, but when he invited Jane Mason to join him there during the summer of 1935, she declined. Feeling rejected by Jane, who told him she had spent much of the winter in Richard Cooper's beautiful African home and that she cared about the Britisher, and disappointed with the response to the serialization of *Green Hills of Africa*, Hemingway poured a great deal of anxious thought into a situation he believed Jane was responsible for creating—an unflattering psychoanalytic essay her psychiatrist Lawrence Kubie had written about him. (The essay on Hemingway was one of a series Kubie was publishing about living American writers, Faulkner, Caldwell, Hemingway.)[1] Kubie saw Hemingway as a man fundamentally harmed by women—whether by his mother or other women in his early life. Because of his feelings of loss and violation, Kubie speculated, Ernest had had bad relationships with not only women but with men. Difficult to befriend, Hemingway had lived a life fueled by his need to excel—hence, his fiction about supermen, people who were far from human. Even when those figures did excel, however, they found little happiness. The only real friendships in Hemingway's fiction were between male characters.

In the pattern he would adopt as more and more critics wrote about his writing, Hemingway here replied furiously—to Kubie and then to Jane Mason about what he assumed to have been her part in the debacle. She asked Kubie not to publish the Hemingway essay—although his other pieces had already appeared in *The Saturday Review of Literature*—and he promised he would not.

Neither did the lukewarm response to *Green Hills of Africa* improve Hemingway's mood. In fact, that mood continued to worsen through 1935. The year had begun with an unfortunate accident as Katy and Dos, with Mike Strater, were on the *Pilar* with him heading out for tuna, and Ernest, while shooting bullets into a shark, shot himself in both legs. The party returned to Key West for a week while he healed, although Katy raged for months at the chances he took with firearms. Hemingway's long friendship with both Katy Smith and Dos Passos suffered because of his bravado and its consequences.[2] As he had in 1934, Ernest kept his distance from Pauline during much of the summer although in 1935 they spent July together—with the children—on Bimini and then returned to Key West in the late summer.

Hemingway was dedicating himself to his fishing, and to writing about the African safari, as one way to avoid the literary politics of the mid-1930s. Although Fitzgerald's long-awaited novel, *Tender Is the Night*, had finally been published in 1934, most of the books being reviewed were proletarian. Collective novels—ones that spelled out the evils of a capitalistic system that privileged the owner class above the working class, like Tom Kromer's *Waiting for Nothing*, Albert Maltz's *Black Pit*, and Nelson Algren's *Somebody in Boots*—were getting the enthusiastic reviews. Even Sherwood Anderson (*Puzzled America*) and Sinclair Lewis (*It Can't Happen Here*) had climbed aboard the bash-America bandwagon. And it hurt Hemingway even more that Dos Passos was following up *The 42nd Parallel* and *1919* with a third prose behemoth, *The Big Money*. (Hemingway liked Dos Passos' novels, and he wrote to him in 1932, "Don't let a fool like Cowley [Malcolm] tell you the Camera Eye isn't swell."[3])

Hemingway had been arguing against taking political positions in literature for years. In 1932, he had written Paul Romaine that he did not intend to take "the Leftward Swing" (which he called "so much horseshit"). Hemingway's manifesto was, rather, that he did not "follow the fashions in politics, letters, religion." He also railed against communism.[4] A few months later, he wrote to Guy Hickok somewhat wryly, that in the coming elections the United States had "a big choice" between "The Paralytic Demagogue," "The Syphilitic Baby," "The Sentimental Reformer," and "The Yes-Man of Moscow" (referring to Roosevelt, Hoover, Thomas, and Foster, representing the Democratic, Republican, Socialist, and Communist parties).[5] Several years after that, in response to Gingrich's suggestions about what he might write for *Esquire*, Hemingway announced that he had "no romantic feeling" for the American scene.[6] He had somewhat obliquely defended his art to

Perkins, responding to criticism saying that he was just reporting what had happened, "I'm a reporter and *an imaginative writer.*" Defending his great short stories—among them "Hills Like White Elephants"— Hemingway said he knew how fine his fiction was, but his role was not to praise it.[7]

As the political carping grew more pervasive, Hemingway wrote to friends, among them the Russian critic Ivan Kashkin in August of 1935— preparatory to the publication of *Green Hills of Africa*—that he was, of necessity, a professional writer. He said he wrote the *Esquire* columns to eat; the safari book, however, is "the best I can write." Writers now cannot be coerced into being political: the writer is by nature and trade "an outlyer like a Gypsy." To Kashkin he repeated, "I cannot be a communist now because I believe in only one thing: liberty."[8]

Despite the criticism of *Green Hills of Africa*, Hemingway had inadvertently protected himself by publishing other works that Marxist critics thought showed appropriate sentiments. In April of 1934, *Cosmopolitan* published the first section of what would become *To Have and Have Not*, the Harry Morgan story entitled "One Trip Across." In the story of the boat captain who is gypped out of his fee by a wealthy white man (ignorant of both marlin fishing and fair play), Hemingway uses the poverty of the simple man to excuse his agreeing to smuggle Chinese illegals into Cuba. The execution-style murders that open the segment foreshadow the killings Morgan will have to make to protect his boat. (The second of the Morgan stories appeared in *Esquire.*) In the September 1935 issue of *Esquire*, in contrast to all Hemingway's columns about fishing and big game hunting, he wrote "Notes on the Next War: A Serious Topical Letter." With a poignant beginning (Hemingway in World War I, lying wounded, promising himself he would do whatever he could the rest of his life to prevent war), the author predicted that the second world war would begin in 1937 or 1938—because of the greed of capitalism and the propaganda machine fueled by it. In his analysis of the "demagogues and dictators who play on the patriotism of their people" to make good, honest people believe that war could change people's behaviors, Hemingway stated again that war is run by "executives" who want profits.[9] ("The Malady of Power: A Second Serious Letter," a later *Esquire* essay in November of 1935, reinforced Hemingway's argument, and in the January 1936 *Esquire*, his condemnation of the Italian invasion of Ethiopia, strangely titled "Wings Over Africa: An Ornithological Letter," appeared.)

The most influential of Hemingway's writings, "Who Murdered the Vets?" which appeared in the September 17 *New Masses*, was clearly the most passionate. After a monstrous hurricane struck Matecumbe Key to the east of Key West, nearly 500 men died by drowning. Working for the CCC doing construction for government projects in a desolate area, these World War I vets were poorly paid for the work they did in the blistering tropical heat. That they had never been able to re-establish themselves after they had returned from service in Europe was one crime on the government's hands, according to Hemingway; that they were not warned about the impending storm (or evacuated) was the greater crime. Because Hemingway had gone to help the survivors, he knew the story and all its sad details, and he emphasized in particular the inadequate shelter of the makeshift government barracks in which the men were forced to live. (In Hemingway's letter to Perkins, he claimed the deaths were between 700 and 1000; that not a building remained standing; and that 30 miles of railway had blown away—and yet trains had earlier been ready to evacuate the men, had Washington not nixed that effort.)[10]

Absorbed in trying to write new fiction, and now faced with horrifying proof that the most democratic government in the world had feet of clay, Hemingway made fewer fishing trips in the fall. Pauline decided they would celebrate Christmas in Key West rather than making what had become their annual trek to Piggott. Then, soon after the holidays, in January, 1936, Ernest wrote to his mother-in-law Mary Pfeiffer that he was having trouble staying interested in anything. He had never before had this kind of black mood. When it hit hardest, he said he took the *Pilar* out and drove it on his own, night or day. He had come to have more sympathy for people who went through such depressions. He had never understood the toll an emotional down period could take.[11] Especially visible symptoms were his constant insomnia and his shortness with the staff members who had always been his friends—Carlos Gutierrez on the *Pilar*, for instance.

Somewhere during this sustained period of what Hemingway (to his friends) called "the black ass," he had written more on the Harry Morgan stories which would become *To Have and Have Not*, and two of his finest stand-alone stories, "The Snows of Kilimanjaro" and "The Short Happy Life of Francis Macomber." Arnold Gingrich liked the Morgan stories and urged him to work them into a novel. Both the other stories, appearing in August and September, 1936 ("Kilimanjaro" in *Esquire* and "Macomber" in *Cosmopolitan*, for the munificent sum of $5000) received almost more notice than had *Green Hills of Africa*.

Of "The Snows of Kilimanjaro," Hemingway noted years later that he had used up much material in that single story—he implies, too much.[12]

It is true that in the story, he spreads a variegated table of scenes, memories, dialogue, metaphors, and intensities. The forbidding mountain that overlooks the wasteful life of the rich—the gangrenous writer and his fashionable and careless wife, Helen—is the dominant metaphor, as the title suggests. Unlike the country described in his earlier "Big Two-Hearted River," the African terrain in this story is frightening; there will be no recovery here for the wounded writer. The irony accrues from the fact that Harry Walden, the dying man (who, as a literary aside, was never able to read Thoreau's *Walden*) has not been injured in any brave exploit but has rather been careless of a scratch that could easily have been sterilized. Now dying from his infection, he visits his past life, seeing what might have been good and possible in the midst of his defeat. As he accomplishes this kaleidoscopic mental journey, moving in and out of consciousness, he engages his concerned wife in an aggressively hostile dialogue. In effect, he blames her and her family money for the state he now finds himself in—not only being on safari and far from medical attention, but being in a spiritual wasteland, a tundra of lost ambition, comforted too often by the easy life that her money has made possible. Still writing morally, Hemingway lamented the loss of this ability in the surfeit of easy living. That Helen does not take offense at her husband's bitter comments is perhaps the saddest note in the story: she married him, she wanted him, to serve as her partner in her familiar social circumstances. He is her trophy, just as she and he had planned to bring back animal trophies from this safari.

As the manuscript for the story shows, it was at one time even longer. There is an entire page describing the hateful hyena, particularly as it moves closer to the dying man, crouching on his chest as he lies, unable to defend himself or even to speak. The omnipresence of death is physically embodied in the hyena's presence. Another early section is longer, when the author in thinking to himself how much he had never written—what a waste his life had been—thought that he had never written about Paris. He had, however, written of other countries and of his boyhood.[13]

The other truly fine, if more enigmatic, story from early 1936 is "The Short Happy Life of Francis Macomber." Vitriolic over his now-concluded romance or friendship with Jane Mason, Hemingway drew the character of Margot Macomber—another wealthy and vengeful woman, much more vengeful than Helen in the "Kilimanjaro" story—who is a good shot and a good lover, and a woman who has stayed married because she knows that she can control her mild husband in every circumstance. Deflating Francis Macomber once again as Margot conspicuously begins an affair with the white hunter, she also eggs him into dangerous situations as he hunts. She knows he lacks bravery, she knows he cannot shoot well, she knows she is still in control. The denouement of the story occurs in a single flash—the shot from Margot's gun as she shoots at her husband, or at the wild boar, or at a point somewhere between the two. Although Hemingway later said there are few instances of wives who shot husbands on safari,[14] the various kinds of ambiguities in the narrative, coupled with the various kinds of ambiguities in Hemingway's mind as he began the self-critical process that wanted to blame Jane Mason for rejecting him along with the Pfeiffers' money for much of the waste of his last four or five years, kept the story from any simple denouement.

A kind of despair had shadowed Hemingway, but later in 1936, happy to see two such fine stories in print, he felt as though his luck was improving. Though he hesitated to think that he might never have enough stories for a fourth collection, and was cheered because these two new stories were some of the best writing he had done, he could see little promising fiction ahead. Grinding on month after month to fulfill the advance Gingrich had given him toward buying the *Pilar*, Hemingway's letters too took on a bitter tone that surprised some of his friends. For others, his disinterest in them—or even in what he was himself doing—only confirmed the changes they had been witnessing in Ernest during the mid-1930s.

For Scott Fitzgerald, who kept track of Ernest chiefly through his correspondence with Perkins, all of Ernest's writing seemed to be a personal attack on him. Scott Donaldson gives the fullest account of the machinations Perkins had to employ to get Ernest to change the phrase "poor Scott Fitzgerald" in the "Kilimanjaro" story to something less recognizable—and illustrates Hemingway's clear meanness. For instance, the manuscript of *To Have and Have Not* included insulting portraits of both the Masons as well as comments about the deaths of Hart Crane and Harry Crosby and the writing of both Dos Passos and Fitzgerald. Attacking friends in print seemed to be Ernest's new sport.[15]

After the "poor Scott Fitzgerald" reference had appeared in the *Esquire* (August 1936) printing of "The Snows of Kilimanjaro" (if Gingrich had objected, it would not have been in the story at all; Gingrich, who was also publishing Fitzgerald's "Crack-Up" essays, knew how damaging Hemingway's words would be), Fitzgerald himself wrote to Hemingway. The sorrow he expressed could have softened Ernest, but it instead angered him. Fitzgerald was, in effect, showing himself to be a weak man (and particularly a weak husband, perhaps a worse characterization in Hemingway's mind). Even though *Scott's* feelings were hurt, *he* wanted to make amends. Part of Hemingway's reaction to this letter may have stemmed from the fact that he had found the first two of Scott's "Crack-Up" essays unsettling—not only demeaning, but perhaps echoes of his own feelings of inadequacy. There was, obviously, no reason for Fitzgerald to write a pacifying letter. He was not at fault. The fault clearly was Hemingway's and that he would not easily recant showed the disintegration of at least parts of his personality, the winsome self that had so enabled him to "take Paris" in the early 1920s.

Fitzgerald's anxiety increased over time. When "Snows" appeared in Edward J. O'Brien's *The Best Short Stories 1937*, his name still appeared as part of the text. Fitzgerald then wrote to Perkins that, before Hemingway's *First Forty-Nine Stories* collection was to appear in fall, 1938, the change had to be made. "It was a damned rotten thing to do," Scott reminded Max. On target for the first time, Scott realized that his friendship with Ernest was at an end. (Under pressure from Perkins, Hemingway replaced "poor Scott Fitzgerald" with "poor Julian." But along the way, he tried to use the shorter—but still identifiable—phrase, "poor Scott.")[16]

The correspondence Hemingway received from Harry Wheeler, manager of the North American Newspaper Alliance (NANA) in late November, 1936, offered a welcome corrective to what had seemed to him to be the literary world's pettiness. Would Mr. Hemingway be interested in going to Spain to cover the Civil War? Wheeler asked. News media around the world picked up the possibility of Ernest's becoming a war correspondent. Hadley wrote in January, 1937, that she was interested in his plans to go to Spain.[17] As much as she could, Pauline warned him that to go was probably to endanger his life, and he did have children (not to mention a wife who loved him). To put Pauline off, Ernest took the *Pilar* to Cuba and there urged American torero Sidney Franklin to come to Spain with him. He returned home telling his wife that were he to go, he would have company.

Despite what he told Pauline, from the first news items about the Civil War, Hemingway had assumed he would go. Not only was Spain his country, but he believed in elected government. He also saw that the incipient conflicts between the free world and Fascism were no longer remote. When the Nationalists defamed the election of the Loyalists, arguing that the military and the religious forces (not to mention their backing from Fascism) were representative of the people's beliefs, Hemingway could see that rhetoric bore little relation to truth. (He had friends on both sides of the conflict.) But when the slaughter of civilians began, for the first time in the history of mechanized warfare, he could see that he could not simply stand by. After the massive German bombing of Guernica, April 26, 1937, few American intellectuals stayed neutral.[18]

Politics sometimes fade, however, against the backdrop of sunny ocean comfort. What might have brought Ernest to the point of signing the contract with NANA might not have been exclusively political. In late December, walking into Sloppy Joe's Bar, Hemingway saw the beautiful blonde writer who had recently been pictured on the cover of the *Saturday Review of Literature*. The next day, Martha Gellhorn, her mother, and her brother were once more at the bar; this time, she introduced herself to the great Hemingway. Late for dinner—then and frequently during the several weeks Marty spent in Key West—Ernest saw that he had a great deal in common with this much-touted young American writer. Her *The Trouble I've Seen*, stories about unemployed people in the States during the mid-1930s—something of an oral history treatment of the aged, young, middle-aged, and children—had been widely reviewed and promoted by such figures as Eleanor Roosevelt and the President himself. Nine years younger than he, Martha Gellhorn was at the start of an enviable writing career. Both *New Yorker* and *Harper's Bazaar* had recently taken her short stories. Perhaps Hemingway was doing a bit of celebrity chasing himself.[19] Gellhorn had spent the spring in both France and Germany, observing the Nazi support of the Nationalists, and she had already pledged her support to the Loyalists in Spain. Of course she would go to that country.

For Ernest, this beautiful young woman's unerring decision making was a welcome change from the philanderings, and obfuscations, of Jane Mason, the woman to whom he had given several years of attention. In fact, Hemingway had just spent the week before the holidays in a meeting with his and Scribner's lawyer, Maurice Spieser ("Moe") and Arnold Gingrich, trying to determine how libelous his depiction of Jane was in the character of Helene Bradley in the manuscript for *To Have and Have Not*. Because Ernest often used his fiction as pay-back, he had developed the Harry Morgan stories into a class-conscious narrative. Harry and his wife Marie were unlucky and lower class, having to work outside the law to make their living. Set against the Morgan plotline was the wasteful, expensive existence of Tommy and Helene Bradley, the rich couple who led totally unproductive lives. Not without reason, Perkins had worried that Ernest's vitriolic portrait of the woman who had abandoned their romance might well involve Scribner's in a lawsuit.

As the days passed in the meeting and the vetting process, Ernest grew more and more angry. He was beginning to suspect that his friend and publisher Arnold Gingrich had now become Jane Mason's lover, at least when she was in New York. At one point in the deliberations,

Hemingway muttered, "Goddamn editor comes down to Bimini and sees a blonde and he hasn't been the same since."[20]

His own plans—not only to go to Spain but to help fund what he and Dos Passos, MacLeish, and Lillian Hellman were calling "Contemporary History" so that they could make a film about the conflict in Spain— seemed of far more importance, and far more interest, than the publishing of *To Have and Have Not*.[21]

13
Martha Gellhorn and Spain

When in the autumn of 1934 Harry Hopkins hired Martha Gellhorn to investigate how the welfare system really worked, he probably had not thought about the kinds of work the seasoned reporter would do for his new agency, the Federal Emergency Relief Administration (FERA).[1] Typical of her approach to investigative journalism, Gellhorn found people and stories, and processed information at top speed: she did not do quantitative work, she did reporting based on people.

Altruistic in all senses of the word, Gellhorn thought a person's character was the basis for all humane understanding. As one of the four children of a prosperous St. Louis gynecologists' family, Martha had never had financial difficulties. She had finished three years of college at Bryn Mawr, where her mother had graduated decades earlier. As the family's only daughter, Martha was expected to finish her degree, but she grew restless. She worked first for the *New Republic* and some city papers; then on freelance writing gigs she traveled to France where she met young French intellectuals (she worked for an advertising agency, for *Vogue*, and for the United Press). Freelancing for the *St. Louis Post-Dispatch*, she reported on the League of Nations meetings in Geneva and did a series of interviews with political women involved with the League. In Capri, during the summer of 1933, she wrote *What Mad Pursuit*, her novel about three girls from an elite women's college who travel in search of meaning in their privileged lives.[2] Once back in the States, working for the FERA, Gellhorn met Eleanor Roosevelt, who enthusiastically introduced her to the President.

It was to Mrs. Roosevelt that Gellhorn wrote on January 5, 1937, as she was about to end her vacation in Key West. Telling her friend that she had put aside her novel, which seemed, in the face of war, not very significant, she mentioned spending her days with Hemingway, "an odd bird, very lovable and full of fire and a marvelous story teller." She had read the manuscript of his new novel. It seems to be because of his fine storytelling that she gave up her novel. It was a sober letter because, finally, as she wrote Mrs. Roosevelt, "If there is a war then all the things most of us do won't matter any more."[3] With the ingenuousness that was characteristic of Gellhorn, the person to whom she wrote was obviously one of the few people in the world with the power—or with access to that power—to make American life "matter."

Hemingway, the "odd bird" of Gellhorn's phrasing, showed his true colors a few days later. The platonic nature of older-writer-helping-younger-writer changed and when Gellhorn left Key West on January 10, on the very next day Hemingway also left Key West. Finding Martha in Miami, Ernest took her to dinner and then they traveled together by train to Jacksonville, Florida, where she went west to St. Louis, and he continued on to New York.[4] There he met with Perkins about *To Have and Have Not*, signed the North American Newspaper Alliance (NANA) contract, which would pay him the extremely high rates of $500 per cabled story and $1000 for each story sent by mail, and wrote commentary for Prudencio de Pereda's documentary film *Spain in Flames*. He also wrote and phoned Martha, promising he could get her into Spain. (He had given Perkins her story "Exiles" which *Scribner's Magazine* bought.)[5]

After Hemingway returned to Key West from New York, his frantic energy bothered Pauline. She decided that if he were going to Spain, she would go along. Ernest said she could not go but offered as a compromise that perhaps she could join him later in Paris. In his February 9, 1937 letter to the Pfeiffer family, thanking them for Christmas gifts, Hemingway acknowledged his being on the "wrong side" in the Spanish conflict. He planned to leave for Spain soon, to return in May. Calling Spain the "dress rehearsal for the inevitable European war," he apologized for taking the Communist side ("the Reds may be as bad as they say but they are the people of the country versus the absentee landlords, the moors, the Italians, and the Germans").[6] In his simultaneous correspondence with Martha, who was impatient to leave St. Louis, he encouraged her to come to New York and then travel to Paris. But he had already sailed for France with Sidney Franklin and Evan Shipman by the time she reached New York; because of the Franco-British Non-Intervention Pact, she could get no credentials. Finally Kyle Crichton of *Collier's* gave her a letter that identified her as their special correspondent (which was not).[7]

Gellhorn, frustrated at this impasse and angry because Ernest had apparently done nothing for her, flew to France and then took a French train to the Andorran-Spanish border, disembarked, and walked into Spain.

Then she took another train to Barcelona, and from there a press car to Madrid. Although Sidney Franklin claimed to have expedited her trip, and Ernest—when she found him at the correspondents' mess at the Hotel Gran Via—took credit for getting her into Spain, Martha knew that nobody had done anything for her. A few days and weeks passed, with Gellhorn going along with the correspondents but not filing stories herself. When she did send an impressionistic piece to *Collier's*, it was published, as was a second, and Gellhorn then found herself listed on the magazine's roster. And when a shell hit the Hotel Florida's hot water tank, and couples (usually a man and a prostitute) ran from their rooms into the hall, Martha and Hemingway appeared, somewhat blatantly, as a couple.[8]

Not into admitting that even his usual panacea, writing, was failing to keep him steady, Hemingway may have seen his well-paid contract with NANA as the chance to make a fresh start. He knew he was unhappy with *To Have and Have Not*, remarking several years after its appearance that it was never a novel—it was "made of short stories, and there is a hell of a lot of difference."[9] Hemingway was always the writer, trying again and again for some way to reach that fourth and fifth dimension; he may have found a few new routes in Gellhorn's *The Trouble I've Seen*. One of his earliest NANA dispatches, "The Old Man at the Bridge," replicated the understated pathos of the human cost of war. Chary details etched the old man's face in the reader's mind. With no mention of the political forces at work, Hemingway emphasized the waste of human life. Martha's columns, too, collected later in *The Face of War*, gave readers a similarly focused glimpse of the war-torn country. Her description of a little boy killed during a 30-minute shelling of Madrid (which had been under siege for six months) implicated the reader as well as the Nationalists in the grandmother's grief. The old woman had, only a minute before the shell, walked the boy out of the food line toward what she assumed was safety ("Only the Shells Whine").

Madrid under siege was a desperately hungry city. It was hard not to resent the press corps in the hotel for their meals, their drinking, their poker playing—when in the plazas and the streets, the people of Madrid were in food lines that could cost them their lives. If they lived, they would be hungry, ragged, and bereaved for the next decade. The sorrow of the Spanish people in this conflict had been made clear to Hemingway from the first days of his arrival. Meeting his old friend, the painter Luis Quintanilla, Hemingway learned about his imprisonment and the destruction of both his studio and the frescos he had become famous for.[10]

As a way of contributing something more than his presence, Hemingway volunteered to help write material for the money-raising documentary film, *The Spanish Earth*, which was being directed by the talented Dutch communist, Joris Ivens. Working with the film crew, Ernest also saw his participation in the film as a way to spend time with his special friends in the Twelfth International Brigade—Gustav Regler, the political commissar of the Brigade; Werner Heilbrun, a German-Jewish doctor; and the Hungarian general Lucasz. To gather material, in late April, Gellhorn and Hemingway went with a driver to the four central fronts, sometimes sleeping by the roadside. Often shelled, the three of them learned to leap out of the car and hide under whatever cover they could find; Gellhorn, who had never experienced any kind of battle, seemed unflappable. It was Hemingway, still bothered by memories of his wounding years before, who had to steel himself under these attacks. Just as he admired Martha for her readiness to take on random danger, so she admired his calm demeanor during the worst of the shelling.[11]

As Caroline Moorehead discusses in her biography *Gellhorn*, coverage of the civil war was far from objective. Most of the reporters in Spain were anti-fascist, and yet most newspapers did not send two reporters. Hemingway and Herbert Matthews, for example, were silent about the persecutions and executions carried out by the Republicans. Their reporting was, in many respects, one-sided.[12] Caught in his personal political stance in the matter of Dos Passos' friend and translator, Jose Robles Pazos, Hemingway seemed to believe the false reports his "friends" in Republican headquarters had given him. He had told Dos Passos that the man was safe. In fact, Robles had already been executed, probably erroneously.

Back in Key West by mid-May of 1937, Ernest planned to return to Spain as quickly as he could get *To Have and Have Not* to Perkins and finish his work for the documentary. Gellhorn stayed in New York to create interest in both the film and the Spanish Loyalist conflict, but as she wrote him, people's lives there were so far removed from war that nobody seemed interested. All the time he was in Spain, Hemingway had communicated with Pauline by cable—there had been only one letter—although she wrote to him frequently, letters of loneliness and of family news. One piece of news she did not convey was that she was improving the property again. This time she was having a high privacy wall built and adding an in-ground salt water pool (the only one in the area) with a changing house. Surely, with money, there were many ways to keep Ernest at home.

Once he was back in Key West, however, Pauline saw that the Spanish conflict was still uppermost in his mind: cables from Spain, communications about the film, and letters from Gellhorn peppered the slow hot days. Ivens reminded Hemingway that he was to be in New York to speak to the Writers' Congress in early June. The press of his activity for the Spanish conflict erased all other work from his mind. Once again, Hemingway was writing, and working, for a cause.

His appearance on the hot June 5, 1938 Writers' Congress stage was one of the reasons 3500 people crowded into the open session at Carnegie Hall; another thousand had been turned away. Ranging in political views from Russian Communist Party ideologues to liberal intellectuals, the audience thirsted for information about Spain. Archibald MacLeish, as chair of the Congress, read telegrams of support from Thomas Mann, Albert Einstein, Upton Sinclair, and others. Although Hemingway was not a sophisticated political thinker, when he said that writers could not live under a fascist regime, people understood his point of view and his anger. He spoke for only seven minutes, but because he so seldom appeared for any political cause, his presence carried immense weight. (In people's minds, though somewhat foggily recorded, was Hemingway's wounding during World War I—as reinscribed in the pages of his novel *A Farewell to Arms*.) The Hearst papers called the Writers' Congress "a Moscow plot."[13]

Gellhorn and he spent several days at the Hotel Gladstone, and then Hemingway went home. He was to return to New York later in June to record the voice-over narration for *The Spanish Earth*. Before that time, the Twelfth Brigade was decimated—Lucasz and Heilbrun dead, Regler seriously wounded. The loss of friends gave a new bite to Hemingway's voice, which as a rule was less strong than it was on this recording. His bitterness over what was happening to the Loyalists—and to many people he knew well—was to color everything he did that year and the several years to follow.

In Key West, Hemingway gave terse responses to anything connected with the household. Long experienced in running everything alone, Pauline continued to care for the boys, the staff, and the ongoing pool project; she also paid the bills. Gellhorn, meanwhile, had arranged a showing of *The Spanish Earth* at the White House, with both Ernest and Ivens present, for the Roosevelts to view. In early July, Hemingway flew to New York and then to Washington for the showing. From there the men flew to Hollywood to raise money from the film community.[14] By his thirty-eighth birthday on July 21, Ernest was back home (and Pauline's 42nd birthday followed on July 22nd).

Hemingway often wrote to the Pfeiffers in early August, thanking them for the birthday checks he and Pauline received. Despite his being remembered in this way, there is scant mention of Hemingway himself giving gifts. Except for the giving of his stories' or novels' manuscripts, Hemingway seemed to avoid giving presents. Judging from Marcelline's letters, his remembrances to his Oak Park family were monetary, and seemed to be irregular.[15] One of the few gifts in his history is the evening bag he sent Hadley, during the early weeks of their courtship. Otherwise, to his best friends, Hemingway gave invitations—to visit, to stay in his home or on the *Pilar*, to hunt out west. His practices left those closest to him—his wives and children—without much anticipation.

In the case of Pauline, the grudging animosity he felt toward her family's wealth colored his reaction to her gift-giving. Pauline gave appropriate, and sometimes costly, presents. Because Pauline's and Ernest's birthdays were just a day apart, one surmises they did not give gifts—and as their fishing calendar suggested, once they had moved to Key West, they were usually separated during their birthday month, July. (When Martha Gellhorn reminisced about her marriage to Hemingway, she could remember his giving her a gift only once in the duration of that relationship—a set of long-johns and a shotgun so that she would be equipped for their hunting sojourns in the West.[16])

To contrast what appears to have been Hemingway's chary behavior toward his wives with his treatment of good friends, even as he was unable to spend his and Pauline's sixth anniversary together, he had sold stock in order to send John Dos Passos a check for $1000 because Dos Passos was hospitalized with a recurrence of rheumatic fever. His May 15, 1933 letter told Dos Passos he expected no repayment.[17]

During this Key West stay in 1937, there was outright anger between Pauline and Ernest. She could not believe he would return to a country that was clearly slated for destruction. She could not understand his instinct for his own death—and, by implication, his lack of concern for her and their sons. That Hemingway had previously avoided any personal expression of wartime bravery did not fit with his behavior now. Even as he had drawn Frederic Henry's character in *A Farewell to Arms*, the man was a deserter because he had not wanted to die for an unrealistic, and possibly corrupt, cause. In Pauline's view, the Loyalist cause in Spain was similarly unrealistic and corrupt. Politically conservative as the Pfeiffers were, Ernest's support of the Russian and the American Communist parties seemed dangerously unpatriotic. Because he had married into the kind of community that he had derided in *A Farewell to Arms* as being naively patriotic, Hemingway explained to his mother-in-law, to whom he often turned when he could not talk to Pauline, that serving in Spain was, for him, a mystical experience. In his August 2, 1937 letter to Mary Pfeiffer, he said that after two weeks in Spain, he became a different person. He was not a man with a wife, children, a house, a boat: he was a part of the Loyalist fighting machine, and he valued nothing else. While there, he told her, he lost his fear of death and knew that to think of any personal future while the world was headed for destruction was only selfishness.[18]

Returning to New York in early August, Hemingway on August 17 sailed to France on the *Champlain*; Gellhorn sailed on the *Normandie* two days later. Met in Paris by Hemingway and Herbert Matthews of the *New York Times*, Gellhorn found herself a part of what became a powerful newspaper triumvirate. Matthews, particularly, could get top priority clearance for his work; she and Hemingway happily went along as his companions. What they covered was not happy news, however, once they reached Madrid in early September. The Nationalists continued their victorious sweep, but Belchite just below Zaragoza had been taken back by the Loyalists. Matthews, Hemingway, and Gellhorn were the first journalists to be allowed at that site. They observed soldiers rescuing and burying their dead, retrenching for the day ahead, and putting out fires. They then traveled to the Teruel heights, climbing steep hillsides on new military roads, visiting posts no other journalists had reached. They traveled in an open truck with mattresses and cooking utensils, and they usually depended on the largesse of the landowners in whose courtyards they parked the truck overnight.[19] The devastation of what they saw and experienced—so different from Hemingway's context during the World War I—made the year of 1937 a true turning point for his life and art.[20]

Once back in Madrid, Hemingway had time to begin his own writing. The fascist forces were now in the Aragon, so Madrid was comparatively quiet. His choice of creative work, as he followed his usual process of letting new material find its own shape and form, was to write a play. Filled with improbable characters and events, *The Fifth Column* had little to recommend it but a somewhat comic espionage plot, with the Philip Rawlings-Hemingway character acting as a secret agent for the Loyalist side. Exaggeration and mockery undercut whatever truth Hemingway thought he might be creating. That his first work about the Spanish conflict, a war so personally important to him, was satiric was troubling. But the spy plot may have been taking a secondary role to the romance plot, because in *The Fifth Column* (and is there a double reference as well to that elusive fifth dimension Hemingway was still trying for in his prose?)

much of Rawlings' motivation for his actions stems from his genuine love for the Vassar "bitch," the beautiful blonde American correspondent, Dorothy.[21]

Ignorant of all things military, Hemingway's Dorothy may be a wanderer from the Land of Oz, but she is lovely, and she seems to be in love with Rawlings. The play does not end with a permanent romantic pairing, however, as the Rawlings-Hemingway character segues in and out of his memory about his past life and his past loves. When he recalls that other infatuations had died after "the thousand breakfasts come up on trays"—and lists the places he has visited with Pauline or perhaps Jane (not with Martha)—it is clear that once again Hemingway was writing out the dregs of not only his present marriage, but perhaps what he had come to see as the dregs of all his attempts to make a worthwhile human connection with another person. As the play ends, Philip prepares, in good American cowboy style, to move on, to remain a man content to live on his own. The play anticipated by half a dozen years Hemingway's unpublished story, "The Strange Country," in which the male protagonist also decides to go it alone, realizing that reality meant "You made places in your mind that afterwards you could never find and they were better than any places could ever be."[22]

On October 15, 1938, when *To Have and Have Not* appeared in the States, sales—and reviews—were better than Ernest had hoped. Critics argued among themselves about why such a badly written book should be effective: there were comments about politics, there were comments about aesthetics, but it seemed as if Hemingway's novel, perhaps enhanced by the publicity of his work in Spain and the viewing of *The Spanish Earth*, had touched more readers than Scribner's had expected.

Besides the Harry Morgan story, however, and the camaraderie of the men aboard ship, there were two romance plots that readers may have overlooked. The great romance between Harry, deformed and disabled as he had become, and his less-than-respectable wife Marie, shimmered throughout the book. Richard Gordon's misreading of the lusty Marie underlines the fact that one's social position in the world is meaningless: all that matters is the rapport, the enduring love, between a man and a woman. For Gordon, who considers himself a writer, to be unable to appreciate Marie's sensibility is a quick way of damning him as the effete, well-placed, and stupid literary man. But the real criticism of Gordon the writer comes from his bitter wife, Helen, as she leaves him and their marriage. Ambivalent as Helen's act may be, it contributes to the pattern that Hemingway's work was creating. Just as he suggested his uneasiness about a relationship with Dorothy in *The Fifth Column*, so he questioned what kind of marriage Helen Gordon had had. There is a tone of self-reflexive analysis here, and elsewhere in Hemingway's mid- to later 1930s writing.

The complaints that Hemingway harbored against Pauline were, probably, seldom expressed face to face, but they had worked their way through his psyche to appear in his writing. The end of his marriage to Pauline was expressed in both the patient (rich) wife of "The Snows of Kilimanjaro," who was somehow complicit in watching her husband die of inconsequential wounds during his life of upper-class pleasures, and, even more pointedly in the character of Helen Gordon, similarly rich and competent, from *To Have and Have Not*. In the case of Henry Walden, he simply died—one way to end the dissension with that wife. In the case of Helen Gordon, she marched competently on, leaving her writer husband and thereby saving herself, seemingly unaware of what he had thought the real conflicts were. Hemingway as writer often borrowed the often unspoken words of Hemingway as human being. Disconcerting as this practice was, not only for its apparent cowardice but for his partner's need to find a resolution for conflicts, nobody had the power to force Hemingway to change. He lived as a writer in his imagination; he resolved his personal life issues the same way. The closest he may have come was his August 2 letter to Mary Pfeiffer, explaining the very different reality of his life in Spain.

Pauline remembered Ernest's anger once Hadley had brought his affair with her out into the open. As Hadley had also recalled, it was almost as if the affair hadn't existed until she gave language to it. (The assumption was that Hadley had no right to use the language that "belonged" in all ways to Hemingway the great writer.) Even though Hemingway had admitted to Hadley that he loved Pauline (though he was never so forthcoming about the fact that they had been having sex for months), he still seemed to blame his first wife for revealing his secret (*their* secret? *his* private life? And what did that imply about *his* married life with Hadley?). That Hadley was forced to live through months of indecision before her divorce from Ernest might have prepared Pauline for a similar kind of drawn-out ending to her marriage. With Hemingway, history was due to repeat itself. Pauline, however, had endured for years the suspicion of his feelings for and his possible affair with Jane Mason; she felt confident that she could outlast many of his romances. She counted on Hemingway's love of comfort and pleasure and his reliance on her protection—both financial and emotional—to enable him to carry on with his great single love, his writing.

What was different, this time, was the war—and Hemingway's chance to become a part of it. (His unrealistic participation in World War II would echo this behavior pattern.) Going out to catch a tuna or to Africa to shoot a lion were different from fighting in a conflict that meant the death of a beloved country. Part of Hemingway's rage against the Nationalists was a rage against himself for accepting the panacea of sport: the death of Henry Walden in "The Snows of Kilimanjaro" was one way to rid himself of that foolish and unimportant figure, the sportsman. He found it hard to believe that he had ever fallen for the sugar tit of the excitement of the wealthy. He would erase that figure, and go on to live and record more important life experiences. (That he killed off Francis Macomber, who similarly fell for the big game-hunting panacea, echoes his feeling about Henry Walden. In "The Short Happy Life of Francis Macomber," Hemingway was much more interested in the man's death than he was in whether or not his wife had intentionally shot him.)

In the confusion of health problems for both Hemingway and Pauline, of Pauline's coming to Europe and Martha's leaving Spain—and Hemingway's traveling hundreds of miles between lives and between loves—the sorting out of Hemingway's midlife crisis occurred. Through it all, his attention remained on the written word. As he had stated in *Green Hills of Africa*, writing—this "damned serious subject"—was "so difficult" because many factors combined to make the work possible: The writer must have talent, discipline, "an absolute conscience … to prevent faking." As he had said before, the hardest thing for any writer was "to survive and get his work done."[23]

Hemingway's son Gregory wrote years later about the slammed doors, the verbal clashes, the pain during the separation (which was never quite a separation) and the impending divorce. Although he was then a child, he told the story of Hemingway's way of "destroying people with words" and his writing a letter to Pauline titled "How Green Was My Valet" in which Pauline was the "millionairess" and he was the "valet."[24] The dissolution of the marriage continued more than two years longer. Pauline, Martha, the children, and Hemingway traveled in and out of Key West, New York, Spain, Cuba, and France. Through it all, Hemingway wrote out the Spanish Civil War: at least six short stories, dozens of dispatches, the play, and the novel *For Whom the Bell Tolls*. It was December of 1939 before the stubborn Pauline closed the Key West house and moved with the boys to New York.

14
War in Europe and at Home

After nearly four years of being lovers, Martha Gellhorn married Hemingway on November 21, 1940, in Cheyenne, Wyoming. The ceremony was performed by a justice of the peace, and friends gave the couple a celebratory dinner of roast moose.[1] Pauline's divorce was final a few weeks before that time, on November 4, after Hemingway had finally agreed in May to pay her $500 a month alimony. As he had during his break with Hadley and before his marriage to Pauline, Hemingway had worked diligently—almost obsessively—on his writing. Depleted by the emotional arguments that marked not only his relationship with Pauline but increasingly with Martha, he buried himself in the writing that was attempting to mine what he had learned and experienced from being in Spain. Again, it was as if his psyche ran from the personal turmoil, or perhaps the personal turmoil made possible his almost frantic immersion in the writing. Hemingway knew that he needed to score with the Spanish Civil War work, or else he might lose his preeminent place in modern American writing.

Alfred Kazin, reviewing Hemingway's *The Fifth Column and the First Forty-Nine Stories* in 1938 for *New York Herald Tribune Books*, gave his assessment of the reason Philip Rawlings fails as the play's protagonist: "He's Mr. Hemingway's Philip, sick in peace and sick in war, sick in the hearts of too many country-women. It's a good war, yes, but war is what the Hemingway soul has moved through for fourteen years, the war against sobriety and against twentieth century fate."[2] In contrast to what Kazin saw as Hemingway's personal angst (imaged in his drinking and changing sex partners), by going to Spain the writer had managed "to find a little heroism in Madrid."

Kazin's voice of warning—that Hemingway was not able to mature enough as writer to take on his times "in all their complexity" and that

131

8. Hemingway with Martha Gellhorn soon after their wedding, in Sun Valley, Idaho. Martha was the third Mrs. Hemingway.

he remained back in the war trauma of *In Our Time*—was rare in late 1930s reviews. Few critics were disappointed with the writer who was trying to speak truly about slaughter on an international scale. Acclaim for Hemingway's personal involvement in the Spanish Civil War, evidenced through his dispatches and stories for North American Newspaper Alliance (NANA), *Ken*, *Vogue*, and *New Masses* and his work on *The Spanish Earth*, helped to ameliorate what might well have been negative reactions to *To Have and Have Not*, and the Spanish war stories being published in both *Esquire* and *Cosmopolitan* ("The Butterfly and the Tank," "Night Before Battle," "Under the Ridge," "Nobody Ever Dies," and others, published during 1939).

As the shorter works appeared in print, Hemingway had started what would become one of his best novels. He began *For Whom the Bell Tolls* in February of 1939, and worked on it steadily, most of the time living in the Cuban house which Gellhorn had rented and improved. With only brief trips to Key West from Finca Vigia (Lookout Farm), Hemingway finished the novel in July of 1940. When *For Whom the Bell Tolls* appeared in October, a Book of the Month Club selection which sold out in advance of its publication date, Paramount pictures offered $100,000 (and a provision for each copy sold) for its movie rights a few weeks later.[3] With only a few exceptions, reviews of this novel were the best a Hemingway work had ever received: critics claimed that the Hemingway of *A Farewell to Arms* had returned—and was even better, now that his eye was trained on a larger system of world injustice. When in his writing about World War I, Hemingway's message had been that man must find a separate peace, as does Frederic Henry through his and Catherine's desertions, in this novel Robert Jordan insists on a greater notion of participation, self-sacrifice.

Called a "magnificent romance," "uplifting," and "his finest," the novel, according to John Chamberlain, "redeems a decade of futility"[4] during which time Hemingway was writing non-fiction. While there were detractors, usually critics on the left, claiming that Hemingway had not understood what was going on in Spain, the praise overwhelmed the criticism. If critics had been troubled by the personal characteristics of Dorothy Bridges in *The Fifth Column*, they gave up their autobiographical sleuthing when they read *For Whom the Bell Tolls*. They assigned Maria, brutalized and raped by the Fascists yet still welcoming to Jordan, to fantasy, and despite Hemingway's naming the tough Loyalist woman Pilar—which had to suggest Pauline—critics read that character as an almost ungendered survivor of the inhumane civil war.

In reading this novel, politics trumped the biographical. Hemingway's intention was political fairness, showing the travesties and brutalities of the Loyalists as well as the Nationalists. In fact, he had written early in 1940 to Perkins that he was not "A Catholic writer nor a party writer ... not even an American writer. Just a writer."[5] It was Perkins who gave Hemingway the kind of praise he most valued—comments about his craft. In August of 1940, Perkins wrote him about his "amazement" at the book's being so "strange and cunningly contrived"—and so completely effective.[6] As Perkins saw, the unity of *For Whom the Bell Tolls* was unusual, giving importance as it did to every event because of the book's narrative proportion. The novel also showed Hemingway drawing from all his shorter pieces about the war, though never directly and never in an imitative way. "Night Before Battle," for instance, describes a man's last few hours of life, but very differently than does Hemingway's depiction of Jordan's.

Robert Jordan remained the heart of the book for most critics. He was considered a typical Hemingway hero, giving his life so that others could escape. The improbable suggestion that Maria was carrying their child placed the novel in the oldest literary genre known—the epic. Jordan had found his grail in the Spanish conflict, and the embodiment of that religious pursuit was Maria and the fetus she might be carrying. Lionel Trilling wrote with his customary authority that the love between Jordan and Maria was typical of patterns in other of Hemingway's fictions, creating "a rather dull convention in which the men are all dominance and knowledge, the women all essential innocence and responsive passion; these relationships reach their full development almost at the moment of first meeting and are somehow completed as soon as begun."[7]

Far reaching in its implications for Hemingway's personal life, Trilling's comment may have described the way Hemingway had reacted to meeting Martha Gellhorn in Key West. Even as Pauline Pfeiffer had spent her decade of years as Mrs. Ernest Hemingway in creating comfort and sustenance for her writer husband, she was no more submissive or innocent than was Marty Gellhorn; having become resentful over the years about the Pfeiffers' financial resources, Hemingway no longer remembered what he might have considered Pauline's innocence. For Martha, 8 years his junior and so 12 years younger than Pauline, marrying anybody at all was a dramatic change of lifestyle. At ease in the world of powerful men, comfortable with many male reporters and correspondents, Martha thought of her male friends as her true ones.[8] One of her deep friendships was with the young Hungarian photographer, Robert Capa;

it was he who photographed the newlywed Hemingways for a *Life* magazine spread; also a friend of Hemingway's, Capa shared with both writers the joy in doing aesthetic work well. What Gellhorn thirsted after was a community of the talented. Pauline was content to expedite that community; she did not need to be a part of it.

One of the differences between Martha and Pauline that made reconciliation after arguments with Hemingway difficult was Martha's distaste for sex—at least for sex with him. Moorehead quoted Marty's comment to a friend that she had made love with Hemingway as little as possible during their months in Madrid. Her words were direct, her "whole memory of sex with Ernest is the invention of excuses and failing that, the hope it would soon be over."[9] Another difference is somewhat unexpected: although she had had no children herself, Marty seemed genuinely fond of all three of the Hemingway sons (rather than wishing them out of her territory, which was often Pauline's tactic). Each of the boys remembered Marty and her good sportsmanship about learning to do all the athletic things of the Hemingway family with affection.[10]

So far as Hemingway's relationship with Martha Gellhorn, it might be characterized as "wistful." More information accrues from his letters to her mother, Edna Gellhorn, than from those to Marty herself. Like his former mother-in-law Mary Pfeiffer, Edna Gellhorn became a kind of confidante to the troubled, older husband. In the autumn of 1940, for example, Hemingway wrote to Edna that he would like to dedicate *For Whom the Bell Tolls* to Martha but wonders whether he should add the phrase "If I Can Find Her" to the dedication. This is the letter in which he laments Marty's continual need for "adventure." He tells her mother that she plans to leave for Europe in the autumn of 1940, not wanting to become "a dull wife who just forms herself on me like Pauline and Hadley." He said in an aside, "I would argue that but I won't." About Marty's definition of "adventure," he asked Edna, "how can you tell someone that the most exciting adventures come in the head and in two people loving each other ... and not seem selfish saying it?"[11]

As she had with Spain, Martha had already made her plans to travel to China before the world saw clearly why the Pacific rim was filled with danger. As she recalled in her retrospective account of going to China (*Travels with Myself and Another*, naming Hemingway "U. C." for "Unwilling Companion"), soon after their marriage, Martha coerced him into traveling to China with her (by "wheedling until he sighed gloomily and gave in").[12] She described the rough and interminable crossing from Honolulu ("U. C. had a face of black hate") and the grim sightseeing they undertook, one trip a tour of Pearl Harbor, about which

Hemingway said that the popular World War I ploy was to get everyone in a single place "and get the whole lot wiped out,"[13] which happened ten months later. More characteristically, Hemingway talked and drank with people—he reveled in their stories, always looking for interesting experiences—while Martha went off scouring the territory for "real" news. Hemingway's line then, as Martha left, was "M. is going off to take the pulse of the nation."[14]

As Peter Moreira has recently shown, however, Hemingway was on the trip to help the U.S. spy on Chinese government activities. His convivial talking was with such key business and political figures as Carl Blum, U.S. Rubber executive; Major Charles Boxer, head of British intelligence in Hong Kong; Morris Cohen, expert on China and warlords; W. Longhorn Bond, aviation expert; Ramon Lavalle, Argentine diplomat; Rewi Alley, New Zealand industrialist; Emily Hahn, journalist; and others.[15] Moreira believes that the experiences Hemingway had in China intrigued him so much that once he had returned to Cuba, he "spent most of the next four years as a government operative."[16]

Loving all the strange Chinese food, and buying and setting off fireworks in each hotel room, Hemingway paced his trip through China. Yet when they found themselves in the midst of a cholera epidemic, Hemingway spent hours boiling the water and ensuring that Martha was as safe as she could possibly be.

The tenderness that her husband was capable of diminished as the marriage wore on: often separated, the couple had few weeks together that were not interrupted by visitors—her mother Edna, his sons, his Key West friends, even Grace Hall Hemingway. Just as Hemingway was disappointed when the dramatic version of *The Fifth Column* failed in production, so he was disappointed when *For Whom the Bell Tolls* did not receive the Pulitzer Prize for Fiction in 1941. Although rumor was that the novel would win the prize, the Pulitzer jury gave no award for fiction in 1941 and along the way called Hemingway's novel "vulgar, revolting and obscene."[17] To add to Hemingway's own feelings of weariness (and mortality), Scott Fitzgerald's death from heart failure in December of 1940 left a residue of fear behind. And of course, no one as acute politically as Hemingway could deny that World War II was about to begin.

China was just the first of Gellhorn's trips abroad. Most of those trips did not occur, however, until she had spent more than a year living with Hemingway in Cuba, traveling with him to New York, San Francisco, Washington, Key West, and Sun Valley. Until July of 1942, Martha refused all assignments from *Collier's*; then she traveled to Haiti, San Juan,

Puerto Rico, St. Thomas, St. Martin, and Surinam (Dutch Guiana) to do articles for *Collier's* about the way the possible presence of German submarines was affecting life in the Caribbean. Perhaps Gregory's retrospective assessment puts Martha's behavior in the best perspective. He wrote, "Marty never deserted him [Ernest]. She was driven from that house in Cuba, driven away by the return in greater force of papa's megalomania."[18] Megalomania took two forms—concern about his writing prowess, and his need to take an active part in the incipient war.

Soon after Hemingway and Martha were married, on December 28, 1940, they bought the Finca Vigia for $12,500. The way Hemingway felt about the Cuban house, and its setting for his runs with the *Pilar*, was deeply rooted: he loved Cuba and its waters, and its people. Happiest while living there with Marty, he did little writing; in fact, in 1942, he gave the job of writer to his young wife, withdrawing from what he called the competition. Gregory recounted hearing the arguments over Martha's writing, as when Hemingway taunted her, "So you don't think I can write anymore," and calling her "a conceited bitch."[19] One of their long-standing arguments concerned her publishing her 1941 collection of stories, *The Heart of Another*, as *Martha Gellhorn* rather than as (what Ernest had requested) *Martha Hemingway*.

The more militaristic side of Hemingway, developed during the China trip, took an unexpected route. After Pearl Harbor, and as early as spring, 1942, Hemingway had proposed to the American Embassy in Havana (Spruille Braden, the ambassador) his starting a secret intelligence network; with agreement from both Braden and the Cuban Prime Minister, Hemingway was to be funded at $500 a month. In May, 1942, he proposed turning the *Pilar* into a Q-boat in order to hunt German submarines. He had guns installed on the *Pilar* and equipped the boat with grenades; he occasionally took Patrick and Gregory out on his missions during the summer. Hiring a number of jai alai players, fishermen, waiters, a Catholic priest, and others to bring in reports and to help man the boat, Hemingway created what was known as "the Crook Factory,"[20] with headquarters at the small guest house of the Finca Vigia. Remembered for their hard drinking and long hours at sea, the members of the crew of the *Pilar* may have been motivated more by testosterone than by patriotism. In the recollections of Gregorio Fuentes, who captained the *Pilar* for many years, Hemingway would not drink from an opened bottle of liquor; so he "opened a new bottle every day. Gordon's Gin was his favorite."[21] Part of Martha's anger over the men and what she considered their senseless submarine hunting was that they used their occupation as an excuse to drink all day long—and at night at the Finca

Vigia. She recalled a number of unsavory types lurking behind the mango trees; sometimes an unshaven and sloppily dressed Ernest was among them.[22]

Hemingway had been invited to edit a collection of war fiction, so he immersed himself in von Clausewitz and other great military strategists. His introduction suggested that he numbered himself among the latter: he drew plentifully on autobiography ("The editor of this anthology, who took part and was wounded in the last war to end war, hates war and hates all the politicians whose mismanagement, gullibility, cupidity, selfishness and ambition brought on this present war and made it inevitable"[23]). Dedicating the book to his three sons, Hemingway felt that he had made a literary contribution to the war effort: he had no desire to go to Europe.

Martha, however, was ranting against the policy that women correspondents were not encouraged to cover the war. Frustrated with her life in Cuba, and with the "war effort" there, she was pleased when she could spend time with her ailing mother (who wrote to the Hemingways in 1942, "Be glad you two, and hug your happiness tight—it is the only treasure that nor time nor separation can take from you.")[24] It was clear to Hemingway that his wife was restive, even though she was working hard on a new novel, *Liana*, and he increasingly saw her independent behavior as a great contrast to that of his first wife. He had been thinking about Hadley a lot, first of all because their son Bumby enlisted in the Army late in December of his second year at Dartmouth, and second, because Hadley had written during the autumn of 1942 that she had found a trunk of their old letters. If he would like to have them, she would send them. Immersed in what became a nostalgic trip into his early successful writing, Hemingway valorized everything about the Paris years and his young love.[25]

During early 1943, both Hemingway and Martha spent most of their time at the Finca: Hemingway went on his submarine patrol until he called a halt to the Crook Factory in July. Critics suggest that Martha became pregnant during the spring, even though she professed to want no children; Hemingway was angry when she had an abortion.[26] Hemingway's almost unchecked drinking had also caused problems of abuse: Moorehead tells the story of his being too drunk to drive his Lincoln Continental. Yet when Martha took the wheel, he slapped her. Martha then slowly and deliberately drove the car into a tree, got out and walked home, leaving him to handle the wreck.[27] On another night, Hemingway drove the car home without taking Martha with him.[28]

When *Collier's* asked Marty to go to Europe as their war correspondent in the fall, she accepted. She invited Hemingway to accompany her, but he refused. Sailing from New York to Lisbon, she was jubilant: her letters to Hemingway were true love letters, as were his to her. Except for carping about finances, which Hemingway did consistently throughout their relationship, the tone of Marty's letters to him and his to Marty remained complacently stable. She knew, however, that his life consisted largely of drinking. She was hurt by the fact that he had planned to take the *Pilar* out for a three-month journey just as she was leaving for New York. The passive-aggressive model was in place, often for both the Hemingways.

Gellhorn's months in Europe brought her the first news of the Jewish persecutions (beginning in Poland) as well as real understanding of the power of Winston Churchill and the British, and information about the tragic fate of the Italian civilians. She was not the same woman she had been a year earlier. Yet when she returned to the Finca in March of 1944, Hemingway baited her continuously. When she suggested that she and Hemingway share the *Collier's* assignment, he instead wired *Collier's* that he would accept the full assignment: Gellhorn, then, was left without credentials. When Hemingway flew to Europe, slated to receive a hero's welcome in London, she could get no passage of any kind. Eventually she crossed the Atlantic as the only passenger on a freighter loaded with dynamite.[29]

During the months of her absence, Hemingway's letters to both Martha and her mother had remained calm, but his actions showed his brooding anger. Hemingway had realized that he could not stay at home any longer. (During December of 1943, he had written a plaintive letter to Hadley inviting her and Paul Mowrer to visit him at the Finca Vigia, describing his great loneliness.)[30] Early in 1944, he had written to Martha that "We have been away from each other too long" and telling her that he will close up the house, take care of everything, "go to N.Y., eat shit, get a journalism job, which hate worse than Joyce would, and will be over [to Europe]. Excuse bitterness."[31] And in March, 1944, planning to go to New York before going to England, Hemingway wrote angrily to Perkins that he had done nothing *he* wanted for more than two years. Martha, however, "does exactly what she wants to do as willfully as any spoiled child. And always for the noblest motives."[32]

A few days after Hemingway arrived in London, while staying at the Dorchester Hotel, he met Mary Welsh Monks, researcher-correspondent for *Time* magazine. According to Mary's memoirs, he asked her to lunch and then visited her and her roommate a few nights later, telling stories about Oak Park and, upon leaving, telling Mary he wanted to marry her. Assuming he was joking, she replied that he was "very premature."[33] The next week, he was in an auto accident, his knees and head badly cut (the latter requiring 57 stitches). He also had a concussion. Gellhorn heard of his accident and once she had reached London (from Liverpool), went quickly to St. George's Hospital to see him. Surrounded by friends and empty champagne bottles, Hemingway did not welcome her. Despite his physical condition, the drinking parties continued after he had returned to his hotel. Rude and offensive to Gellhorn in public, Hemingway was clearly separating from her. When he began taking Mary Welsh to dinner, his third wife understood that their marriage was over.[34]

15
The Fourth Mrs. Hemingway

For all Hemingway's self-definition as writer ("I loved to write very much and was never happier than when doing it,"[1] he told Perkins), after 1940, he spent great amounts of time worrying about alimony and income taxes, and staying ahead of his financial responsibilities. Keeping the Finca going cost $1000 a month, Pauline's alimony was $500 monthly, and he figured his income tax at something over 62 percent of his net. In May of 1943, for instance, he wrote to Perkins that he had "had to pay $160,000 to the government for writing *For Whom the Bell Tolls*."[2]

From the moment his divorce from Pauline was final, Hemingway seethed anger over her alimony. On August 26, 1941, he berated Perkins because Scribner's had not been paying the monthly $500; they had paid it in June but not July ("That kind of thing is hard on people and it isn't very businesslike ... involved me being delinquent in payments.")[3] Two years later, he called the payment "blood money," which Pauline had demanded, he said, to keep him from being able to write. Everyone knew, Hemingway wrote, that Pauline could just live on her family's wealth but such a style of living would not damage him. Pauline "has the cards stacked" so that Martha had "to keep working as a journalist."[4]

Triggered by both his animosity toward Pauline and the sad aftermath of Fitzgerald's death and impoverished estate, Hemingway in 1943 ranted about the problems of living with a crazy woman (in his case, Pauline; in Fitzgerald's, Zelda). No man could be mean to a woman if she were ill. As he wrote bluntly to Perkins, "A woman ruined Scott."[5] Then, instead of telling that woman to go to hell, he had to care for her during her malady. Men who leave women, Hemingway wrote, ought to simply shoot them because they make trouble forever.

Onto this layered hostility toward Pauline, for whom he also blamed his difficulties in seeing Patrick and Gregory, came Hemingway's pique that his marriage to Gellhorn was far from idyllic. Considering Martha selfish and opportunistic, Hemingway wrote often to Perkins about his unhappiness. There may have been other causes for his depression, however. His health was increasingly poor. Susan Beegel thinks Hemingway already suffered from the hemochromatosis that may have plagued him till his death. Known as the "iron storage disease," this ailment increases its effect as the patient ages. Often, heavy eaters and drinkers are diagnosed between thirty and forty; others, at later ages. Among possible symptoms are liver disease, impotence, sleeplessness, anxiety, diabetes, and high blood pressure.[6]

His mood in a January, 1944 letter to Martha suggests depression over his health, mentioning "bad head aches" and general malaise: "Take not the slightest interest in where am going to go and feel no lilt or excitement. Just feel like horse, old horse, good, sound, but old."[7] Hemingway no doubt attributed his lack of interest (which he mentions twice in the brief letter) to a mental state, but it might well have been physical. He closed the above sentence with the description that the old horse felt that he was "being saddled again to race over the jumps because of an unscrupulous owner." If Martha failed to see herself in that role, Hemingway continued the letter describing how happy he had been on the *Pilar*, planning to write new fiction about his experiences there. But now, if he must come to Europe to cover the war, that plan will be abandoned.

In Hemingway's anger over Pauline's alimony and Martha's absences, expressed in a bevy of letters—including those to Edna Gellhorn and Mary Pfeiffer, the two mothers-in-law—one may also read the effects of a quarter century of alcoholism. It is true that Hemingway seemed to have had an incredible capacity for liquor, but all such a characteristic finally meant was that he was damaging his body at a brisk pace. As he matured, he developed some personal traits that could be identified as alcoholic behavior. He was erratic and increasingly unpredictable. He liked to blame others for whatever happened to him. He also embellished his stories to a ridiculous degree: everything that happens to an alcoholic is hyperbolic (his or her life is of primary importance, sole importance).[8] Much of the alcoholic's expectation lies in the realm of fantasy. No event, no person, could possibly meet those expectations: consequently, the alcoholic is both chronically disappointed and angry.[9]

Many of those traits are evident in one of Hemingway's last letters to Edna Gellhorn. Writing late in 1944, ostensibly to find out where

Martha was, Hemingway told a tale of self-pitying blame: he had been in the hospital with a concussion, he said, and he and the doctor had waited two hours for Martha to come and be given instructions about his care. She never came. All the time he was married to Martha, Hemingway assured her mother, everyone worked for her, doing her typing, taking care of her. But she was unkind, and he saw now that she was just "a bad joke played on me in … 1936," a joke that cost him 500 dollars a month for life and made him give up his children. Rather than Marty's being his "true love and holy grail all mixed together," he saw now that she was "a spoiled, selfish girl with a thyroid deficiency."[10]

Hemingway did more than complain to Martha's mother in this letter; he also told her that his flying missions in the European war during the summer had kept him alive. His head hurt intolerably, but he flew with the R. A. F.—in limited ways—until about the middle of July. He had also been present for the D-Day invasion of June 2, but then had been returned to base on the transport *Dix*.[11] There he began covering the 22nd Infantry Regiment, where he came to know and admire Buck Lanham, its commander. Hemingway traveled with the infantry through Normandy—taking Villebaudon and St. Pois—although never in the kind of heroic action he described in letters to Mary Welsh. In August, they reached Rambouillet (where a number of the French turned themselves over to Hemingway, thinking him to be the leader of the force) and by August 24, were at the outskirts of Paris.[12]

Intermittently serving with Lanham, Hemingway saw Mary Welsh at least once during the French campaign and much more when he was in Paris. Ironically, Martha was in Paris during those weeks, taking care to stay far away from her spouse.[13] He also wrote to Patrick (once on September 15, 1944, and again on November 19, from the Hürtgen Forest) that he was through with Marty because of what he called her "Prima-Donna-ism." "I made a very great mistake on her—or else she changed very much." Ruefully, he added, "I hate to lose anyone who can look so lovely and who we taught to shoot and write so well."[14] Concluding that the marriage was definitely over, Hemingway saw Gellhorn in November—when he refused to discuss divorce—but then in December when he visited her at the Dorchester in London while she was ill with flu, he agreed to that action.[15] By that time, his missives that were truly love letters had won over Mary Welsh Monks. She planned to divorce her Australian husband as soon as she could. In their intimate moments in Paris, however, Hemingway had already shown her his capacity for both insulting verbal behavior and actual physical abuse.[16] Mary seemed to think "taking it," which was a tactic Martha Gellhorn had never accepted, was the way to win the important American novelist. According to Mary's memoirs, their primary arguments were about her work—when she should leave the European front and live with Hemingway in Cuba.[17]

Hemingway was with Buck Lanham and the 22nd Infantry for the last of the major battles of the European sector. From November 16 through December 3, 1944, going up against the German artillery of the Siegfried Line in the Hürtgen Forest campaign, the unit experienced 2678 casualties. Twelve of the dead were officers; hundreds of men were missing. For both Bill Walton and Hemingway, as correspondents, as well as all the military forces, it was a tragic eighteen days.[18] To add to this sorrow, word came that Bumby was Missing in Action. A few months later, Hemingway learned (through Mary's efforts) that his oldest son had been wounded and interrogated (luckily by the boyfriend of the Austrian nurse who had cared for him nineteen years earlier in Schruns) and then hospitalized before being sent to a prisoner of war camp near Hammelburg. Later Bumby was moved to Stalag Luft III in Nuremberg.[19]

Wrapped up completely in the events of the war, Hemingway wrote his faithful letters to Mary, as if their future were assured. Except for the brief paragraphs in his letters to Patrick, Hemingway seemed to feel no need to communicate with any of his family or friends about the demise of his third marriage. Martha, quietly, was accepting that demise with little but distaste. She continued covering the European sector, doing some of the best reporting U.S. readers would see. She had an impassioned romance with James Gavin of the U.S. military, but when he slept with actress Marlene Dietrich, she ended that relationship.[20] With her friend Virginia Cowles, she wrote the play, *Love Goes to Press*, which was a semi-successful comedy about war correspondents and made use of some names and characters from Hemingway's *The Fifth Column*. It was produced on Broadway in 1945. As that year continued, Gellhorn admitted missing the Cuba house, the three Hemingway boys, and Hemingway's companionship. She wondered what was wrong with her that she was destined to be alone. But then, after being among the first press to visit both Buchenwald and Dachau, she came to terms with the German evil in a way she had not previously.

In the summer of 1945, Hemingway began divorce proceedings, charging Martha with desertion. Her August 13, 1945 letter to him asked that he return all her family possessions—linens, silver, and china—and her papers, her clothes, and her gun. She said that she could not use her furniture, or at least not much of it, but when Mary had decided what she wanted to get rid of, Hemingway should let Edna Gellhorn know and she would make arrangements. She admitted missing the boys ("It is a sorrow not to see Bumbi, not to see Mousie's work, not to hear Gigi"), and she wished great success for him in his continued career, saying "the finca will one day become a national monument and be tended by a grateful and admiring government."[21] Gracefully phrased, her wishes for his happy marriage to Mary stressed her hope that "this marriage is everything you have been looking for and everything you needed." She had begun the letter with what appeared to be a comic innuendo about finances, saying "My dear Bug, I may not have been the best wife you ever had, but at any rate I am surely the least expensive don't you think? That's some virtue."[22] The divorce was final on December 21, 1945, but Gellhorn later complained that she had not been sent any possessions for months after that date—and some of her property she never saw again.

Gellhorn lived through 1945 in a manner characteristic of a successful war correspondent, but Hemingway's year was marked by troubles both physical and geographical. Beginning in December of 1944, his series of colds turned into pneumonia, and he frequently coughed up blood. But despite his clear illness, he and Bill Walton flew to Luxembourg (the Germans had launched a successful counterattack); there Buck Lanham's physician put Hemingway to bed with sulfa pills. Once he returned to Paris, Hemingway waited for Mary's arrival from London. She had filed for her divorce in January, but Noel Monks was causing problems. It was in February, 1945, that Hemingway used one of the pair of German machine pistols that Lanham had brought him as a gift to blast away at Monks' photo. After Lanham stopped him from shooting in the room where everyone stood, Hemingway took the photo into the bathroom, where the bullets destroyed not only the photo but the toilet bowl.[23] Lanham was thoroughly disgusted with this dangerous act; Mary almost ended the relationship. Little bothered Hemingway, however, who spent the next few weeks in Paris setting up both Lanham and Bill Walton with Marlene Dietrich (and showing off the petite Mary as the new Mrs. Hemingway).[24] Returning to New York on a military bomber, Hemingway shopped for Patrick and Gregory and then took the boys to Cuba for their spring break. It was after they had left that Hemingway and Pauline traded incivilities by phone. In her March 17, 1945, letter, Pauline reminded him that there was no need to fight over Patrick and Gregory. Hemingway and she needed instead to "respect" each other. "After all," she concluded, "you and I have trusted each other pretty thoroughly for some ten years."[25]

During the spring of 1945, Hemingway experienced his blackest depression, complaining to his friend Jose Luis Herrara about his headaches, his inability to read or concentrate, and other physical ailments. Herrara took him under his care. He explained that two major concussions, virtually uncared for, had done serious damage—damage which was not ameliorated by quantities of alcohol. A subdural hematoma needed rest, and Hemingway's drinking had exacerbated conditions that had already been serious.[26]

In the midst of his new healthy regime, trying hard to put off drinking until lunch, Hemingway received a letter from Marcelline written on April 7, 1945. She told him that Windemere, the Michigan cottage his mother had given him after he established the trust, had been advertised for sale for unpaid taxes from 1942, 43, and 44. Marcelline, with his mother, would pay what was owed.[27] Feeling patronized, Hemingway remained angry. Then, working with a lawn crew and a household staff and spending close to $3000, Hemingway readied the Finca for Mary's arrival. She came on May 2,[28] along with the news that Bumby had been released and would be coming to Cuba for his recuperation. All three of the Hemingway sons arrived in early June. By that time, Mary was feeling more relaxed about what appeared to be her role. As she wrote,

> Ernest and the Finca Vigia and Cuba Bella presented me a variety of challenges: a new language, a new climate, a world of blossoms on trees, vines, shrubs and stalks I didn't know, a large staff and so a new manner of living, new diversions requiring new skills—fishing and shooting—a one-leader boss of operations instead of the complex hierarchy of Time Inc., a new focus of interest and activity. No office.[29]

Once the three Hemingway boys arrived, Mary realized she also had to provide food—a lot of it. In her words, "Ramon, the Chinese cook, and I were developing our private esoteric language, he with his Chinese accent, I substituting *l* for *r* in my babytalk Spanish, words without sentences."[30] Gregory remembered that Hemingway had promised his sons they would like Mary because she was "truly beautiful." But it was the fact that she "brought order to the domestic chaos that Marty had left" that impressed him most.[31]

Her good-humored response to her new life and its new challenges (Mary had never had children) was blunted somewhat on June 20, when Hemingway drove her to the airport in the rain. (Mary was going to Chicago to expedite her divorce proceedings, since that was her permanent U.S. address.) Taking a shortcut to the Havana airport, Hemingway

9. Mary Welsh Monks on her way to becoming the fourth Mrs. Hemingway.

topped a rise and when the car skidded, headed for a high bank beside the road. Mary went through the windshield, and Ernest's forehead crashed into the rearview mirror, while his ribs met the wheel. Because the plastic surgeon was away, Mary had to wait several days for the surgery that would close the myriad cuts and give her face some chance of normalcy. When the surgery was completed and the physician removed the stitches, he told her she was lucky that her face hadn't been paralyzed; fragments of glass had missed a crucial nerve by millimeters.[32]

The accident and the very painful recovery, coupled with the anxiety of making a home in Cuba for Hemingway and his three sons, made Mary re-think her situation. Had she been able to read the correspondence between Martha Gellhorn and Hemingway, she might have made a different decision. Throughout their years together, Hemingway wrote many supportive and loving letters, but the letters of complaint and self pity were also frequent, and the complaints were not always about

Martha's being absent—they were often about money, who was to pay the household staff, why she made so little money, and so on. Given the high expenditures for liquor and entertaining that the household faced, Hemingway's stinginess about paying the gardeners was surely a warning sign of disproportionate anxiety.[33]

Hemingway was a good nurse, so by August 31, when Mary flew to Chicago to expedite her divorce, she was confident she would marry Hemingway. From Cuba, where he needed to maintain a six-months residency for his own divorce (charging Martha with desertion), he wrote impeccable, poignant letters. Several described the ways he and "Small Friend" were alike—modest, Midwestern, well-rooted in places where their grandparents had lived and died. Hemingway commented too that he was writing again (parts of what would become *Islands in the Stream*) and that he and Mary were alike in that they had previously made "exotic" marriages. Now they would rectify that error.[34] When Mary returned, Hemingway celebrated—and he also celebrated the sale of two stories to Hollywood: "The Killers" brought $37,500 and "The Short Happy Life of Francis Macomber," $75,000.[35] Unproductive as his attempts at writing had been since he returned from the war, Hemingway relished such proof of the value of his earlier work.

Mary was learning to shoot (pigeons), to fish, and to deal with Hemingway's macho Cuban friends. Hemingway was writing sometimes inchoate pages toward what would become *The Garden of Eden*. Sons, guests, military acquaintances—all came and stayed over the winter. As the wedding date of March 14, 1946, neared, Mary took a trip to Miami to stay with friends, saying she needed to buy suitable clothes but really considering again whether or not to marry. Sensing her reluctance, Hemingway sent her flowers and loving letters and cables. Part of the Cuban ceremony was a meeting with lawyers to settle the business of property; then came the vows. Later, the two had a violent argument—a "small, furious earthquake of incrimination"—which led to Mary's getting her luggage out of their closet after Hemingway went to sleep.[36] Once again, Hemingway's good humor the next morning put most of Mary's trepidation to rest. As Bernice Kert phrased it, "In the afternoon she loved him, in the evening he was a boor."[37]

During the following fifteen years, the situation only worsened.

16
From Cuba to Italy

Hemingway had never disguised his deep desire to have a daughter. When Mary missed a period in July, even though she was 38, she was as happy as he (Hemingway wrote several of his friends about the very early stage of pregnancy). The fact that they might soon be tied down with an infant made him more eager to take the long trip to Sun Valley (which Mary and he had missed the summer before while they recovered from their crash injuries), so in early August, the Hemingways began the drive across the States. They got only as far as Casper, Wyoming, before the ectopic pregnancy nearly took Mary's life the night of August 18. The very heavy internal bleeding and her collapsed veins had caused the surgeon to tell Hemingway that, unconscious for some time, she was dying; they could not operate. In his letter to Buck Lanham, Hemingway recounted that he got the assistant "to cut for a vein and got plasma going"[1] and finally, Mary had recovered enough for surgery.

After three weeks, much of it in an oxygen tent, Mary with an attentive Hemingway beside her joined the sons in Ketchum, Idaho, a place she later called "a sentimentalist's dream of the Old West."[2] Driving back home after the weeks of hunting, they planned to rendezvous in New Orleans for Thanksgiving, bringing Mary's parents down so that they could meet Hemingway. Charming to the modest couple, he arranged for a day of horse racing and gave the winnings to Mary's mother Adeline. Then after the traditional meal, he and Tom Welsh traded Chippewa stories and amateur naturalist observations about the North Country, the Minnesota and Michigan lands they both knew well.[3]

Mary's confidence that she could handle her sometimes erratic husband grew in part from her childhood. As an only child in Minnesota, she had done everything there was to be done in the family's not-always-profitable

149

lumbering business. Tom Welsh had homesteaded near Bemidji but soon saw the promise in lumbering, so he moved the family to Walker; Mary spent summers on board their boat *Northland*, usually in the pilot house with her father (a man known for his quick temper). On Leech Lake, home of the Chippewas, the *Northland* sometimes carried a crew of 25 men, ransacking the 640 miles of the lake's shoreline for lumber. Mary's life of practicing piano, reading, going to church, and spending an unusual amount of time as her father's "son" led her to become quietly confident. She studied journalism for two years at Northwestern University, devouring the paintings at Chicago's Art Institute. In the summer after her sophomore year, however, she traveled to Boston with her roommate and ended up editor of the "puny" *American Florist*. She did not return to college.[4] Working her way to England, she saw World War II develop. From the midst of the London bureau of *Time, Life*, and *Fortune*, she learned the importance of the media. It was in London, at the Dorchester Hotel, that she met Hemingway.

During Christmas of 1946, Mary and Hemingway were alone, but the three sons and friends arrived soon after; Patrick planned to stay for the term, studying and taking his College Boards. With Mary involved in designing a 40-foot tower which was to house cats, storage areas, her sun deck, and Hemingway's study, life moved peacefully on until mid-April. When word came that her father had collapsed and was in need of surgery, Mary left for Chicago. Simultaneously, Patrick became delusional. (The causes of his long "breakdown" were sometimes thought to be his bumping his head in a minor car accident, or being anxious about taking the College Boards, or harboring some virus.) Tied into his bed, he needed constant supervision. Ernest sat with him as long as he could day and night. After a few days, Pauline came from Key West, writing immediately to Mary as if in apology. Patrick's condition was very serious. It was a month before he could speak. Hemingway told a friend that during the months of his illness, Patrick had gone from 160 pounds to 98 pounds. His convalescence, like his recovery, was lengthy.[5]

When Mary returned from Chicago in mid-May, Pauline and she became friends. Then, no sooner had Pauline returned to Key West than Mary caught undulant fever and ran temperatures up to 105 for days. As she recovered, Pauline invited her to Key West. Patrick's constant care was wearing everyone down though Hemingway did make it to Havana to accept the Bronze star for his meritorious service as a war correspondent.[6] In the next month, as Patrick improved, Hemingway's blood pressure was found to be 215 over 125, so the house began a health regime of exercise and comparatively little drinking.[7] Out west for the autumn,

Hemingway was told he could not hunt deer. Doctors thought that the climbing would be too dangerous for him in this condition.

As the Hemingway family survived unusual illnesses together, Hemingway knew deep grief when Max Perkins died suddenly from pneumonia, and even more grief when Katy Smith Dos Passos was decapitated in an accident; the car had been driven by her husband. Hemingway knew disappointment when the deal for $300,000 he had expected from the sale of four short stories fell through because Mark Hellinger died. Hemingway had been working, somewhat dispiritedly, on several projects, but Patrick's illness had completely changed his priorities. It had also depleted his energy. Enroute to Sun Valley in later fall, he visited Marcelline and the Hemingway family cottage in Michigan while Mary and Pauline remained with Patrick in Cuba. Mary arrived in Idaho in October, and they had a successful autumn (Hemingway borrowed $12,000 from Charles Scribner to get ready for the year's taxes; he knew it was financially imperative that he finish some fiction).[8]

Driving back to Cuba in January, Hemingway and Mary spent most of the year enjoying the Finca, although Hemingway claimed he missed the household noises when he tried to write in the tower. Everyone remained worried about Patrick, who had grown even more insistent that he be accepted at Harvard. As Pauline wrote to Hemingway in January, 1948, the specialist who was caring for Patrick thought "the memory lapses and the bad spelling" would correct themselves. What he saw as positive was that Patrick was "cheerful and interested in things."[9]

Hemingway, however, worried a great deal about Patrick, as well as about his own writing. He was helpful to Malcolm Cowley, who spent several weeks in Cuba working up a story for *Life*, but in June he declined an invitation to become a member of the American Academy of Arts and Letters. That same month, *Cosmopolitan* sent the young staffer A. E. Hotchner to Havana to persuade Hemingway to write a literary essay for them and, partly because of Perkins' death, Hemingway began confiding in Hotchner, who would eventually become a kind of informal agent for him.[10]

During the summer of 1948, the family took several cruises on the *Delicias*, one in celebration of Patrick's entering Harvard in the fall. Then Hemingway, after celebrating his forty ninth birthday, decided to return to Italy—in part to please Mary, who had learned so well to live with not only Hemingway but his three sons and at least one former wife, and in part because fall hunting in Sun Valley seemed less exciting than it had been. On the *Jaqiello*, the Hemingways sailed from Havana and docked at Genoa. Although they had not chartered the Hungarian-captained yacht, there were so few other passengers that Mary remembered the great privacy.[11] Then they hired a car and driver and headed for Stresa on Lake Maggiore and then on to both Como and Bergamo. The beauty of the countryside was enhanced by the fact that Ernest Hemingway was truly famous in Italy.

They had not planned to be gone from Cuba for eight months, but the exhilaration of being in such a welcoming country, and being able to live as well as they wanted for comparatively little cost, drew them through the winter and into the spring. In October, when they had found the Cortina d'Ampezzo, they rented the Villa Aprile for a stay to begin on December 15. Hemingway's memories of the long European ski season lay at the heart of his nostalgia for his expatriate years. The magic center of their autumn, however, was Venice, where they stayed at the Gritte Palace Hotel. Presented with a scroll making him Cavaliere de Gran Croce at Merito in the Knights of Malta, Hemingway felt in command of the country. He drove out to see Fossalta, the site of his World War I wounding; then, writing seriously, he moved to Torcello Island, north of Venice in the lagoon.[12] Sometimes Mary was there. At other times she traveled with friends, once meeting art critic Bernard Berenson. Impressed with that acquaintance, and remembering that Martha Gellhorn had been close to Berenson, Hemingway began writing to the venerable man on questions both aesthetic and sexual. The correspondence grew with increasing frequency—particularly during 1952 and 1953.[13]

In early December of 1948, at a hunt attended by some of Italy's finest families, Hemingway met Adriana Ivancich. Beginning what was to be his rhetoric of courtship whenever he could be near the beautiful dark-eyed eighteen-year old, Hemingway was soon professing his love for her. (As Hemingway's letters to Adriana from the States during the following year, 1950, showed, his voice with her was arch in its courtliness, fervently repetitious in its professions of love ["I do not, and cannot, ever love anyone as I love you"][14]; claiming that he thought of her every minute, he devised a system of signatures to prove that he and Adriana were the same person: "A. E. Hemingstein-Ivancich" or "A. Ivancich"— with the salutation to Adriana of "Hemingstein."[15])

Mary, traveling with Ernest back in Cortina both before and after Christmas, referred to Adriana and her friend Giovanni as their "constant" companions. There were other young women: those Mary called "his [Ernest's] vestal virgins."[16] But the convivial period was brief. On January 20, Mary broke her right ankle skiing and was in a cast until March.

In February Hemingway took to bed with a chest cold for two weeks and then developed erysipelas in his eye. Because his doctor feared the virus would spread to his brain, he was hospitalized in Padua. The winter of skiing dwindled into spring and it was late March before the Hemingways returned to Venice. There they met Gianfranco Ivancich, Adriana's brother, who had taken a position in Cuba and was moving there.[17]

In April, Hemingway began writing a long story of duck hunting in Europe, the genesis for the novel that would be published late in 1950 as *Across the River and Into the Trees*. On April 30, the Hemingways sailed from Genoa back to Havana, and their friends began visiting them at the Finca once again. In June, Buck Lanham went with Hemingway and Gregory to fish the Bahamas. Gregory's sudden illness led to their returning to Key West for an emergency appendectomy (of the boys, it had been Gregory—Gigi—who had fought sea sickness throughout his life).[18] As Hemingway had with a family cruise before Patrick started college at Harvard, he had planned this celebratory time with his youngest son before he entered St. John's College that fall.

On June 25, in Paris, Bumby married Byra (Puck) Whitlock, and then they moved to Berlin: Bumby had re-enlisted. In Cuba, Hemingway was working hard on the love story in *Across the River and Into the Trees*, more intent on creating the beautifully innocent Renata than on developing plot. The Hemingways were returning to Europe in the late autumn. Before they left Cuba, Hemingway took a long fishing trip while Mary visited her parents in Chicago—and bought the full length, natural ranch mink coat that Hemingway railed about. In a fragmentary manuscript titled "The Mink Jacket," Hemingway wrote about a nightmare, about how "niggardly" he had become—saying he had given up pigeon shooting, turned off lights, and ate just a sandwich for lunch. Then he segued to an argument about his failure to give his wife a "decent Christmas" present (she had wanted a mink coat; he had given her a Polaroid land camera and a bird book). The following pages recount his father's suicide "for debt" and draw scenes from his hardy boyhood—he and his father in the snowy world, his father rubbing snow on his frost bitten ears.[19]

In mid-November, the Hemingways flew to New York, where Lillian Ross interviewed Hemingway for her *New Yorker* profile. They had dinner with Marlene Dietrich, Charles Scribner, Hotchner, and others, and then sailed to Paris on the *Ile de France*. Working in the mornings in his suite at the Ritz, Hemingway finished *Across the River and Into the Trees*. In the afternoons they went to the racetrack. With Hotchner, recently arrived to take the novel back to *Cosmopolitan* for the serialization he had arranged (the fee to Hemingway was $85,000), they drove with Peter and Jige Viertel to the south of France, the five of them in their rented Packard, Hemingway in the front passenger seat serving as tour guide. They saw Saulieu, Avignon, Aigues-Mortes, Aix-en-Provence, and the Riviera, and went from Nice back to Paris by train.[20] (In Hemingway's increasingly candid letters to Hotchner, he described Mary's incessant scolding about his flirtation with Jige.)[21]

Spending time in Venice early in 1950, the Hemingways repeated the winter of 1949. Adriana and other worshipful Italian women surrounded Papa. The Hemingways went back to Cortina to ski in February, and again Mary broke an ankle—this time her left. Assessing how the right ankle had healed, the orthopedic surgeon rebroke that ankle in order to better set it. It was mid-March before Mary was out of casts and could return to Venice. There, seeing the great affection that had developed between Adriana and Ernest, she packed for their return to the States—but Hemingway would not return to Cuba until she invited Adriana and her mother to visit them at the Finca.[22] Mary had no choice but to make the invitation, graciously. It was accepted.

Back in New York after crossing on the *Ile de France*, the Hemingways spent some time at the Sherry-Netherlands, surrounded by Lillian Ross, Hotchner, Marlene Dietrich, and others. Patrick came to town with his fiancé Henrietta Broyles from Baltimore, asking for his father's blessing. Mary, however, spent one of those days alone being tested and consoled by her gynecologist. After undergoing a "painful test" to discover that her remaining fallopian tube was so "occluded" that she would never conceive, she returned to the hotel suite filled with partying people. The only hope was surgery, and the specialist could not promise success even with that process. As Mary wrote in *How It Was*, "I kept my grief to myself." When people finally left, she talked the matter over with Hemingway, who urged her not to have the surgery—and they did not discuss their situation again.[23]

In her account of this in her memoir, Mary used a fast-paced, objective style. She began the poignant section about her visit to the doctor's office—alone—with the phrase, "Hoping to begin the production of a baby." Her account of the aftermath of this knowledge and their return to the Finca—where Hemingway wrote to Adriana constantly—took only a few pages. (His first letter to Adriana was dated April 10, 1950. He was living in expectation of Adriana and her mother's visit. He clearly had stopped thinking of Mary, and his relationship with Mary, in any constructive way.) As Mary told the story of her decision to leave

Hemingway, when her old friend Bea Guck arrived in late April, Hemingway busied himself with fishing—avoiding the women as much as possible. One day he invited Mary and Bea to have lunch on the *Pilar*, but when they arrived, he was gone. When he did come back, he was accompanied by one of his fishing friends, who brought along his Cuban prostitute. After Bea left, Mary composed a long, and direct, letter to Hemingway, telling him the marriage was over. She emphasized his "insolence and arrogance," his being "increasingly unthinking of my feelings"—and "undisciplined" in his own living. She reminisced about the way they had loved each other in 1944 and told him that she had understood that so long as he could write, he would be happy and secure in the relationship. She had maintained his residence, she had stabilized his life—yet "Both privately and in public you have insulted me and my dignity as a human being." Worse, Hemingway had never showed any remorse for his behavior. As a result, she was ending the marriage.[24]

Mary closed the letter by saying she would stay on a while, continuing to run the Finca. The reader must interpolate context for her willingness to stay: was Hemingway's support of her parents' modest retirement a factor? Was her own need to find work a consideration (she wrote to Charlie Scribner in October that she would need a job and hoped he would help her find one)? Her husband's reaction to her ultimatum as described in Mary's cryptic autobiography was far from compelling: Hemingway made no apology, and he showed no remorse. He appeared in her bedroom early the next morning and said only, "Stick with me, kitten. I hope you will decide to stick with me."[25]

In *How It Was*, Mary never explained why she decided to stay. She noted that Hemingway gave her carte blanche to make the improvements she had wanted for the Finca, and he designed some fishing tournaments and other activities he thought she would like. She closed the chapter by describing their cat population—how it grew so large, and who the chief cats were—and by mentioning that she did try to get control of their heavy expenditures. Keeping a journal for a six-week period, she realized she had captured only about half of the costs of the Finca. Of course, the *Pilar* was three times as costly to maintain as the house, and, as she noted wryly, "I never knew how high my husband's monthly bills ran at the Floridita, or how much he gave away to its little squad of hard-luck hangers on."[26]

One of the most dramatic of the summer events may have been a determinant in Mary's staying. The couple took several fishing trips in early summer, and it was on June 12, 1950, that Hemingway instructed Scribner that he was to dedicate *Across the River and Into the Trees*

"To Mary with love" (no other dedication of his career was made with "love").[27] The second fishing trip on July 1 may have been the decisive one. It was heavy weather and Mary and Hemingway, with Gregorio and Roberto, had hardly set out when Hemingway fell hard against the large clamps that held the gaffs in place. The rush of arterial blood from the deep scalp wound (his head was cut to the bone) required pressure bandages and a quick return to shore. To Hotchner, Hemingway wrote, "If Roberto hadn't been there I probably would have bled out."[28] In Mary's account, the sheer quantity of the bright red blood was frightening. No doubt she continued to see through his bravado to the frailties in Hemingway's psyche. It was hard to miss his pattern of continuing, serious physical injuries.[29]

Another contretemps for the Hemingway family was the occasion of Patrick's marriage to Henrietta. In his first April letter to Adriana, Hemingway had said that he would not attend the ceremony ("I will [not] go to any weddings at which you are not present").[30] In Pauline's scolding undated missive to him, she said "They [the sons] have had to take *four* of yours, and I think they have been damn cooperative and well mannered about it. What if you DON'T like them. You can act as though you do." Earlier in the letter she had said that *he* was the one who liked "money and titles." She also had written to Patrick's doctor about whether or not Henrietta's family should be told about Patrick's previous illness.[31] Giving his family less and less of his attention, by late summer, Hemingway had moved into a quasi-fantasy world: waiting for Adriana to visit Cuba, waiting for the reviews of *Across the River and Into the Trees* (for which Adriana had designed the book jacket, as she had for two of his magazine publications). He was sure this was his best book to date. Posturing to everyone in person or by mail, Hemingway was setting himself up for the hard fall as the truly bad reviews came in. (Such adjectives as "dreadful," "without feeling," "dull," full of "silly writing," "dreamlike," "sad, nostalgic, autumnal," "egregiously bad," and "parodic" were plentiful.)

There were, of course, some good reviews. The best of those took into consideration the writer's oeuvre, and emphasized the strength of the descriptions of war and of the aging old soldier. But many of the reviews also described the wide division between reviews, as if to say the autobiographical elements (the writer aging along with the colonel) ameliorated some of the long stretches of narrative plateau while the characters talked. None of this response made Hemingway happy. Mary left to help her parents move from Chicago to Gulfport, Mississippi. Hemingway wrote to her about his bad cramps and a blood clot in his right leg, a condition worrisome enough that his doctor took him off all medications.[32] Then in one of Louella Parsons' gossip columns, she broke the story that the Hemingways were divorcing. Supposedly, Ernest was in love with an Italian countess. Quickly writing to Mary and phoning her father, Hemingway denied that any of the Parsons' column was true.[33]

A great many angers surfaced in the late summer of 1950. Hemingway wrote to Gigi, for example, that his father was never "the little poor boy" who stole the silver from the "wonderful rich family" (the Pfeiffers). Whereas Uncle Gus did buy the Key West house for $12,000, he had spent $60,000 improving it. Since his separation from "Mother"(Pauline) he has paid her "some 66,000 dollars."[34] To Charles Scribner, Hemingway complained that his publisher was absent—and silent—when *Across the River* was taking its beating.[35]

Even after Adriana and her mother arrived in Cuba on October 18, Hemingway erupted in anger at Mary. Her clothes were wrong, she was "sabotaging" him with Adriana; then he called her a "hangman" and threw wine in her face. Refusing to eat, he put his full dinner plate on the floor for the cats. He threw a heavy Venetian ashtray on to the tile floor, shattering it, as he did her typewriter.[36] After weeks of this behavior, Mary did not write to him. Instead, she confronted him in his bedroom. Once more she told him she would stay and do the best she could. She would stay until he—when sober—asked her to leave. As she wrote in *How It Was*, "He never asked me to leave."[37]

17
Old Men, Prizes, and Reports of Hemingway's Death

In January, 1951, Hemingway began writing *The Old Man and The Sea*. Gregory Hemingway, I think rightly, attributed his father's returning pristine writing ability to what he identified as his great love for Adriana. Because Gregory believed that it had been years since Hemingway had had "the old effortless elemental naturalness," he saw that the "platonic affair" with Adriana had brought his father back to creative life.[1]

Adriana and her mother Dora had lived in the guest house of the Finca since their arrival in October, 1950. After nearly two months, her mother could no longer ignore the gossip that the character of Renata in *Across the River* was based on her daughter. She moved Adriana out of the Finca guest house and into a Havana hotel. In February, Mary Hemingway took Dora and Adriana on a tour of Florida; then the mother and daughter took a train to New York. Hemingway wrote to Hotchner, sending him a substantial amount of money to take Adriana out to clubs and plays while she was in New York. Not wanting to be linked with her, Hemingway repeated to Hotch that he and Adriana were "business partners. Bookmakers."[2] Then the Ivanciches sailed back to Italy, arriving home on February 23, 1951. Hemingway continued to write long letters, but the correspondence suggests that Adriana did not answer so often as she had previously. (According to his correspondence in the Hemingway Archive at the John F. Kennedy Library, Hemingway continued to write to Adriana until 1955.)

Supplementing Gregory's analysis, Hemingway knew that the careful fluidity he had achieved in what would be *The Old Man and the Sea* (the work he kept calling "Part 4" of a larger manuscript) was also the result of his decades of practicing his craft. He wrote to Charlie Scribner that the novel was "prose that I have been working for all my life." It "should read easily and simply and seem short and yet have all the dimensions of the visible world and the world of a man's spirit."[3] William Faulkner's review of *The Old Man and the Sea* echoed those words, saying that the novella was Hemingway's "best," that in it he had had found "a God, a Creator," and that he had been able to draw the characters with both pity and love.[4]

When Hemingway finished drafting the novella in the remarkably short time of eight weeks, he put the manuscript in his bank vault and began reworking the much longer text that would become *Islands in the Stream*. Both works describe the joys of living on the water; both foreground loving relationships between men and their sons. In *The Old Man and the Sea*, Santiago loves—and loves to fish with—the boy Manolin, although they are not biologically related. Happy with his existence, comfortable with his relationships with his sons, in 1951, Hemingway did not understand that the publication of this novella was going to change his life.

The year 1951, in fact, seemed anything but miraculous. On June 28, Hemingway's mother died in a Memphis hospital; she had not known her children for many months.[5] During the summer, Hemingway was angry about requests from such literary critics and would-be biographers as Charles Fenton, Carlos Baker, Philip Young, Harry Burns, and others. He spent his birthday alone on the *Pilar* while Mary vacationed for the month of July on the mainland. Then on September 30, Pauline wired Hemingway stating that Gregory was in trouble in Los Angeles. She was in San Francisco and would go down to see what the situation was, and would call him.[6]

She called Hemingway at midnight on October 1. The argument they had then was long and accusatory. Pauline went to bed but had such abdominal pain that her sister Jinny took her to St. Vincent's hospital, where she died at 4 a.m. on the operating table. The condition Pauline had been under medical care for—volatile blood pressure, terrific headaches—turned out to be a tumor of the adrenal medulla, till then undiagnosed. That condition had led to a ruptured blood vessel and to her blood pressure going from 300 to 0. Pauline died of shock.[7]

Jinny wired Hemingway the following morning. Hemingway was silently grieving, as was Mary. Even though *Time* reported that Pauline had died after a long illness, people who had known her were stunned. Hemingway received a flood of letters of condolence. In the words of long-time Key West friend, the poet Elizabeth Bishop, Pauline "was the wittiest person, man or woman, I've ever known."[8] An even greater fallout from Pauline's death at only fifty-six was the enmity that resulted between Gregory and his father. Gregory blamed Hemingway for upsetting his mother during the long phone call while Hemingway blamed Gregory's misbehavior in Los Angeles for setting off the chain of fatal events.[9]

Hemingway later wrote to Hotchner that much of the year of Pauline's unexpected death had been devoted to the aftermath of her loss.[10] Except for Scribner's death early in 1952, that year kept Hemingway more pleasantly occupied. When in the autumn *The Old Man and the Sea* was published entire in a single issue of *Life* magazine, Ernest found himself immediately famous on a popular level. More than five million copies of the magazine sold on newsstands in two days for 20 cents each. One surmises that for every copy sold, at least two people read the novella. It also was a Book-of-the-Month Club selection, described in the group's brochure as "superbly placid and superbly exciting."[11] Praise came to Hemingway from around the world (Bernard Berenson compared it to a Homeric epic[12]). Mary recalled Hemingway's getting "30 to 40 letters a day ... [all of] bright cheer."[13] Only Gregory criticized the novella as "sentimental."[14] In December, Leland Howard came to the Finca to discuss a movie, perhaps starring Spencer Tracy.

In a few months, too, the prize winning began with Hemingway's acceptance of a Medal of Honor from the Cuban government "in the name of the professional marlin fisherman." (Despite Fulgencio Batista's seizure of power early in March, 1951, with a military coup, the Hemingways were not worried about their residence.)[15] In May of 1953, *The Old Man and the Sea* won the Pulitzer Prize for Fiction, Hemingway's first. In March of 1954, he accepted the $1000 Award of Merit from the American Academy of Arts and Letters. On July 21, 1954, Cuba awarded Hemingway its highest honor, the Order of Carlos Manual de Cespedes. Then on October 18, 1954, he received word that he had won the Nobel Prize in Literature. There was no higher honor for any writer, and Hemingway was suitably modest about receiving it.

Hemingway did not go to the major presentation ceremonies. He also had not gone to New York in the autumn of 1952, when the novella had first appeared (although Mary had). What was happening to Hemingway's emotional health in the aftermath of completing—and then publishing—his novella was predictive of what was about to happen to his usually strong physical health. That fall, Hemingway spent much of his energy planning another African safari. Patrick, who had graduated from Harvard *magna cum laude*, had moved with his wife to Tanganyika, where the couple was negotiating to buy a large farm. Going on a hunting safari to southern Kenya would allow Mary to have the fascinating experience he and Pauline had so relished in the 1930s, and it would also permit Ernest a visit with Patrick. In the midst of his diligent planning, he realized that he could combine the trip to Africa with a journey to Europe, seeing Adriana and her family and also returning to Pamplona for the fiesta bullfights. Hemingway's plans were that they be ready for a late June sailing.

In April, 1953, *The Old Man and the Sea* began its extraordinary financial payoff. When Spencer Tracy arrived in Havana to film fishing sequences for the movie, the film company paid Hemingway $25,000 in advance royalties and then another $25,000 to supervise the photography of the marlin fishing. (The work was not without anxiety, however; he wrote to Hotch that he had installed "a giant bulldozer to serve me the shit I have to eat each day."[16]) That same month, *Look* magazine offered him a large advance for a series of essays he was to write for them about his African safari the coming autumn.

The Hemingways flew to New York and then sailed on the *Flandre* to Le Havre in late June, where Gianfranco Ivancich met them with a car and chauffeur. By July 4, they were in Pamplona, seeing the Fiesta of San Fermin for the first time in years. There, Hemingway became a champion of Antonio Ordónēz, the son of Nino de la Palma, and when the fiesta had finished, he and Mary visited the bullfighter and his brother-in-law Luis Miguel Domingúin at the Villa Paz ranch. They returned to Paris and then on to Marseilles, and on August 6, sailed to Mombasa on the *Dunnottar Castle*. In Mombasa, they were met by Philip Percival, who had been Hemingway's guide 20 years before on his first safari. The safari began on September 1, 1953.[17]

In the midst of truly successful shooting (particularly by Mary, somewhat to Hemingway's surprise), Hemingway wrote to Hotch that Mary had been "wonderful," "damned good." He reported that he was himself down to 190 pounds, in the prime of condition.[18] Hemingway told Hotchner only some of the romantic events that comprised one narrative of his "African book"—his courtship of Debba—but he did recount Mary's leaving the safari in order to Christmas shop in Nairobi. As a postscript to this letter, Mary raved, "No place and nothing we've done compares with this life of Safari." Her memories in *How It Was* were similarly ecstatic: spending nearly a hundred pages of the 550 page book on this safari year, she called the time "the most exciting, instructive and prolonged holiday of my life."[19] Drawing from her extensive journals, Mary included a number of passages that described the rare events and beauties of their three seasons in Africa. For example, "we roamed among the game, everything from little bush babies and bat-eared foxes, through all the antelope to lion, buffalo, rhino and elephant."[20] In the "opalescent morning," she found every day an inspiration to live with zest and excitement. Her love of the terrain under Mount Kilimanjaro colored all her memories.

During the last week of January, 1954, with the safari officially over, Mary and Hemingway took a flying tour of the area: the trip was Hemingway's Christmas gift to his wife. On January 23, as the Cessna 180 was enroute from Entebbe to Murchison Falls, it struck a telegraph wire and crashed. The survivors made their way to a ridge top to spend the night, awaiting rescue and hoping to be ignored by elephants. Unfortunately, when the crash site was observed and there was no movement, the news report went out that Hemingway and his party were lost. The world press carried such headlines as "Hemingway Dead in Crash." (Sunny Hemingway in Michigan was contacted by the Chicago papers, but she told them that Ernest had gotten out of many serious situations and she expected that he would be found alive.[21]) The Hemingways' endeavor was further complicated the next day, when their second plane crashed after it had burst into flames on take off and Hemingway, too large to crawl out the window, butted the back exit open with his head.[22] This was the crash that badly injured Hemingway. He described his injuries to various people as including a ruptured kidney, spleen, liver, and a collapsed lower intestine; a full concussion— complete with double vision and loss of vision in his left eye and loss of hearing in his left ear; first-degree burns on face, arms, and head; and two crushed vertebrae.[23] Writing in Mary's diary, Hemingway called his state " 'semi-unbearable suffering.' "[24] He kept himself functioning by living on gin, against doctors' orders, but his behavior was erratic and, often, abusive. As Carlos Baker described the writer's pain in those weeks, "he vomited often, his lower backbone felt like a red hot poker, and he carried his broken head like an egg." As Baker saw it, Hemingway was close to dying.[25] The already severe burns were augmented several weeks later when a brushfire at the Nairobi fishing camp caused second-degree burns over the front of Hemingway's body, when he stumbled and fell into the flames.

Following the second crash, the Hemingways were driven to Entebbe, where Patrick joined them. Then on January 28, 1954, Hemingway was flown to Nairobi; Mary and Patrick followed the next day by commercial airliner. Typical stories in the world press now included the *Washington Post* headlined feature, "Hemingways Survive Two Plane Crackups," a relatively comic narrative of the macabre narrow escapes. Dated January 26, the story did not include mention of Hemingway's serious injuries.[26]

Barely able to travel, Hemingway spent the rest of his days in Africa resting, and on March 10, he and Mary sailed from Mombasa for Venice, resuming their lives there at the Gritti Palace Hotel.[27] Although Hemingway greeted his friends—including Adriana—and told stories, he was still frantic with pain and often vented his frustration on Mary. Upon reaching Venice, Hemingway had lost 20 pounds, his hair had turned white, and he was still suffering from internal bleeding.[28] To relieve Mary of coping with him, he planned a trip for her through Europe. She left on April 14, and on May 2, Hotchner arrived in Venice to drive with Hemingway to Pamplona, where he steeled himself to attend a few bullfights. Then he and Mary sailed from Genoa to Havana on board the *Francesco Morosini*, by this time using alcohol sparingly and eating very little. Much of Hemingway's life in the Finca was also spent resting, after swimming mornings in the pool.

It took Hemingway more than two years to recover from his injuries in the African plane crash; the amount of pain and worry was incalculable. He eventually found his daily rhythm as he worked on the African safari book (a truncated version of which appeared posthumously as *True at First Light* and then in a complete version as *Under Kilimanjaro*), and it could be that only such a massive and continuing project was his means to recover comparative health.

After 13 months away from Cuba, there was an immense amount of work to be done at the Finca: Mary did most of it. She also traveled to Gulfport to put her parents in a care facility, since they could no longer manage living by themselves: Hemingway wrote her then, sympathetically, about her father's ailments—and his eventual demise—" 'dying is such a worthless business.' "[29] Receiving the Nobel Prize for Literature in the autumn of 1954 seemed to be only another imposition. Glad as Hemingway was to have the extra $35,000, he complained about the publicity, the phone calls, and the constant visitors. He wrote his acceptance speech (and recorded it), sending it to Sweden—because he was too ill to travel—with American Ambassador John Cabot, who accepted the prize for him.[30]

Except for some occasional fishing on the *Pilar*, Hemingway rested. Whenever he tried to make a public appearance, he became ill. After accepting the highest Cuban honor in the fall of 1955, he developed a cold and took to his bed on November 20, 1955. He did not leave that bed until January 9, 1956. His red corpuscle count was very low. The only activity he did with regularity was writing on the African book, which by winter had reached 700 pages.

Somewhat surprisingly, his physical vigor eventually returned. In the spring of 1956, heartened by the winter visit of the Spanish bullfighters Ordóněz and Domingúin, Hemingway planned a return to Europe. First, in April, he and Mary flew to Peru for some work toward the filming of *The Old Man and the Sea* and some fishing. Then they tentatively planned another safari to Mombasa, where Hemingway's son Patrick would be their white hunter. September 1, 1956, they sailed to Le Havre on the *Ile de France* and were driven to Spain for the bullfights in both Madrid and Zaragoza. Drinking far too much, Hemingway was battling both high cholesterol and high blood pressure, yet he took offense when one of his doctors told him his health was so fragile that he could never return to Africa (the trip was postponed anyway once Nasser closed the Suez Canal in November).[31] In a kind of stalemate, Hemingway was dissatisfied with Europe, though he and Mary returned to Paris and in the Ritz Hotel, found the trunks of material Hemingway had left there decades earlier. January 24, 1957, the Hemingways sailed for New York on the *Ile de France* before returning to Cuba. There Hemingway worried a great deal about political conditions. It was clear that change was going to be necessary if he were to continue the life, and the work, he loved most.

18
Endings

Beset with worries about money, the comparatively wealthy Hemingway blamed his often unreasonable fears on the looming specter of federal income taxes. Another cause for his almost constant worry was the existence of his FBI file. Sometimes discussed in biographies as evidence of his growing paranoia, the file had existed since 1942, when Hemingway began his "Crook Factory" spying activities in Cuba. By the 1950s, nobody in the United States was complacent about what behavior might have been considered unpatriotic—and Hemingway knew many people who had been questioned by the House UnAmerican Activities Committee. A later document from his file, dated 1959, summarized his role in the Spanish Civil War and the reception of his 1940 novel, *For Whom the Bell Tolls*; it also commented on Hemingway's reaction to Castro's takeover of Cuba.[1]

During the remainder of 1957 and 1958, after their return from Peru and Europe, Hemingway and Mary lived quietly in Cuba, Hemingway working away on the Paris sketches which would comprise *A Moveable Feast* and rewriting *The Garden of Eden*. The Castro revolution occupied much of 1958 and in early 1959, after the Batista government fell, the Hemingways decided to buy a home in Ketchum, Idaho. The major event of 1959 was Hemingway's return to Spain in order to follow the *mano a mano* rivalry between Spain's two leading matadors, his friends Antonio Ordóñez and Luis Domingúin.[2] On April 26, the Hemingways sailed from New York on the *Constitution*, and it was in Madrid at the San Isidro bullfights that Valerie Danby-Smith, a young news stringer, asked Hemingway for an interview.[3] From that time on, the novice Irish reporter with the beautiful complexion was a part of their traveling group.

So too were the wealthy Bill and Annie Davis, the American couple whose palatial home near Málaga—La Consula—became Hemingway's headquarters; Hotchner, flown in from New York; and on occasions, Peter Buckley. The Davis estate had been equipped for Hemingway's comfort, even to the slanted writing board he preferred to work at rather than a desk. Bill Davis had met the Hemingways when they docked, taking them and their 21 pieces of luggage directly to La Consula.[4] Then as they followed the bullfight circuit from place to place, sometimes getting only a few hours sleep at night, the car arrangement was that Valerie Danby-Smith sat in the center of the front seat between Davis, who drove, and Hemingway. Hotchner with all the food, drink, luggage, and paraphernalia occupied the back seat. Anne Davis drove the second car, with Mary as her passenger. At times, especially after Mary had broken her toe and was walking with a cane, the women did not accompany the party.[5]

Early in the 1959 season, as Hemingway was zealously taking notes for the story *Life* magazine had contracted with him to write, Ordónēz was severely gored. Then La Consula became the shelter for him and his wife Carmen as well. During the 1959 season, both Ordónēz and Domingúin were gored on two different occasions and, as Mary pointed out, such injuries made Carmen's life almost unbearably painful (she was Domingúin's sister as well as Ordónēz's wife).[6]

The spectacular event during the 1959 *mano a mano* season was the birthday party Mary planned and gave for Ernest (and Carmen) at La Consula (she had taken on a writing assignment to make the money for the flamenco dancers, the booths for target shooting, the fireworks, and the immense displays of food and drink). At one point, Hemingway shot the ash off a lighted cigarette in Antonio Ordónēz's mouth;[7] otherwise, he behaved more circumspectly than he had during the previous month. Whereas their friends had been aware of Hemingway's mistreatment of his wife during the summer, other guests such as Buck Lanham were sobered to see how cruel Ernest, on the occasion of his sixtieth birthday, had become to the long-suffering Mary.[8] As Valerie Danby-Smith remembered, there was "a darker, meaner side" to Hemingway.[9]

Returning to Cuba in advance of Hemingway, so that she could ready both the Finca and the Ketchum house for the Ordónēz's visit, Mary once more wrote her husband a long letter, complaining that she seemed completely unnecessary to his life. He cabled her to take no action, and when he arrived with Antonio and Carmen, the Finca was ready for festivities. The party then traveled West. After the Spanish couple flew back to Europe, Mary and Hemingway were hunting on a snowy November day with George Saviers when she fell and splintered her left elbow. Although Saviers performed extensive surgery as soon as they could get to a major hospital, Mary was in great pain for some time. To his wife's dilemma, Hemingway only muttered that he was being treated like a servant and being asked to do numerous chores—both while Mary was hospitalized and then after she was at home—that interrupted his writing and his life.[10] Mary's pain, and Hemingway's inconvenience, were not to end yet. In December, Dr. Saviers saw that the arm was not healing properly, so he rebroke it and started over.[11]

Working on the *Life* story of the summer bullfights, which now reached to 65,000 words rather than the 10,000 contracted, Hemingway wired Valerie Danby-Smith to come to Cuba to serve as his secretary. (She recalled his telling her "if I did not come, he would have no reason to go on."[12]) The months of spring and summer passed, and then Hemingway decided that he had to return to Spain in order to do some fact-checking. Mary, still in pain from her broken arm and its surgery, begged off. Part of Hemingway's being unsettled may have stemmed from the warning Phil Bonsall, the U.S. ambassador to Cuba, gave him one night at dinner (before he was recalled). Bonsall told Hemingway he would have to choose between Cuba and the States, and that he should probably "voice his displeasure at Castro's government."[13]

When Hemingway left the States on August 4, flying first to Paris and then to La Consula (a period of weeks the Davises remembered as "nightmarish"),[14] it was clear to everyone who knew him that his health, both physical and mental, had deteriorated dramatically. Because he wrote regularly to Mary, who had remained in New York, that he was having nightmares and feared a crack up, Mary sent Valerie to Spain. She could barely control his temper tantrums, nor could she alleviate his clear paranoia. On October 8, Hemingway flew to New York and then took the train to Ketchum. By this time, Mary had talked with the sons, close friends, and especially George Saviers. Opinions differed, but the Mayo Clinic seemed to be an appropriate choice for Hemingway's treatment.

He was at the Mayo Clinic in Rochester, Minnesota, under an assumed name, from November 30 of 1960 through January 22, 1961, when doctors were satisfied that the electroshock treatment had alleviated his depression, the condition which posed the greatest risk. Back in Ketchum, however, Hemingway found writing impossible.[15] On April 21, he planned suicide with his shotgun, but Mary intervened and he was sedated and hospitalized locally. Two days later he repeated the episode while at home to pack clothes for re-admission to Mayo.[16] Bernice Kert reports that while the plane that was taking him back to Minnesota had landed to refuel, Hemingway walked quickly toward another plane's revolving propellers.[17] During this April week, the news was filled with the United State's disastrous Bay of Pigs invasion of Cuba, which had been made on the Hemingways' favorite site for duck hunting.

With Hemingway safe at the Mayo Clinic, Mary waited a few weeks to visit. She was on the edge of nervous collapse herself. Looking toward finding a place to continue his care, she was amazed when the staff at Mayo called her in to release Hemingway to her. She knew this "enormous mistake" meant the end for her husband.[18] With Charles Brown driving them back to Ketchum in a rental car, the Hemingways traveled the 1700 miles with anxious fear. They arrived home on June 30, 1961. On the morning of July 2, Hemingway died a suicide. Like his father before him, Hemingway did not trust his death to any kind of luck.

*   *   *

At the end of Hemingway's life, he began to resemble the way his father had looked and behaved in 1928. And like Clarence, who managed to keep his medical practice going even as he burned financial papers and hid out in his room upstairs, Ernest too kept his public career afloat. During the last years of his life, he made the final trips to Spain for his second bullfight book, and as Valerie Hemingway wrote in her memoir *Running with the Bulls*, in most circumstances, Ernest Hemingway seemed competent to make the trips—so long as good friends such as Annie and Bill Davis surrounded him, housed him, drove him, and protected him.

Once back from Spain in October of 1960, however, he seemed to crumble. The change was visible. Even as he and Mary tried to resume their life in Idaho, once their friends went back to their own existences, nothing was left of Ernest. Writing away on the Spanish trip log, hundreds of pages over the word count his publishers had requested and already declared "finished" at 120,000 words (in May, 1960), he turned doggedly every day to the project. True to the caveat of those early modernist writers who were his true forefathers, a man is known and judged by his work, and only his work. Consequently, Hemingway once more built his daily existence on his writing.

Friends recalled that Ernest would sometimes stand for not just the morning but the entire day in front of the writing board where he worked. Stymied, frozen, horrified to find that he could write hardly at all, the man who lived for the perfection of style groped for the memory of how to physically write.[19] Exhausted with the strain of waiting to compose, the tired Hemingway would finally allow himself to be called down, or drawn down, to either lunch or supper. He could barely eat whatever meal it was.

10. Late in Ernest's life, a dinner scene at the Finca in Cuba: Ernest with one of his many cats, and Mary.

On other days, he managed to write. If most of what he composed was tangential to the main idea he was following, the quality of his writing did not matter. He was ecstatic to be writing. He was angry if anyone interrupted him—and, by necessity, it was usually Mary who had to do the interrupting. The animosity between them had grown so extreme that she often thought of leaving him, and their life, and her existence as Mrs. Ernest Hemingway out of sheer weariness and worry. She knew what his end would probably be, and she also was convinced that that end was inevitable. All she could do—so long as she stayed—was to ask his many friends for help. During the days, she was seldom alone in the house with him. In her memoir written some years later, she makes her staying seem matter-of-fact. But it was really the greatest gift she could have given this man she had once loved with all her being.

The fear that Hemingway knew as a teenager returning from the World War I's horrific wounding became his primary mode of living: fear of the government—either its income tax arm or its FBI investigators—set against fear of exposure by the media (to which he had once said, gruffly, that even boxers were allowed to retire); fear of the loss of prowess of physical effort (shooting, fishing, walking, seeing, having sex, eating, drinking, bicycling); and especially, fear of becoming another. The memory of his father's transformed appearance during his last visit to Oak Park in the fall of 1928, just weeks before Clarence's suicide, haunted him. This was his family line. This was the inheritance that his grandfather Anson Hemingway had perpetrated on his sons and the inheritance he, Ernest, had passed on to his own increasingly fragile sons—witness his disappointment in especially Gregory, and even Patrick. Only John, the Bumby of his and Hadley's union, seemed whole and competent. During the late years of his career, when he wrote with love of Hadley and the Paris years, it was partly to honor their son. During those same years, his bitterness toward the unwitting Pauline, mother of both the less satisfactory boys, stemmed from the same kind of obsession. In his increasing debility, Hemingway's sons, like the memory of his father, came to haunt him.

For the man who had created his own celebrity, based always, primarily, on his power to write, his fear of what new stories the media would create about his failings, his failures, his idiosyncratic behaviors, his outrageous angers, was also real. For him to use the name of his doctor in Idaho when he went for treatment at the Mayo Clinic was more than just a precaution. It was a lifeline back to his old life, the life that was really his and that he would not easily relinquish. *Ernest Hemingway* was not going to fail in this life: *Ernest Hemingway* had won the Nobel Prize for Literature, and his words—whether spoken or written—were revered worldwide. That single honor had made up for years of frustration and angry competition, for in addition to learning how to write better than nearly anyone in the twentieth century, Hemingway had had to manage his own publishing history. And then he had had to manage his own fame. He had to become the world's most influential critic as he pointed readers to what was expert about a scene, what was fluid and real about characters' interaction, what was accurate about the description of the natural world. Every word he had written was careful and astute. Every word. Every interview he had given existed for a purpose. Every critique of someone else's work was done to honor the profession of writing.

The way Hemingway's deteriorating mental condition played out in his life differed from its manifestations in his father's life, however. For Ernest—husband to four wives and partner in other romantic infatuations—his physical health depended on his being in love. Increasingly in his late years, the chosen "daughters" of his friendship were meant to be the tantalizing—and probably available—sexual objects of his fantasy life. Their responses, however, could never admit to that fantastic element. They needed to play the role straight; they needed in their adoration, their deft touches of the hand on his shoulder, their willingness to come into the shelter of his arms for a close embrace, to be convincing.

No record of this kind of sensibility exists except for that recounted in Valerie Hemingway's recent book, when her candor makes clear how dependent Ernest had become on her, an unaware nineteen-year-old Irish girl who met him and Mary during their 1959 sojourn in Spain, traveled with the Hemingways, and then lived with them in Cuba; then, finally, she was sent to rescue Hemingway during the last trip to Spain— always as Ernest's secretary. Playing out his misguided belief that he and Valerie were in the midst of an unconsummated love, perhaps the greatest love of his life, and one that would eventually lead to marriage, Hemingway brought Valerie innocent tokens of luck. He bought her a rabbit's foot, and books she should know. He read her palm. He touched her gently at the close of an evening, and sometimes, in the dark of the Cuban hillside, he wrapped her within his arms for a bear hug. Occasionally, too, during lunch, he played with her sandaled feet caught under his bare feet beneath the luncheon table. The immensity of his love had to have some physical component—but he would never have violated her, and both of them understood that.[20]

According to Valerie Hemingway's account, Hemingway also made her part of his suicide plan. Here too the reader must wonder if this fervid conversation had been a part of his somewhat inexplicable earlier relationship with Adriana Ivancich, the protected daughter of the elite Italian family, the model for Renata in *Across the River and Into the Trees*. When he had first met Valerie, Hemingway told her about Adriana and said that every ten years he fell in love. For the aging writer to continue to live, he said, he must have the love of a beautiful young woman as a totem.[21] Life was volition. He could end it at any time, but he chose not to end it so long as his life were given meaning by the great love he had found with this younger, beautiful woman. Susceptible to this immense flattery from a Nobel Prize winner, what woman of her late teens would have been able to resist the appeal—especially when Ernest seemed to be healthy and well, the center of his friends' attention and of his wife's concern. Most important of all, he was a writer who was a person still writing, as he was in both these instances. He wrote the novel about Venice for Adriana, and he wrote and wrote on the Spanish trip for Valerie, partly because he was able to legitimate her presence by paying her a salary and therefore keeping her with him for her secretarial work. At the close of the 1959 Spanish trip, Hemingway insisted she join him and Mary in Cuba. He needed her work—but more, he needed her presence.

On the rare times that he discussed his eventual suicide, with Valerie and—one supposes—with Adriana, Ernest was never threatening. He did not say that the young woman must continue to love him, to accompany him (or, in Adriana's case, to come to the States and visit him), or else he would die. He said instead that it was his great love which kept him alive, and that if that love ended, then he would have no reason to remain alive. As Valerie described the scene, Hemingway told her he could work well only when she was around. By phrasing his needs in this way, Hemingway put his love partner under no obligation. Better, he kept the romance where it was most viable, in the realm of imagination. For the kind of pact he was creating, secrecy was implicit. Nobody but the love partners would know that their love existed. Even Mary, the wife, was not to know of the relationship—or especially Mary was not to know of the relationship. If there were times when Mary's anger over his foolishness about either Valerie or Adriana became evident, he was able to pacify her into complacency. After all, his feeling for these young girls was not sexual, at least not visibly sexual; and there was no betrayal of his and Mary's marriage bed. Words, words, Ernest Hemingway had been a master of them for his entire life. He was not about to founder on them here in the last years of his existence.

What Ernest seemed to want from these young women was not physical, sexual comfort, but kindness. As Gregory Hemingway wrote in his memoir, "Not to touch, not to kiss, not to make love with."[22] Hemingway wanted only to be allowed to follow his fantasy life, and have someone pretend involvement, but to do so without destroying his present life and marriage. The scars from Ag's rejection had healed differently than had those from Gellhorn's blunt dismissal. In the first case, he had loved desperately the older woman who had given him reason to think she loved him; in the latter, he had loved desperately the younger woman who had loved him in return. To counter the rejection from Ag, he had married two older women—both of whom had truly loved him. But there had been no way to counter his rejection from the beautiful Martha Gellhorn, younger, sophisticated, talented in the same way he was. That was the rejection that marked his last years, and marrying Mary Welsh was not an answer. Mary was neither so beautiful nor so talented, and she was much more eager to become Mrs. Ernest Hemingway than he had been to have her assume that role. Hemingway, then, was still looking for the beautiful young mate, the replacement for the courageous and independent third wife—the only one of his wives who had wanted out of her marriage to him. It was his psychological need to put her, or someone like her, back into that space.[23]

Hemingway led his life straddling the two important streams of energy that comprised it. The one stream that was crucial, that he could not exist without, was his writing, his craft with words, his hunger to find the power to express what lay—always unconsciously and always surprisingly—somewhere within his mind. The second stream, one that he kept even more hidden because he was somehow ashamed of that physical and emotional need, was the current of exquisite sexual closeness, a highly elaborate concept of romantic love that had more in common with courtliness than it did with orgasmic fulfillment. Wherever he found that completion, whether in his marriages or in his flirtatious friendships or in his paternal relationships with beautiful young women, Hemingway was at rest for a time. The women with whom he shared those idylls were all trustworthy. They embarked on these dreamlike fantasies with Hemingway as though they believed in them as much as he seemed to. After all, he asked so little. What he asked, finally, was their complicity in his dream of happiness. The great writer, working away mornings, lunching and playing the rest of the day with his beloved, a comforting almost faceless muse who made the life—and the work—possible.

Notes

1 " 'Fraid a Nothing"

1. Carlos Baker, *Ernest Hemingway, A Life Story* (1969), 5; please consult Baker's recounting of the child's verbal development.
2. Susan Beegel, "Eye and Heart: Hemingway's Education as a Naturalist," *Historical Guide to Ernest Hemingway* (2000), 53–92.
3. Baker, *Ernest Hemingway*, 3; see also Kenneth Lynn, *Hemingway* (1986).
4. Marcelline Hemingway, *At the Hemingways* (1962, 1999), 3.
5. Michael S. Reynolds, "Hemingway's Home: Depression and Suicide," *Ernest Hemingway: Six Decades* (1987), 9–11. Peter Griffin (*Along with Youth*, 1985) recounts Clarence's taking the five-year-old son on a seven-mile hike, at the end of which both the boy's shoes and socks were bloody (10).
6. Ernest Hemingway. "Fathers and Sons," *Complete Short Stories of Ernest Hemingway*, 376.
7. See Scott Donaldson, *By Force of Will* (1977), Michael S. Reynolds, *The Young Hemingway* (1986), and Reynolds, "Hemingway's Home," 14–16.
8. Reynolds, "Hemingway's Home," 14–16.
9. Leicester Hemingway, *My Brother, Ernest Hemingway* (1962), 117; see Hemingway, *At the Hemingways*, 31.
10. See her scrapbooks for Ernest at the Hemingway Room, John F. Kennedy Library.
11. Beegel, "Eye and Heart," 69–80.
12. Leicester Hemingway, *My Brother*, 38.
13. Donaldson, *By Force of Will*, 144. As Griffin tells the story, however, Ernest had that first date at the end of his senior year *(Along with Youth)*, 22.
14. Henry S. Villard in *Hemingway in Love and War: The Lost Diary of Agnes von Kurowsky*, ed. Villard and James Nagel (1989), 114.
15. Jeffrey Meyers (*Hemingway: A Biography*, 1985) quotes from a Bill Horne letter that while the Croce di Guerras was not difficult to get, the Medaglia d'Argento al Valore was, 31.

2 Eighteen and Fear—and Agnes

1. Henry S. Villard, "Red Cross Driver in Italy," *Hemingway in Love and War: The Lost Diary of Agnes von Kurowsky*, ed. Villard and James Nagel (1989), 1–46; see 27–28.
2. Hemingway's September 21, 1918 letter to Marcelline, *At the Hemingways*, 288–89. Agnes Von Kurowsky wrote in her August 27 diary entry, "All I know is 'Ernie' is far too fond of me" (*In Love and War*, 73).
3. Hemingway's November 28, 1918, letter to Marcelline, *At the Hemingways*, 297–98.
4. Bernice Kert, *The Hemingway Women* (1983), 64–65.

5. See *Hemingway in Love and War*, Part III, Agnes Von Kurowsky Letters to Ernest Hemingway, 92–168.
6. Agnes to Hemingway, *In Love and War*, 96.
7. Hemingway to Marcelline, November 25, 1918, *At the Hemingways*, 299–300.
8. Agnes to Hemingway, March 7, 1919, *In Love and War*, 163–64.
9. Hemingway, *At the Hemingways*, 178; his younger sister Sunny said that the pain was not only in his legs and feet: bits of shell splinters had also damaged his fingers (Madelaine Hemingway Miller, *Ernie*, 1975), 85.
10. Hemingway, *At the Hemingways*, 183; she also mentioned her brother offering her a drink (as he had Sunny) from the bottles he kept in his room.
11. Baker, *Ernest Hemingway*, 58. Marcelline recalled that the Hemingways were told to invite their friends as well, because the Italian group would bring food for at least fifty people—which they did (*At the Hemingways*, 186).
12. Baker, *Ernest Hemingway*, 60–61.
13. Constance Cappel Montgomery, *Hemingway in Michigan* (1966), 159.
14. Ibid., 160–62.
15. Max Westbrook, "Grace under Pressure: Hemingway and the Summer of 1920," *Ernest Hemingway: Six Decades of Criticism* (1987), 19–40.
16. Miller, *Ernie*, 67.
17. Ibid., 67–68.
18. Grace Hall Hemingway to Ernest, July 24, 1920, in Baker, *Ernest Hemingway*, 72.
19. Letter quoted in Constance Montgomery, *Hemingway in Michigan*, 176.
20. Hemingway, *At the Hemingways*, 206.

3 "Dear Ernesto"

1. Hadley Richardson to Hemingway, Hemingway Archive, John F. Kennedy Library (the source for all her correspondence used in this chapter), this letter dated November 5, 1920.
2. Gioia Diliberto, *Hadley* (1992), 29.
3. Ibid. See also Bernice Kert, *The Hemingway Women*, 83–85.
4. Ibid., 11–12.
5. Hadley to Hemingway, November 5 and November 11, JFK Hemingway collection.
6. Ibid., November 11, 1920, JFK Hemingway collection.
7. Ibid., December 11, 1920, JFK Hemingway collection.
8. Ibid., January 2, 1921, JFK Hemingway collection.
9. Ibid., December 11, 1920, JFK Hemingway collection.
10. Ibid., November 25, 1920, JFK Hemingway collection.
11. Ibid., January 1, 1921, JFK Hemingway collection.
12. Ibid., January 9, 1921, JFK Hemingway collection.
13. Ibid., two letters, January 12, 1921, JFK Hemingway collection.
14. Ibid., January 15, 1921, JFK Hemingway collection.
15. Ibid., January 18, 1921, JFK Hemingway collection.
16. Ibid., January 16, 1921, JFK Hemingway collection.
17. Ibid., February 24, 1921, JFK Hemingway collection.
18. Ibid., March 4, 1921, JFK Hemingway collection.
19. Ibid., March 16, 1921, JFK Hemingway collection.

20. Hadley to Grace Hemingway, July 12, 1921, JFK Hemingway collection.
21. Hadley to Hemingway, July 8, 1921, JFK Hemingway collection.
22. Ernest to Marcelline, August 11, 1921, *At the Hemingways*, 314–15.
23. Gioia Diliberto, *Hadley*, 78.
24. Leicester Hemingway, *My Brother*, 72.
25. Hadley Richardson Hemingway to Gertrude Stein and Alice B. Toklas, various, JFK Hemingway collection.
26. Michael S. Reynolds, *Hemingway: The Paris Years* (1989), 4–15.
27. Ibid., 7.
28. Hemingway to Clarence Hemingway, May 2, 1922; within the year, March 26, 1923, he told his father that he had traveled thousands of miles by R. R.—"Been to Italy 3 times. Back and forth Switzerland-Paris 6 times … . Sure have a belly full of traveling" (*Letters of Ernest Hemingway*, ed. Baker, 66 and 81).
29. Peter Griffin, *Less Than a Treason* (1990), 18–19.
30. Linda Wagner-Martin, *"Favored Strangers": Gertrude Stein and Her Family* (1995), 166–78.
31. Baker, *Ernest Hemingway*, 92.
32. Ibid., 92–94.
33. Diliberto, *Hadley*, 130 (Hemingway supposedly told Bill Smith he had been unfaithful, but Hadley said that he would not have had time).
34. Baker, *Ernest Hemingway*, 72; Diliberto, Ibid.
35. Ibid., 131–37.

4   The Route to *In Our Time*: The Arrival

1. Bernice Kert, *The Hemingway Women*, 111.
2. Michael Reynolds, *The Young Hemingway*, 163–64, 238–39.
3. Madelaine Hemingway Miller, *Ernie*, 25–26.
4. Ernest Hemingway, "Indian Camp," *Complete Short Stories*, 68.
5. Hemingway to F. Scott Fitzgerald, May 28, 1934, *Letters*, 407.
6. See Linda Welshimer Wagner, *Hemingway and Faulkner: inventors/masters* (1976), 15–52.
7. See Gertrude Stein, *The Autobiography of Alice B. Toklas* in *Gertrude Stein, Writings 1903–1932*, ed. Catharine Stimpson and Harriet Chessman. (1998), 261–63.
8. Hemingway, "A Man's Credo," *Playboy*, 10, no. 1 (January 1963), n.p.
9. Hemingway to Leicester Hemingway, August 3, 1938, 1–2. Harry Ransom Humanities Research Center, Hemingway Collection, University of Texas, Austin.
10. Hemingway, Manuscripts of "The Doctor and the Doctor's Wife," Hemingway Archive, John F. Kennedy Library.
11. See Linda Wagner-Martin, "'I like you less and less': The Stein Subtext in *Death in the Afternoon*," *A Companion to Hemingway's Death in the Afternoon*, ed. Miriam B. Mandel (2004), 59–77.
12. Hemingway to Gertrude Stein and Alice Toklas, August 15, 1924, *Letters*, 122.
13. Gregory S. Sojka, *Ernest Hemingway, The Angler as Artist*, 141, 87.
14. Hemingway, "My Old Man," *Complete Short Stories*, 160.
15. Robert Knoll, *Robert McAlmon*, 227–28.

16. Hemingway to Edmund Wilson, October 18, 1924, *Letters*, 128–29. Here he spoke of the arrangement intending "to give the picture of the whole between examining it in detail. Like looking with your eyes at something, say a passing coast line, and then looking at it with 15X binoculars. Or rather, maybe, looking at it and then going in and living in it—and then coming out and looking at it again." Similarly, in a 1923 letter to Ezra Pound about the structure of the vignettes in the earlier *in our time*, Hemingway explained the patterning of the arrangement (Bruccoli, "'Yr Letters Are Life Preservers,'" *Paris Review*, 106–07).
17. Hemingway called himself this, as told by Sylvia Beach, *Shakespeare & Company* (1959), 77.
18. See Madelaine Hemingway Miller *(Ernie)*, Leicester Hemingway *(My Brother, Ernest Hemingway)*, Marcelline Hemingway *(At the Hemingways)* and, of the biographies, Reynolds and Baker.
19. Hemingway to F. Scott Fitzgerald, July 1, 1925, *Letters*, 165.
20. Hemingway, "The End of Something," *Complete Short Stories*, 81.
21. Ibid., "Hills Like White Elephants," *Complete Short Stories*, 213.
22. Irwin D. Yalom and Marilyn Yalom, "Ernest Hemingway—A Psychiatric View" (1971), 485–94.

5 Of Babies and Books

1. Ezra Pound, "Small Magazines," *The English Journal*, 19, no. 9 (November 1930), 700.
2. Michael Reynolds, *The Paris Years*, 118–20.
3. "A French Officer," 409A, Hemingway Archive, John F. Kennedy Library. The selection continues, relating all the housekeeping events Hemingway is responsible for ("the kitchen to clear up again the palos to empty again other things to do and then there is an hour to work before noon.")
4. Gioia Diliberto, *Hadley* (1992) 150–52.
5. Thomas Hermann, *Quite a Little About Painters* (1997), 41; evidently *Le Coup de Des* was purchased then. Masson shared a studio later with Joan Miro, whose *The Farm* was one of the best of Hemingway's early purchases. In this year Ernest and Hadley also bought some sketches from Tami Koume, a Japanese artist Pound admired.
6. The Hemingway biographers mention that Clarence Hemingway had returned five copies of the book *in our time* just before his son's visit, Marcelline had written a note to the publisher saying that the book wasn't suitable for holiday gifts. When Ernest discovered the situation, he changed the story so that it was his mother who returned the books; it was supposedly Grace's sense of propriety that had been offended (Reynolds, *Paris Years*, 157).
7. Reynolds, *Paris Years*, 177.
8. Ibid., 178–80.
9. See both Reynolds, *Paris Years*, 194–97 and Peter Griffin, *Less Than a Treason*, 72. As Griffin tells the story, Hemingway experienced van Gogh's own disillusion at the hollowness of what he had considered his great friendship with Gauguin—and wrote to Ezra Pound that Arles was no place for a writer.
10. Griffin, *Less Than a Treason*, 76–77.
11. Janet Flanner in Diliberto, *Hadley*, 168.
12. Ibid.

13. For a full discussion of Stein's relationship with the Hemingways, see my *Favored Strangers*, 166–92.
14. Ibid., 171.
15. See Hemingway to Gertrude Stein, August 15, 1924, in Baker, *Letters*, 122.
16. See *Ernest Hemingway, The Critical Reception*, ed. Robert O. Stephens, 30–51; see conjoined commentary in reviews of both *The Torrents of Spring* and *Men Without Women*.
17. See my "Intertextual Hemingway" in *Historical Guide*, 173–94.
18. Ibid. Consider also Hemingway's sneeringly critical comments about both Willa Cather's *One of Ours* and Virginia Woolf's *Jacob's Room*, each war novel well received by critics and readers but denigrated by Hemingway because the authors were women who had not seen war.
19. See my "The Secrecies of the Public Hemingway" in Svoboda and Waldmeir, *Hemingway: Up in Michigan Perspectives*, 149–56; also consider Hemingway's first book review (for the Toronto paper) of Rene Maran's 1922 novel *Batouala, A Negro Novel*, a book about the primitive rituals of South African blacks, much of it in a jungle. The novel includes festivals, ritual dancing, feasting, and sex.

6   Pauline Pfeiffer and Hadley Richardson Hemingway

1. Carlos Baker, *Ernest Hemingway*, 159–64; see correspondence between Hemingway and Max Perkins in *The Only Thing That Counts*, 32–53.
2. See my *Zelda Sayre Fitzgerald, An American Woman's Life*.
3. Gioia Diliberto, *Hadley* (1992), 186ff.
4. Bruccoli, *Some Sort of Epic Grandeur*, 146–50 and see Donaldson, *Hemingway vs. Fitzgerald*.
5. "Racial and Sexual Coding in Hemingway's *The Sun Also Rises*," *Hemingway Review*, 1991, 39–41.
6. Diliberto, *Hadley*, 205–10; Bernice Kert, *Hemingway Women*, 172–78; Baker, *Ernest Hemingway*, 160–65.
7. Pauline Pfeiffer to Ernest and Hadley Hemingway, January 14 and 16, 1926; Pfeiffer collection, Hemingway Archive, John F. Kennedy Library.
8. Michael S. Reynolds, *Hemingway: Paris Years* (1989), 343.
9. Hadley to Hemingway, May 21, 1926, Hemingway Archive, John F. Kennedy Library.
10. Ibid.
11. Hadley to Hemingway, August 20, 1926, Hemingway Archive, John F. Kennedy Library.
12. Pauline to Hemingway, October 2, 1926, Ibid.
13. Hadley to Hemingway, September 17, 1926; Hadley to Hemingway, August 20, 1926; Pauline to Hemingway, October 2, 1926.
14. John Dos Passos, *The Best Times, an Informal Memoir (1966)*, 223.
15. Pauline to Hemingway, October 1, 1926, Hemingway Archive, John F. Kennedy Library.
16. Ibid., October 2, 1926, Hemingway Archive, John F. Kennedy Library.
17. Ibid., October 29, 1926, Hemingway Archive, John F. Kennedy Library.
18. See Reynolds, *Hemingway Chronology*, 40–47; Bruccoli, *The Only Thing That Counts*, 36–56.

19. Hadley to Hemingway, October 16, 1926, Hemingway Archive, John F. Kennedy Library.
20. Ibid., November 16, 1926, Hemingway Archive, John F. Kennedy Library.
21. Pauline Pfeiffer to Hadley Hemingway, October, 1926, Hemingway Archive, John F. Kennedy Library.
22. Hemingway to Hadley, November 18, 1926, Hemingway Archive, John F. Kennedy Library.
23. Hadley to Hemingway, letters undated except for January, 1927, Hemingway Archive, John F. Kennedy Library.
24. Marcelline Hemingway, *At the Hemingways*, letter from Marcelline to Ernest, February 7, 1927, 319. Leicester Hemingway's *My Brother* describes in greater length the "shame" his parents felt at the divorce (102–03).
25. Madelaine Hemingway Miller, *Ernie: Hemingway's Sister "Sunny" Remembers*, (1975), 3, 103 and 104.

7   Marriage in the Midst of *Men Without Women*

1. Diliberto quotes from his November 12 letter to Pauline that he would commit suicide in order "to remove the sin out of your life and avoid Hadley the necessity of divorce" (*Hadley*, 240).
2. Ernest Hemingway, page 13 of "James Allen," (529a), Hemingway Archive, John F. Kennedy Library.
3. Ibid., 15–16.
4. Ibid., 17.
5. Pauline Pfeiffer to Hemingway, March 20, 1927, Hemingway Archive, John F. Kennedy Library.
6. Hemingway, "James Allen" (529a), Hemingway Archive, John F. Kennedy Library.
7. Pauline Pfeiffer to Hemingway, Dec. 3, 1926, Hemingway Archive, John F. Kennedy Library.
8. Hemingway to Max Perkins, Dec. 6, 1926, *The Only Thing That Counts*, 53.
9. Ibid.
10. Hemingway to Hugh Walpole, April 14, 1927, Hemingway file, Harry Ransom Humanities Research Center, University of Texas, Austin.
11. Hemingway, "My Own Life," *New Yorker*, 11 (February 27, 1927), 23–24.
12. See Hemingway's February 5, 1927, letter to Grace Hall-Hemingway, where he tells her she does not understand his work, and has no right to criticize it (*Letters*, 243–44).
13. Hemingway, "Now I Lay Me," *Collected Short Stories*, 281–82.
14. Nancy R. Comley and Robert Scholes, *Hemingway's Genders* (1994), 35–36. Perhaps the best-known earlier commentary on Hemingway's "feminism" is Robert E. Gajdusek's essay, most recently included in his 2002 *Hemingway in His Own Country*, 331.

8   *A Farewell to Arms*

1. Virginia Woolf, "An Essay in Criticism," *New York Herald Tribune Books*, 4 (October 9, 1927), 1, 8.
2. Madelaine Hemingway Miller, *Ernie: Hemingway's Sister "Sunny" Remembers*, (1975), 103.

3. Pound to Hemingway, March 11, 1928, in Baker, *Ernest Hemingway*, 190.
4. Hemingway to Max Perkins, April 21, 1928, *The Only Thing That Counts*, 71.
5. Pauline to Hemingway, July 8, 1928, Hemingway Archive, John F. Kennedy Library.
6. Baker, *Ernest Hemingway*, 198–99; Madelaine Hemingway Miller, *Ernie*, 109–10.
7. Madelaine Hemingway Miller, *Ernie*, 110 and 112.
8. *A Farewell to Arms* manuscript, Hemingway Archive, John F. Kennedy Library.
9. "An Interview with Ernest Hemingway," *Paris Review*, ed. Wagner, *Ernest Hemingway: Five Decades of Criticism* (1974), 25.
10. Madelaine Hemingway Miller, *Ernie*, 118.
11. Ibid., 119–20.
12. Hemingway to Max Perkins, April 3, 1929, *The Only Thing That Counts*, 97. Matt Bruccoli *(Some Sort of Epic Grandeur)* attributed the coolness to Pauline's dislike of the Fitzgeralds (271).
13. There are many accounts of Fitzgerald's critique; the best is found in Donaldson's *Hemingway vs. Fitzgerald*, 126–30; see also Bruccoli, *Some Sort of Epic Grandeur*, 271–74. The correspondence in question has been published, and other notes are in the Hemingway Archive, John F. Kennedy Library.
14. Archibald MacLeish to Hemingway, September 1, 1929, quoted in *Hemingway and Faulkner, In Their Time*, 49.

9   The Bullfight as Center

1. Donaldson, *Hemingway vs. Fitzgerald*, 133–34.
2. See Wagner-Martin, *Zelda Sayre Fitzgerald, An American Woman's Life*.
3. Ernest Hemingway, "Introduction," *Kiki's Memoirs*; see Wagner-Martin, *Hemingway Review* 9 (Spring 1990), 176–77.
4. Madelaine Hemingway Miller, *Ernie*, 119.
5. Bernice Kert, *The Hemingway Women*, 211.
6. Ibid., 227.
7. Baker, *Ernest Hemingway*, 210 & 213.
8. Ibid., 217.
9. Quoted in Madelaine Hemingway Miller, *Ernie*, 122.
10. Gaston Bachelard, *The Poetics of Space*, 1969, quoted in J. Gerald Kennedy, *Imagining Paris* (1993), 7.
11. Baker, *Ernest Hemingway*, 206.
12. Clifton Fadiman, "A Letter to Mr. Hemingway," *New Yorker* (October 28, 1933), 74–75, in *Ernest Hemingway, The Critical Reception*, 136.
13. See *A Companion to Hemingway's Death in the Afternoon*, Miriam B. Mandel's collection of new essays on *Death in the Afternoon* (England: Camden House, 2004). She uses as jacket a reproduction of *El Torero*, the Juan Gris painting which Hemingway had purchased and used as frontispiece of the original printing.

10   Hemingway as the Man in Charge

1. Baker, *Ernest Hemingway*, 200. Hemingway wrote to Perkins (November 20, 1929) that he was trying to support "9 dependents," but the federal government allowed him only two for income tax purposes (*The Only Thing That Counts*, 129).
2. Bernice Kert, *Hemingway Women*, 230.

3. Madelaine Hemingway Miller, *Ernie*, 125.
4. Ibid., 127.
5. Hadley to Hemingway, January 26, 1930, Hemingway Archive, John F. Kennedy Library.
6. Michael Reynolds, *Chronology of Hemingway's Life*, 63.
7. Hemingway to Perkins, April 27, 1931, *The Only Thing That Counts*, 157.
8. Ibid., April 4, 1932, *The Only Thing That Counts*, 162.
9. Ibid., February (early) 1933, *The Only Thing That Counts*, 180.
10. Perkins to Hemingway, December 10, 1929, *The Only Thing That Counts*, 134.
11. Thomas Hermann, *"Quite a Little About Painters,"* 43.
12. Ibid., 44, 42, 43; Hermann noted that Gris's *Guitar Player* was always hanging in Hemingway's bedroom, no matter where they lived.
13. See Marilyn Elkins' "The Fashion of Machismo" in *Historical Guide to Ernest Hemingway*, 102–03.
14. Kert, "Jane Mason and Ernest Hemingway," *Hemingway Review* 21 (2002), 111–14. Unlike her extremely wealthy husband, Jane Mason had not been raised with a fortune. Born Jane Welsh in Tuxedo Park, New York June 24, 1909, she took the name of Kendall when her mother, a beautiful southerner, divorced Welsh to marry the millionaire Kendall. At eighteen, Jane married Mason and despite some talent for sculpting and painting, spent her time entertaining, gambling, and shopping. The Masons were soon to adopt two small boys, but the staff would care for them much of the time.
15. Quoted in Kert, Ibid., 112–13.
16. Hadley to Hemingway, May 16, 1931, Hemingway Archive, John F. Kennedy Library.
17. Ibid., June 15, 1931, Hemingway Archive, John F. Kennedy Library.
18. Reynolds, *Chronology of Hemingway's Life*, 64.
19. Kert, *The Hemingway Women*, 248.
20. Ibid., 242. Alane Salierno Mason ("To Love and Love Not," 111) suggests that the writing might be that of Carol Hemingway.
21. Kert, *The Hemingway Women*, 233, 243.
22. Ibid., 227.
23. Baker, *Ernest Hemingway*, 228.
24. Patrick Hemingway, comments at the January, 1984, Key West Literary conference on Hemingway.
25. Leicester Hemingway, *My Brother, Ernest Hemingway*, 112.
26. Ben Stoltzfus, *Lacan & Literature*, 1996, 14–15.
27. Ibid., 15.
28. Ibid., 100–01.

11   *Esquire* and Africa

1. Hemingway to Perkins, July 26, 1933, *The Only Thing That Counts*, 193.
2. See the listings of essays and stories in Reynolds' *Chronology of Hemingway's Life*, and in Baker, *Ernest Hemingway*. Baker counts more than thirty contributions to *Esquire*.
3. Bernice Kert, *The Hemingway Women*, 247–48.
4. Ibid., 249; quoting Bumby (Jack Hemingway) in Kert essay, *Hemingway Review* (2002), 113. Alane Salierno Mason places their sexual intimacy in the summer of 1934 ("To Love and Love Not," 149).

5. Alane Salierno Mason, Ibid., 146.
6. Kert, *Hemingway Review* essay, 113. Dos Passos had told Kert that Hemingway had boasted to him that Jane had jumped out a window "for unrequited love of him."
7. Kert, *The Hemingway Women*, 249–50.
8. Baker, *Ernest Hemingway*, 246–51.
9. Hemingway to Mrs. Paul Pfeiffer, October 16, 1933, *Letters*, 397.
10. Alane Salierno Mason, "Introduction to Jane Mason's *Safari*," *Hemingway Review* 21 (2002), 14.
11. Kert, *The Hemingway Women*, 254–61, and see *Green Hills of Africa*.
12. Baker, *Ernest Hemingway*, 251–56.
13. Pauline Hemingway to Sunny, quoted in Madelaine Hemingway Miller, *Ernie*, 124.
14. The Hemingway party thought the place exquisite; Jane Mason several years later called it "one of this world's lovely places" (quoted in Alane Mason, *Hemingway Review* (2002), 15, from Jane's letter to the Hemingways, May 17, 1935).
15. Kert, *The Hemingway Women*, 262; Kert's account is relatively complete since she makes use of Pauline's log, written during the safari.
16. Baker, *Ernest Hemingway*, 258. In various accounts of this episode, no mention is made of where Pauline ate her dinner.
17. Ibid., 260–66.
18. Hemingway, *Green Hills of Africa*, 26–27.
19. Scott Donaldson, *Hemingway vs. Fitzgerald*, 193.
20. See Nancy Comley and Robert Scholes, *Hemingway's Genders*, 1994.

12   Hemingway in the World

1. Kert, *The Hemingway Women*, 270–72; as Alane Salierno Mason told the story, it took influence from Archie MacLeish (now an editor at *Fortune*) to keep Kubie from publishing the essay ("To Love and Love Not," 149).
2. Baker, *Ernest Hemingway*, 271–72.
3. Hemingway to John Dos Passos, October 1932, *Letters*, 375.
4. Hemingway to Paul Romaine, July 6, 1932, Ibid., 363.
5. Hemingway to Guy Hickok, October 14, 1932, Ibid., 372–73.
6. Hemingway to Arnold Gingrich, July 15, 1934, Ibid., 409.
7. Hemingway to Perkins, November 16, 1933 (italics in original), Ibid., 400–01.
8. Hemingway to Ivan Kashkin, August 19, 1935, Ibid., 418–19.
9. Baker, *Ernest Hemingway*, 275.
10. Hemingway to Perkins, September 7, 1935, *Letters*, 421–22. Filled with bitterness, Hemingway continued that he was with a group who found 69 bodies as yet undiscovered. His blame falls on Hopkins and Roosevelt who sent those bonus marchers down into such a wasteland to get rid of them.
11. Hemingway to Mary Pfeiffer, January 26, 1936, *Letters*, 435–36. He also said candidly, "It makes me more tolerant of what happened to my father."
12. In "The Art of the Short Story, and 9 Stories to Prove It," he commented on the story carrying "the most load any short story ever carried" and yet "it still takes off and flies" (7), Hemingway Archive, John F. Kennedy Library.
13. And see Robert Gajdusek, *Hemingway in His Own Country*, 359ff.

14. Hemingway, "The Art of the Short Story, and 9 Stories to Prove it," Hemingway Archive, John F. Kennedy Library. His statement is "the incidence of husbands shot accidentally by wives who are bitches and really work at it is very low" (6).
15. Donaldson, *Hemingway vs. Fitzgerald*, 202.
16. Ibid., 202–04.
17. Hadley Mowrer to Hemingway, January 19, 1937, Hemingway Archive, John F. Kennedy Library.
18. Kert, *The Hemingway Women*, 278–80.
19. Caroline Moorehead, *Gellhorn, A Twentieth-Century Life* (2003), 104–07.
20. Kert, *The Hemingway Women*, 280–81.
21. Moorehead, *Gellhorn*, 104.

13   Martha Gellhorn and Spain

1. Kert, *The Hemingway Women*, 287.
2. Ibid., 285–86.
3. Quoted in Kert, Ibid., 291–92.
4. Ibid., 292.
5. Baker, *Ernest Hemingway*, 299–300.
6. Hemingway to the Pfeiffers, February 9, 1937, *Letters*, 457–58.
7. Baker, *Ernest Hemingway*, 300.
8. Moorehead, *Gellhorn*, 118. This biographer notes that Hemingway's liaison with Martha met with disapproval from Sidney Franklin, who liked Pauline immensely, and from others.
9. Hemingway, *New York Times* interview, 1940, in *Conversations with Ernest Hemingway* (1986), 20.
10. Baker, *Ernest Hemingway*, 301–02.
11. Ibid., 305.
12. Moorehead, *Gellhorne*, 124–26.
13. Ibid., 130.
14. Ibid., 132.
15. Marcelline Hemingway, *At the Hemingways*; see 336, 339, 348.
16. Kert, *The Hemingway Women*, 306.
17. Hemingway to Dos Passos, May 15, 1933, *Letters*, 389.
18. Hemingway to Mary Pfeiffer, August 2, 1937, Ibid., 460–61.
19. Baker, *Ernest Hemingway*, 317–20; Moorehead, *Gellhorn*, 133–38.
20. James H. Meredith, "Hemingway's Spain, 1937," "Hemingway in Andalusia" conference, June 25–30, 2006.
21. The improbability of Hemingway's savage portrait of Dorothy being aimed at Gellhorn has finally led some critics to see the character as reminiscent of Jane Mason, with her history of incomplete projects ("pampered, idealistic, restless" and "breezily exchanging one man for another," in the words of Alane Salierno Mason, "To Love and Love Not," 151). That Jane was herself writing a play (*Safari*) might have prompted Hemingway to start this project.
22. Hemingway, "The Strange Country," *Complete Short Stories*, 638.
23. Hemingway, *Green Hills of Africa*, 26–27.
24. Gregory Hemingway, *Papa, a Personal Memoir* (1976), 6 & 23.

14   War in Europe and at Home

1. Moorehead, *Gellhorn*, 173.
2. Alfred Kazin, "What Spain Has Made of Ernest Hemingway," *New York Herald Tribune Books*, 14 (October 16, 1938), 5.
3. Perkins wrote Hemingway October 31, 1940, that 200,000 copies had been printed for the Book of the Month sales, with Scribner's printing 160,000 copies for general sale. The book was selling over 20,000 copies each week (*The Only Thing That Counts*, 299–300).
4. John Chamberlain, "Hemingway Tells How Men Meet Death," *New York Herald Tribune Books*, 17 (October 20, 1940), 1.
5. Quoted by Perkins to Hemingway, February 14, 1940, *The Only Thing That Counts*, 280.
6. Perkins to Hemingway, August 13, 1940, Ibid., 286.
7. Lionel Trilling, "An American in Spain," *Partisan Review* 8 (January–February 1941), 63–67.
8. Moorehead, *Gellhorn*, 143–44.
9. Quoted in Moorehead, *Gellhorn*, 135–36.
10. Gregory Hemingway, *Papa, a Personal Memoir*, 91; Baker, *Ernest Hemingway*, 375; Diliberto, *Hadley*, 270.
11. Hemingway to Edna Gellhorn, addressed as "Dear Mother," September 28, 1940, Hemingway Archive, John F. Kennedy Library.
12. Martha Gellhorn, *Travels with Myself and Another* (1979), 20.
13. Ibid., 22.
14. Ibid., 24.
15. Peter Moreira, *Hemingway on the China Front* (2006), xv, 56.
16. Ibid., xvi.
17. "Out of Oak Park by Madrid," *The Monthly Letter of the Limited Editions Club*, September 1941, 1–4, in Stephens's *Ernest Hemingway, Critical Reception*, 268.
18. Gregory Hemingway, *Papa*, 91.
19. Ibid., 91–92.
20. Norberto Fuentes, *Hemingway in Cuba* (1984), 421; Moorehead, *Gellhorn*, 186–87.
21. Fuentes, *Hemingway in Cuba*, 101; Baker, *Ernest Hemingway*, 372–76; Patrick Hemingway recalled the summer of 1942, with he and Gregory on board the *Pilar*, in his introduction to Hemingway's *True at First Light*, 9–10.
22. Moorehead, *Gellhorn*, 187.
23. Hemingway, "Introduction" (for the 1955 edition," *Men At War* (1942)), 5.
24. Edna Gellhorn to Marti and Hemingway, 1942, Hemingway Archive, John F. Kennedy Library.
25. Diliberto, *Hadley*, 267; Hadley Mowrer to Hemingway, September 21, 1942, Hemingway Archive, John F. Kennedy Library.
26. Moorehead, *Gellhorn*, 198.
27. Ibid.
28. Baker, *Ernest Hemingway*, 380.
29. Kert, *The Hemingway Women*, 391–93.
30. Diliberto, *Hadley*, 269; Hemingway to Hadley Mowrer, December 23, 1943, Hemingway Archive, John F. Kennedy Library.

31. Hemingway to Gellhorn, January 1, 1944 (noted at top of page, written December 9–11, 1943), Hemingway Archive, John F. Kennedy Library. Later in the letter, he admitted "I know how good your reasons are and ... how much I need to see and partake and be a part of history, fk history I always said."
32. Hemingway to Perkins, March 12, 1944, *The Only Thing That Counts*, 332.
33. Mary Welsh Hemingway, *How It Was* (1976), 95–96.
34. Moorehead, *Gellhorn*, 216–17.

15 The Fourth Mrs. Hemingway

1. Hemingway to Perkins, February 25, 1944, *Letters*, 557.
2. Ibid., May 18, 1943, *The Only Thing That Counts*, 323.
3. Ibid., August 26, 1941, *The Only Thing That Counts*, 310.
4. Ibid., May 18, 1943, *The Only Thing That Counts*, 324.
5. Ibid., November 16, 1943, *The Only Thing That Counts*, 327.
6. Susan Beegel, "Hemingway and Hemochromatosis," *Hemingway: Seven Decades of Criticism* (1998), 375–88.
7. Hemingway to Gellhorn, January 31, 1944, Hemingway Archive, John F. Kennedy Library.
8. In conversation with Gellhorn at a 1987 Michigan State University conference on the Spanish Civil War, I was told that she had believed that most of Hemingway's narratives were intentionally inflated. Once she started to see that he believed much of his storying, she saw the extent of his illness: she cut her losses and began to think of separating. (Some of Gellhorn's comments were about my recent biography of Sylvia Plath, just published that autumn, in which she wondered why Plath had stayed with a man who obviously made her unhappy. Gellhorn stated that she would have left long before the infidelity.)
9. See Matts Djos, "Alcoholism in Ernest Hemingway's *The Sun Also Rises*: A Wine and Roses Perspective on the Lost Generation," *Casebook on The Sun Also Rises* (2002), 139–52. Another section of the Djos' essay also applies: "alcoholics have a higher level of anxiety, dependence, and defensiveness ... a remarkable degree of moodiness, impulsivity, hostility, and distrust."
10. Hemingway to Edna Gellhorn, September 21, 1944, Hemingway Archive, John F. Kennedy Library. In an August 28, 1940, letter from him to Martha, he analyzed her personality after she began taking thyroid ("there is a time when you are almost crazy"), and then she thinks their life is "worthless, you enchained, me a son of a bitch." Hemingway Archive.
11. Baker, *Ernest Hemingway*, 393–98.
12. Ibid., 404–410, and see Baker, 428, for description of the charges against Hemingway for taking military action although he was a correspondent; eventually, charges were dropped.
13. Moorehead, *Gellhorn*, 225.
14. Hemingway to Patrick, September 14, 1944, *Letters*, 571.
15. Moorehead, *Gellhorn*, 230.
16. Kert, *The Hemingway Women*, 414–16; see Baker, *Ernest Hemingway*, 440–42.
17. Mary Hemingway, *How It Was*, 102–03. That Martha Gellhorn includes a similar speech in her play, *Love Goes to Press*, between Philip and the character

named Jane Mason—when he falls in love at first sight—suggests that she had also heard this line from Hemingway.

18. Baker, *Ernest Hemingway*, 436–38.
19. Ibid., 443; Diliberto, *Hadley*, 269.
20. Moorehead, *Gellhorn*, 245.
21. Gellhorn to Hemingway, August 13, 1945, Hemingway Archive, John F. Kennedy Library.
22. Ibid. See Kert, *The Hemingway Women*, 422–23.
23. Baker, *Ernest Hemingway*, 439 & 443; Mary Hemingway, *How It Was*, 147.
24. Baker, *Ernest Hemingway*, 444.
25. Pauline Hemingway to Hemingway, March 17, 1945, Hemingway Archive, John F. Kennedy Library.
26. Baker, *Ernest Hemingway*, 447.
27. Marcelline to Hemingway, April 7, 1945, *At the Hemingways*, 356–57. The letter was particularly irritating to him because in 1937, he had written vituperatively to Marcelline about what he had misread as her request to use the cottage. Luckily, she had replied tactfully, but Hemingway's insults about the family and herself were hard to forget. He later apologized (*At the Hemingways*, 349–50).
28. Baker, *Ernest Hemingway*, said May 2, landing in Havana; Mary Hemingway said early June, landing in Miami. Both agree that the meeting was tense, with Hemingway scrubbed and slimmer, nervous about whether or not Mary would like his Cuban life. Mary recalled a lot of anxiety, and her gradually learning to keep quiet about anything that troubled her (*How It Was*, 154–57; *Ernest Hemingway*, 448).
29. Mary Hemingway, *How It Was*, 156.
30. Ibid., 160.
31. Gregory Hemingway, *Papa, a Personal Memoir*, 95; see Norberto Fuentes, *Hemingway in Cuba*, 23.
32. Mary Welsh, *How It Was*, 166 & 168.
33. See Gellhorn-Hemingway correspondence at both Boston University (the Gellhorn Archive) and John F. Kennedy Library (the Hemingway Archive). As Hemingway had written to her on August 28, 1940, she doesn't have to marry him if she has changed her mind. He gives her permission to have as many men friends as she wants "and go anywhere with them;" she doesn't have to come West to hunt with him; she can go on all her trips. However, there is a financial text to this letter as well. If Gellhorn has decided not to marry him, he needs to know quickly so that he can "pare back Pauline's settlement" (Hemingway Archive, John F. Kennedy Library).
34. See Hemingway to Mary, April 19, September 7, September 9, September 13, September 15, September 17, 1945; Hemingway Archive, John F. Kennedy Library.
35. Baker, *Ernest Hemingway*, 454.
36. Hemingway, *How It Was*, 183.
37. Kert, *The Hemingway Women*, 423.

16 From Cuba to Italy

1. Mary Hemingway, *How It Was*, 189, quoting from Hemingway's letter to Lanham.
2. Ibid., 191.

3. Ibid., 196.
4. See *How It Was*, 1–29.
5. Ibid.; see Rodger L. Tarr, "Hemingway's Lost Friend: Norton S. Baskin," *Hemingway Review* 25 (Spring 2006), 135–39; letter from Baskin, 138.
6. Baker, *Ernest Hemingway*, 461.
7. *How It Was*, 197–207.
8. Baker, *Ernest Hemingway*, 463.
9. Pauline to Hemingway, January 21, 1948, Hemingway Archive, John F. Kennedy Library.
10. A. E. Hotchner, "Preface," *Dear Papa, Dear Hotch, The Correspondence of Ernest Hemingway and A. E. Hotchner* (2005), ix–x.
11. *How It Was*, 222.
12. Baker, *Ernest Hemingway*, 468.
13. James D. Brasch, "'Christ, I Wish I Could Paint': The Correspondence between Ernest Hemingway and Bernard Berenson," *Hemingway in Italy and Other Essays*, ed. Robert W. Lewis (1990), 49–68.
14. Hemingway to Adriana Ivancich, April 15, 1950, Hemingway Archive, John F. Kennedy Library.
15. Hemingway to Adriana, June 16, 1950, and April 10, 1950, Hemingway Archive, John F. Kennedy Library.
16. *How It Was*, 253.
17. Baker, *Ernest Hemingway*, 470–74.
18. Gregory Hemingway, *Papa*, 21–22.
19. A later section of this fragment describes Hadley's first attempts to breastfeed Bumby, the mixed pleasure and pain of the process. #575A, Hemingway Archive, John F. Kennedy Library.
20. Baker, *Ernest Hemingway*, 480.
21. Hemingway to Hotchner, Nov. 11, 1950, *Dear Papa, Dear Hotch*, 85. There are many confidences about his life in this correspondence; for instance, October 3, 1949, Hemingway reported that Mary got her mink coat, 47.
22. *How It Was*, 255–60.
23. Ibid., 260–61. To Hotchner, however, Hemingway wrote, "the hell with love when you can't have children" (*Dear Papa*, 90, Dec. 7, 1950 letter); he had earlier referred to Casper, Wyoming, "where Miss Mary lost our kid" (*Dear Papa*, 48, October 3, 1949).
24. *How It Was*, 262–64.
25. Ibid., 264.
26. Ibid., 268.
27. Baker, *Ernest Hemingway*, 484.
28. Hemingway to Hotchner, July 4, 1950, *Dear Papa*, 79.
29. *How It Was*, 269.
30. Hemingway to Adriana, April 10, 1950, Hemingway Archive, John F. Kennedy Library.
31. Pauline Pfeiffer Hemingway to Hemingway, undated, Hemingway Archive, John F. Kennedy Library.
32. *How It Was*, 273.
33. Ibid., 275; Baker, *Ernest Hemingway*, 487.
34. Hemingway to Gregory Hemingway, August 15, 1950, Hemingway Archive, John F. Kennedy Library. (His alimony figures, at $500 a month, would not bear scrutiny.)

35. Hemingway to Charles Scribner, September 9, 1950, *Letters*, 712–14.
36. *How It Was*, 279–81; Baker, *Ernest Hemingway*, 487.
37. *How It Was*, 281.

17   Old Men, Prizes, and Reports
of Hemingway's Death

1. Gregory Hemingway, *Papa*, 4.
2. Hemingway to Hotchner, February 7, 1951, *Dear Papa*, 116.
3. Hemingway to Scribner, October 5, 1951, *Letters*, 738.
4. William Faulkner, "Review of *The Old Man and the Sea*," *Shenandoah* 3, Autumn 1952, in *Ernest Hemingway: Six Decades of Criticism*, 273.
5. Madelaine Hemingway Miller, *Ernie*, 130–31.
6. Kert, *The Hemingway Women*, 463–64. Whether Gregory's trouble had to do with taking drugs (he says the former) or cross-dressing remains unclear.
7. Baker, *Ernest Hemingway*, 496; *How It Was*, 290; Gregory Hemingway, *Papa*, 6–8.
8. Quoted in Brett Candlish Millier, "Elusive Mastery," *Elizabeth Bishop, The Geography of Gender* (1993), 243; in Millier's biography, *Elizabeth Bishop: Life and the Memory of It* (Berkeley: U of California P, 1993), she speculates that the friendship between Pauline and Bishop, which probably began in the late 1930s after Bishop and Marjorie Carr Stevens had bought a house on Whitehead Street in Key West, may have been sexual. At least, it continued many years. As late as 1948, Pauline wrote, asking Bishop (now in New York) whether or not she and Tom Wanning were engaged (201). For several months in the winter of 1947, Bishop lived in Pauline's Key West house while she was gone (180).
9. Gregory Hemingway, *Papa*, 7–8, 10–12.
10. Hemingway to Hotchner, July 21, 1952, *Dear Papa*, 131; see, for example, Hemingway's letter to Scribner (October 2, 1951, *Letters* 737) and his letter of thanks for his sympathy to John Dos Passos, October 30, 1951 in which he reminisces about his "haunted past" (Hemingway Archive, John F. Kennedy Library).
11. Quoted in Robert Stephens, *Ernest Hemingway, The Critical Reception*, 339.
12. Quoted in James Brasch, "'Christ, I Wish I Could Paint'," *Hemingway in Italy*, 58.
13. *How It Was*, 306.
14. Baker, *Ernest Hemingway*, 506.
15. Ibid.
16. Hemingway to Hotchner, March 10, 1953, *Dear Papa*, 142.
17. Baker, *Ernest Hemingway*, 508–25; *How It Was*, 342–90; Reynolds, *Chronology*, 122–25.
18. Hemingway to Hotchner, December 22, 1953, *Dear Papa*, 148–49.
19. *How It Was*, 308ff.
20. Ibid., 348.
21. Madelaine Hemingway Miller, *Ernie*, 136.
22. Rescued by riverboat, the Hemingways were taken to Butiaba on Lake Albert. A local pilot there agreed to fly them to Entebbe, but it was that small plane that burst into flames on take off. Reynolds, *Chronology*, 125.

23. Reynolds, *Chronology*, 126 and see *The Final Years*, Reynolds' fifth volume of the Hemingway biography.
24. Quoted in *How It Was*, 389.
25. Baker, *Ernest Hemingway*, 521–22.
26. News story included in Bruccoli's *Conversations with Ernest Hemingway*, 74–76.
27. Typical of Hemingway's behavior is Mary's account of his calling her a "thief" in the dining room of the *Africa*. *How It Was*, 400.
28. Kert, *The Hemingway Women*, 478; *How It Was*, 394ff.
29. Quoted in *How It Was*, 403.
30. Baker, *Ernest Hemingway*, 528–29.
31. Ibid., 536–37.

18 Endings

1. Baker, *Ernest Hemingway*, 538 & 543; Kert, *The Hemingway Women*, 488; and see Professor Yasushi Takano materials, "Hemingway in Andalusia" Conference, June, 2006.
2. *How It Was*, 474; Kert, *The Hemingway Women*, 490.
3. Valerie Hemingway, *Running with the Bulls* (2004), 5, 25.
4. *How It Was*, 462–63.
5. Kert, *The Hemingway Women*, 490–93.
6. *How It Was*, 467–68.
7. Valerie Hemingway, *Running with the Bulls*, 40.
8. Kert, *The Hemingway Women*, 491–92; Baker, *Ernest Hemingway*, 547–50; *How It Was*, 470–73.
9. Valerie Hemingway, *Running with the Bulls*, 31.
10. Kert, *The Hemingway Women*, 493.
11. *How It Was*, 480.
12. Valerie Hemingway, *Running with the Bulls*, 82.
13. Ibid., 106.
14. Kert, *The Hemingway Women*, 498.
15. Baker, *Ernest Hemingway*, 558; and see, in the Hemingway Archive at the John F. Kennedy Library, Hemingway's poignant two-page handwritten piece about being able to write "in the daytime" (#786).
16. Baker, *Ernest Hemingway*, 562; *How It Was*, 497–98.
17. Kert, *The Hemingway Women*, 501.
18. Baker, *Ernest Hemingway*, 562.
19. Ibid., 558.
20. Valerie Hemingway; *Running with the Bulls*, 59, 67, 78, 82–85, 105; as she remembered, she thought his protestations of love were a part of "his childish fantasy life" (85).
21. Ibid., 38.
22. Gregory Hemingway, *Papa*, 109.
23. Valerie Hemingway, *Running with the Bulls*, comments about Hemingway's "rage and ridicule" for Martha, 131.

Bibliography

Primary bibliography

Hemingway, Ernest. *Across the River and into the Trees*. New York: Scribner's, 1950.
——. *The Complete Short Stories of Ernest Hemingway*, ed. Finca Vigia. New York: Scribner's, 1987.
——. *Conversations with Ernest Hemingway*, ed. Matthew J. Bruccoli. Jackson: University Press of Mississippi, 1986.
——. *Dear Papa, Dear Hotch*, ed. Albert J. DeFazio III. Columbia: University of Missouri Press, 2005.
——. *Death in the Afternoon*. New York: Scribner's, 1932.
——. *A Farewell to Arms*. New York: Scribner's, 1929.
——. *The Fifth Column and the First Forty-Nine Stories*. New York: Scribner's, 1938.
——. *For Whom the Bell Tolls*. New York: Scribner's, 1940.
——. *The Garden of Eden*. New York: Scribner's, 1986.
——. *Green Hills of Africa*. New York: Scribner's, 1935.
——. *Ernest Hemingway: Selected Letters, 1917–1961*, ed. Carlos Baker. New York: Scribner's, 1981.
——. *Hemingway: The Viking Portable Library*, ed. Malcolm Cowley. New York: Viking, 1944.
——. *in our time*. Paris: Three Mountains Press, 1924.
——. *In Our Time*. New York: Boni & Liveright, 1925.
——. "An Interview with Ernest Hemingway," *Paris Review*, Spring 1958, in *Ernest Hemingway: Five Decades of Criticism*, ed. Linda Welshimer Wagner (1974), 21–38.
——. *Islands in the Stream*. New York: Scribner's, 1970.
——, ed. *Men at War*. New York: Crown Publishers, 1942.
——. *Men Without Women*. New York: Scribner's, 1928.
——. *A Moveable Feast*. New York: Scribner's, 1964.
——. "My Own Life" (subtitled segment: "The True Story of My Break with Gertrude Stein"), *New Yorker* (12 February 1927), 23–24.
——. *The Old Man and the Sea*. New York: Scribner's, 1952.
——. *The Spanish Earth*. Cleveland: J. B. Savage, 1938.
——. *The Sun Also Rises*. New York: Scribner's, 1926.
——. *Three Stories and Ten Poems*. Paris: Contact, 1923.
——. *To Have and Have Not*. New York: Scribner's, 1937.
——. *The Torrents of Spring*. New York: Scribner's, 1926.
——. *True at First Light*, ed. Patrick Hemingway. New York: Scribner's, 1999.
——. *Under Kilimanjaro*, ed. Robert W. Lewis and Robert E. Fleming. Kent, Ohio: Kent State University of Press, 2005.
——. *Winner Take Nothing*. New York: Scribner's, 1933.

Secondary bibliography

Baker, Carlos. *Ernest Hemingway, A Life Story*. New York: Charles Scribner's Sons, 1969.

Beegel, Susan. "Eye and Heart: Hemingway's Education as a Naturalist," *Historical Guide to Ernest Hemingway*. New York: Oxford University Press, 2000, 53–92.

——. "Hemingway and Hemochromatosis," *Hemingway Review* 10 (Fall 1990), 57–65.

Berenson, Bernard. *Sunset and Twilight, from the Diaries of 1947–1958*, ed. Nicky Mariano. New York: Harcourt, Brace and World, 1963.

Brasch, James. "'Christ, I Wish I Could Paint': The Correspondence between Ernest Hemingway and Bernard Berenson." *Hemingway in Italy and Other Essays*, ed. Robert W. Lewis. New York: Praeger, 1990, 49–67.

Brasch, James and Joseph Sigman. *Hemingway's Library: A Composite Record*. New York: Garland, 1981.

Braudy, Leo. *The Frenzy of Renown, Fame and Its History*. New York: Oxford University Press, 1986.

Bruccoli, Matthew J. *The Only Thing That Counts. The Ernest Hemingway/Maxwell Perkins Correspondence, 1925–1947*. New York: Scribner, 1996.

——. *Some Sort of Epic Grandeur, The Life of F. Scott Fitzgerald*, 2nd edition. Columbia: University of South Carolina Press, 2002.

——. "'Yr Letters Are Life Preservers': The Correspondence of Ezra Pound and Ernest Hemingway," *Paris Review* 163 (Fall 2003), 96–124.

Burwell, Rose Marie. *Hemingway, The Postwar Years and the Posthumous Novels*. Cambridge, MA: Cambridge University Press, 1996.

Comley, Nancy R. and Robert Scholes. *Hemingway's Genders*. New Haven: Yale University Press, 1994.

Crowley, John. *"The White Logic": Alcoholism and Gender in American Modernist Fiction*. Amherst: University of Massachusetts Press, 1994.

Curnutt, Kirk. *Literary Topics: Ernest Hemingway and the Expatriate Modernist Movement, II*. Farmington Hills, MI: Gale, 2000.

Diliberto, Gioia. *Hadley*. New York: Ticknor & Fields, 1992.

Donaldson, Scott. *By Force of Will*. New York: Viking, 1977.

——. *Hemingway vs. Fitzgerald: The Rise and Fall of a Literary Friendship*. Woodstock, NY: Overlook Press, 1999.

Dos Passos, John. *The Best Times, an Informal Memoir*. New York: New American Library, 1966.

Eby, Carl. *Hemingway's Fetishism: Psychoanalysis and the Mirror of Manhood*. Albany: State University of New York Press, 1999.

Fuentes, Norberto. *Hemingway in Cuba*, trans. Consuelo E. Corwin. Secaucus, NJ: Lyle Stuart, 1984.

Gajdusek, Robert E. *Hemingway in His Own Country*. Notre Dame, IN: University of Notre Dame Press, 2002.

Gellhorn, Martha. *Love Goes to Press* (introduction); play by Martha Gellhorn and Virginia Cowles. Lincoln: University of Nebraska Press, 1946, 1995.

——. *Travels with Myself and Another*. London: Allen Lane, 1978.

Griffin, Peter. *Along with Youth*. New York: Oxford University Press, 1985.

Griffin, Peter. *Less Than a Treason, Hemingway in Paris.* New York: Oxford University Press, 1990.

Hemingway, Carol. "Jane Mason's *Safari*," *Hemingway Review* 21 (Spring 2002), 117–20.

Hemingway, Gregory. *Papa: A Personal Memoir.* Boston: Houghton Mifflin, 1976.

Hemingway, Hilary and Jeffry P. Lindsay. *Hunting with Hemingway.* New York: Riverhead, 2000.

Hemingway, Leicester. *My Brother, Ernest Hemingway.* New York: World, 1962.

Hemingway, Marcelline. *At the Hemingways, with Fifty Years of Correspondence between Ernest and Marcelline Hemingway.* Moscow, Idaho: University of Idaho Press, 1999 (original publication 1962, Boston: Little, Brown, by Marcelline Hemingway Sanford).

Hemingway, Mary Welsh. *How It Was.* New York: Alfred A. Knopf, 1976.

Hemingway, Patrick. "*Islands in the Stream*: A Son Remembers," *Ernest Hemingway: The Writer in Context,* ed. James Nagel. Madison: University of Wisconsin Press, 1984, 13–18.

——. "Introduction" to *True at First Light.* New York: Scribner's, 1999, 7–11.

Hemingway, Valerie. *Running with the Bulls, My Years with the Hemingways.* New York: Ballantine, 2004.

Hermann, Thomas. "*Quite a Little About Painters*," *Art and Artists in Hemingway's Life And Work.* Tubingen: A. Francke Verlag, 1997.

Kennedy, J. Gerald. *Imagining Paris: Exile, Writing, and American Identity.* New Haven: Yale University Press, 1993.

Kennedy, J. Gerald and Jackson R. Bryer, eds. *French Connections, Hemingway and Fitzgerald Abroad.* New York: St. Martin's, 1998.

Kert, Bernice. *The Hemingway Women.* New York: W. W. Norton, 1983.

——. "Jane Mason and Ernest Hemingway: A Biographer Reviews Her Notes," *Hemingway Review* 21 (Spring 2002), 111–16.

Knoll, Robert E. *Robert McAlmon.* Lincoln: University of Nebraska Press, 1957.

Kubie, Lawrence. "Ernest Hemingway: Cyrano and the Matador." *American Imago* 41: 1 (Spring 1984), 9–18.

Lynn, Kenneth. *Hemingway.* New York: Simon & Schuster, 1987.

Mason, Alane Salierno. "An Introduction to Jane Mason's Safari," *Hemingway Review* 21 (Spring 2002), 13–21.

——. "To Love and Love Not," *Vanity Fair* (July 1999), 108–18, 146–52.

Mason, Jane. *Safari. Hemingway Review* 21 (Spring 2002), 23–110.

Mellow, James. *Hemingway: A Life Without Consequences.* New York: Houghton Mifflin, 1992.

Meredith, James H. "Hemingway's Spain, 1937," *Hemingway in Andalusia Conference* (June 25–30, 2006).

Miller, Madelaine Hemingway. *Ernie: Hemingway's Sister "Sunny" Remembers.* New York: Crown, 1975.

Millier, Brett Candlish. "Elusive Mastery," *Elizabeth Bishop, The Geography of Gender,* ed. Marilyn May Lombardi. Charlottesville: University of Virginia Press, 1993, 233–43.

Moddelmog, Debra A. *Reading Desire, In Pursuit of Ernest Hemingway.* Ithaca: Cornell University Press, 1999.

Montgomery, Constance Cappel. *Hemingway in Michigan.* New York: Fleet, 1966.

Moorehead, Caroline. *Gellhorn, A Twentieth-Century Life.* New York: Henry Holt, 2003.

Moreira, Peter. *Hemingway on the China Front.* Dulles, VA: Potomac, 2006.

Reynolds, Michael S. *Hemingway: The American Homecoming.* Cambridge: Basil Blackwell, 1992.

——. *Hemingway: An Annotated Chronology.* Detroit, MI: Omnigraphics, 1991.

——. *Hemingway: The Final Years.* New York: Norton, 1999.

——. *Hemingway: The Paris Years.* Cambridge, MA: Basil Blackwell, 1989.

——. "Hemingway's Home: Depression and Suicide," *Ernest Hemingway: Six Decades of Criticism*, ed. Linda Wagner-Martin. East Lansing: Michigan State University Press, 1987, 9–17.

——. *The Young Hemingway.* Cambridge, MA: Basil Blackwell, 1986.

Rovit, Earl and Arthur Waldhorn, eds. *Hemingway and Faulkner, in Their Time.* New York: Continuum, 2005.

Smith, Paul. *A Reader's Guide to the Short Stories of Ernest Hemingway.* Boston: Hall, 1989.

Sojka, Gregory S. *Ernest Hemingway, The Angler as Artist.* New York: Peter Lang, 1985.

Spilka, Mark. *Hemingway's Quarrel with Androgyny.* Lincoln: University of Nebraska Press, 1990.

Stephens, Robert O. *Hemingway's Nonfiction, The Public Voice.* Chapel Hill: University of North Carolina Press, 1968.

——, ed. *Ernest Hemingway: The Critical Reception.* New York: Burt Franklin, 1977.

Stein, Gertrude. *The Autobiography of Alice B. Toklas.* In *Gertrude Stein, Writings 1903–1932*, eds. Catharine Stimpson and Harriet Chessman. New York: Literary Classics of the United States, 1998, 653–913.

Stoltzfus, Ben. *Lacan & Literature, Purlioned Pretexts.* Albany: State University of New York Press, 1996.

Strychacz, Thomas. *Hemingway's Theaters of Masculinity.* Baton Rouge: Louisiana State University Press, 2003.

Svoboda, Frederick J. "The Great Themes in Hemingway: Love, War, Wilderness, and Loss," *Historical Guide to Ernest Hemingway.* New York: Oxford University Press, 2000, 155–72.

Tarr, Rodger L. "Hemingway's Lost Friend, Norton S. Baskin," *Hemingway Review*, 25 (Spring 2006), 136–39.

Villard, Henry S. and James Nagel, eds. *Hemingway in Love and War: The Lost Diary of Agnes von Kurowsky, Her Letters and Correspondence of Ernest Hemingway.* Boston: Northeastern University Press, 1989.

Wagner-Martin, Linda. (alternate name, Linda Welshimer Wagner). "At the Heart of *A Farewell to Arms*," *Hemingway's Italy, New Perspectives*, ed. Rena Sanderson. Baton Rouge: Louisiana State University Press, 2006, 158–66.

——. *Ernest Hemingway's A Farewell to Arms, A Reference Guide.* Westport, Conn.: Greenwood Press, 2003.

——. *"Favored Strangers:" Gertrude Stein and Her Family.* New Brunswick, NJ: Rutgers University Press, 1995.

——. "Hemingway: The First 75 Years," *Al Majal* (Arabic USIS Magazine), 66 (1975), 26–32.

——. *Hemingway and Faulkner: inventors/masters.* Metuchen, NJ: Scarecrow, 1975.

——. "Hemingway's Search for Heroes, Once Again," *Arizona Quarterly* 44: 2 (Summer 1988), 58–68.

Wagner-Martin, Linda. "'I like you less and less': The Stein Subtext in *Death in the Afternoon*," *A Companion to Hemingway's Death in the Afternoon*, ed. Miriam B. Mandel. Suffolk: Camden House, 2004, 59–77.

——. "The Intertextual Hemingway," *A Historical Guide to Ernest Hemingway* (2000), 173–94.

——. "'Proud and friendly and gently': Women in Hemingway's Early Works," *Ernest Hemingway, The Papers of a Writer*, ed. Bernard Oldsey. Boston: Garland, 1981.

——. "Racial and Sexual Coding in Hemingway's *The Sun Also Rises*," *Hemingway Review* 10.2 (1991), 39–41.

——. "The Romance of Desire in Hemingway's Fiction," *Hemingway and Women: Female Critics and the Female Voice*, ed. Lawrence Broer and Gloria Holland. Tuscaloosa: University of Alabama Press, 2002, 54–69.

——. "The Secrecies of the Public Hemingway," *Hemingway: Up in Michigan Perspectives*, ed. Frederick J. Svoboda and Joseph J. Waldmeir. East Lansing: Michigan State University Press, 1995, 149–56.

——. and Michael Reynolds, "Hemingway and the Limits of Biography, An Exchange on the 'Jimmy Breen' Manuscript," *Hemingway: Up in Michigan Perspectives*, ed. Frederick J. Svoboda and Joseph J. Waldmeir. East Lansing: Michigan State University Press, 1995, 105–126.

——, ed. *Ernest Hemingway: Five Decades of Criticism*. East Lansing: Michigan State University Press, 1974.

——, ed. *Ernest Hemingway: Six Decades of Criticism*. East Lansing: Michigan State University Press, 1987.

——, ed. *Hemingway: Seven Decades of Criticism*. East Lansing: Michigan State University Press, 1998.

——, ed. *Hemingway's The Sun Also Rises: A Casebook*. New York: Oxford University Press, 2002.

——, ed. *A Historical Guide to Ernest Hemingway*. New York: Oxford University Press, 2000.

Woolf, Virginia. "An Essay in Criticism," *Granite and Rainbow*. London: Hogarth, 1927, 1958, 85–92.

Yalom, Irvin D. and Marilyn Yalom. "Ernest Hemingway—A Psychiatric View," *Archives of General Psychiatry* 24 (June 1971), 485–94.

Index

Adams, Nick (fictional character), 22, 37, 40–41, 69, 73, 91, 101
Agassiz group, 1, 6
Aiken, Conrad, 39
Albeniz, I., 23
Algren, Nelson (*Somebody in Boots*), 113
Alley, Rewi, 136
American Academy of Arts and Letters, 151, 160
Anderson, Sherwood (*Dark Laughter*), 28, 39, 50, 54–57, 94, 113 (*Puzzled America*, 113)
Arnold, Ruth, 4
Audubon, John James, 102
Austen, Jane, 52

Bach, Johann Sebastian, 23
Bachelard, Gaston, 90
Baker, Carlos, 159, 162
Batista, Fulgencio, 160, 165
Beach, Sylvia (Shakespeare & Company), 28, 39
Beau Brummel (Clyde Fitch), 7
Beegel, Susan, 7, 142
Benchley, Robert, 58–59, 71
Berenson, Bernard, 152, 160
Best Short Stories, 1937 (Edward J. O'Brien), 118
Bird, Bill, 29–30, 46–47, 49–50, 113
Bird, Sally, 30, 49
Bishop, Elizabeth, 159
Blum, Carl, 136
Boltons (family), 33–34
Bolton, Prudy, 8, 33–34
Bond, W. Longhorn, 136
Bone, John, 28–31, 47–48
Boni & Liveright, 49–50, 56–58, 63
Bonsall, Phil, 167
Boxer, Charles, 136
Boyd, Ernest, 59
Braden, Spruille, 136
Bradford, Ruth, 25

Braque, Georges (*Still-life with Wine Jug*), 98
Breaker, George, 25, 49
Breaker, Helen, 25
Brown, Charles, 168
Browning, Robert, 23
Broyles, Henrietta, 154, 156
Brumback, Ted, 10, 17–18
Buckley, Peter, 166
bullfighting, 47, 86–95, 99, 161–66
Bump, Marjorie, 16
Burns, Harry, 159

Cabot, John, 163
Caldwell, Erskine, 112
Capa, Robert, 134–35
Castro, Fidel, 165, 167
Cather, Willa, 39, 52, 77 (*One of Ours*, 77)
Cézanne, Paul, 37, 52
Chamberlain, John, 133
Charles, Mrs. Joseph (Auntie), 8, 16, 26
Chesterton, G. K., 23
Chicago, 2, 6, 15, 18–21, 25–26, 38–39, 69, 146, 148
Chopin, Frédéric, 23
Churchill, Winston, 139
Cohen, Morris, 136
Collier's, 122–23, 136–37, 139
Comley, Nancy (*Hemingway's Genders*), 75–76, 111
Connable, Mrs. Harriet, 16–17
Connable, Ralph, 16–17
Connally, Marc, 58
Conrad, Joseph, 50–51
Cooper, Richard, 107–10, 112
Cosmopolitan, 133, 151, 154
Cowles, Virginia (*Love Goes to Press*), 144
Cowley, Malcolm, 113, 151
Crane, Hart, 95, 117
Crane, Stephen, 35
"Crook Factory, The," 137–38, 165

Crosby, Caresse, 88
Crosby, Harry, 88, 90–91, 95, 117
Cuba, 133; see Finca Vigia
Cummings, E. E. (*Enormous Room, The*), 39, 87

Daughters of the American Revolution (DAR), 6
Davis, Anne, 165–68
Davis, Bill, 165–68
Danby-Smith, Valerie; see Hemingway, Valerie Danby-Smith
Dell, Floyd (*Moon Calf*), 23
Dickens, Charles, 23
Dietrich, Marlene, 99, 109, 144–45, 153–54
Dilworth, Jim, 8
Dinesen, Isak, 109
Domingúin, Luis Miguel, 161, 164–66
Donaldson, Scott, 4, 117
Dorman-Smith, E. E. ("Chink"), 29, 31, 45, 48–49
Dos Passos, John, 39, 49, 57, 61–62, 71, 79, 82, 88–89, 95, 110, 113, 117, 120, 124, 126, 151, (*1919*, 113), (*Big Money, The*, 113), (*42nd Parallel, The*, 113)
Dos Passos, Katy; see Smith, Katy
Dreiser, Theodore (*An American Tragedy*), 34–35
Du Bois, W. E. B., 39
Du Maurier (*Trilby*), 23

Eastman, Max, 29
Einstein, Albert, 125
Eliot, T. S. (*The Waste Land*), 35, 39, 53
Ellis, Havelock, 23
Esquire, 94, 104–105, 109, 113–15, 133

FBI, 165, 170
Fadiman, Clifton, 93
Faulkner, William, 23, 112, 159
Fenton, Charles A., 159
Finca Vigia (Lookout Farm), Cuba, 133, 137–39, 141, 144, 146, 151, 153–55, 158, 163, 165–66

Fitzgerald, F. Scott, 23, 34, 39, 40–41, 50, 55–60, 64, 82, 88, 94–95, 97, 110, 113, 117–18, 136, 141, ("Crack-Up," 117–18), (*Great Gatsby, The*, 55), (*Tender Is the Night*, 84, 113)
Fitzgerald, Zelda Sayre, 50, 57–58, 60, 82, 88, 106, 141
Flanner, Janet, 50
Flechtheim, Alfred, 98
Ford, Ford Madox, 48–51, 54, 79 (*Good Soldier, The*, 54)
Fossalta de Pave, 10–11, 152
Franklin, Sidney, 118, 122–23
Fuentes, Gregorio, 137, 156

Gavin, James, 144
Gellhorn, Edna, 119, 135–36, 138–39, 142–43
Gellhorn, Martha; see Hemingway, Martha Gellhorn
Gilberts (family), 33
Gingrich, Arnold, 94, 106, 113–15, 117, 119–20
Glasgow, Ellen, 39
Gogh, Vincent van, 49
Gordon, Caroline, 88
Goya, Francisco de, 98
Greco-Turkish War, 30
Green Hat, The (Michael Arlen), 70
Gris, Juan (*Guitar Player, The*) (*Torero, The*), 98
Guck, Bea, 155
Guthrie, Pat, 55
Gutierrez, Carlos, 101, 115

H. D., 39
Hahn, Emily, 136
Hall, Ernest ("Abba"), 2–3, 5–6
Harry Ransom Humanities Research Center, University of Texas, 5
Heilbrun, Werner, 124–25
Hellinger, Mark, 151
Hellman, Lillian, 120
Hemingway, Anson, 170
Hemingway, Carol, 96

Hemingway, Dr. Clarence, 1–7, 10–11, 15–18, 23–24, 27–29, 33–35, 38, 48, 65, 78, 80–81, 85, 87, 90–91, 93, 153, 168, 170
Hemingway, Ernest,
  alcoholism, 87–88, 138, 142–48, 162–67
  ambition as writer, 22–23, 34–45, 46–56, 68–76, 84, 86–7, 94–5, 133–35, 141–44, 151, 153–58
  autobiographical writing 40–41, 87, 114
  "black ass," 87, 115; see illnesses
  Catholicism and other religious beliefs, 5–6, 62–3
  "deaths" of, 162–63
  family relationships, 1–10, 14–18, 27–8, 39–40, 48, 80–1, 90, 102–103, 170
  illness (wounding, shell shock, accidents, depression, hemochromatosis), 11–16, 25, 29, 78–9, 108–10, 115, 142, 145–48, 150–51, 153, 156–57, 162–64, 167–73
  journalism, 9–10, 28–31
  masculinity, 9–11, 17–18, 41–2, 96–8, 99, 104, 108–11, 113–17, 135
  musical training, 5, 12
  politics, 104, 113–16, 118–19, 122–26, 128, 137–39, 164
  racial considerations, 2, 32–35, 58, 73–75
  rhetoric of courtship, 140, 152, 171–72

Works

Books

Across the River and Into the Trees, 95, 153, 155–56, 158, 172
Death in the Afternoon, 70, 92, 94–95, 97–98, 101, 105, 110
Farewell to Arms, A, 76–86, 88–94, 96, 98, 110–11, 125–26, 133

Fifth Column, The, 127–30, 133, 136, 144
Fifth Column and the First Forty-Nine Stories, The, 131–32
First Forty-Nine Stories, The, 118
For Whom the Bell Tolls, 130, 133–36, 141, 165
Garden of Eden, The, 31, 67, 103, 148, 165
Green Hills of Africa, 95, 108–11, 113–15, 130
in our time, 10, 46, 50, 84
In Our Time, 32–33, 35, 37–38, 40–42, 45, 46, 49–51, 55–56, 71–72, 74, 98, 133
Islands in the Stream, 31, 100, 148, 159
Men at War, 138
Men Without Women, 45, 69, 71–75, 77, 92, 98
Moveable Feast, A, 84, 100, 165
Old Man and the Sea, The, 158–61, 164
Sun Also Rises, The, 52–58, 63–64, 69–70, 77–78, 84, 94, 97–98
Three Stories and Ten Poems, 46
To Have and Have Not, 95, 114–15, 117, 119–20, 122–24, 128–29, 133
Torrents of Spring, The, 54–57, 63–64, 71, 98
True at First Light, 163
Under Kilimanjaro, 163
Winner Take Nothing, 91–92, 106

Short Fiction, Poetry, and Prose

"After the Storm," 92–93
"Alpine Idyll, An," 71
"Banal Story," 72
"Battler, The," 72
"Big Two-Hearted River," 37, 52, 74–75, 84, 91, 116
"Butterfly and the Tank, The," 133
"Canary for One, A," 69
"Cat in the Rain," 42–45
"Clean, Well-Lighted Place, A," 90–91
"Cross Country Snow," 34, 42
"Doctor and the Doctor's Wife, The," 32, 35–38, 74, 91
"End of Something, The," 41–42, 44

"Fathers and Sons," 4, 91
"Fifty Grand," 72–73
"God Rest You Merry, Gentlemen,"
    91–92
"Hills Like White Elephants," 73, 114
"Homage to Switzerland," 92
"How Green Was My Valet," 130
"In Another Country," 69–70
"Indian Camp," 32–35, 38, 48–49, 51,
    91
"James Allen" (ms), 66, 69
"Killers, The," 69, 72, 148
"Light of the World, The," 92
"Malady of Power; A Second Serious
    Letter, The," 114
"Mink Jacket" (ms), 153
"Mother of a Queen, The," 91–92
"Mr. and Mrs. Elliot," 42
"My Old Man," 31
"My Own Life," 71
"Natural History of the Dead, A," 92,
    94
"Night Before Battle," 133–34
"Nobody Ever Dies," 133
"Notes on the Next War: A Serious
    Topical Letter," 114
"Now I Lay Me," 73, 75, 77, 84–85
"Old Man at the Bridge, The," 123
"Out of Season," 42, 44, 51
"Sea Change, The," 91–92
"Short Happy Life of Francis
    Macomber, The," 106, 115–18,
    130
"Snows of Kilimanjaro, The," 95,
    115–18, 130
"Soldier's Home," 22, 35–37, 39, 53,
    74–75, 84
"Strange Country, The," 128
"Summer People," 40
"Ten Indians," 8, 32–35
"Three Day Blow, The," 34, 41
"Three Shots," 32
"Undefeated, The," 72, 75
"Under the Ridge," 133
"Up in Michigan," 31
"Very Short Story, A," 75
"Way You'll Never Be, A," 92, 101,
    105–106

"Who Murdered the Vets?" 114–15
"Wings Over Africa: An
    Ornithological Letter," 114
Hemingway, Grace Hall, 1–7, 9–10,
    15–18, 25, 27–28, 35–36, 45, 65,
    72, 75, 80, 85, 89–90, 96, 102,
    111, 136, 146, 159
Hemingway, Gregory, 100–102,
    105–107, 109, 125, 130, 135–38,
    153, 157–60, 167, 170, 172–73
Hemingway, Hadley Richardson, 5,
    18–32, 42, 45–66, 75, 78, 90, 94,
    97, 99–100, 107, 118, 126, 129,
    131, 135, 138–39, 170
Hemingway, John Hadley Nicanor
    (Bumby), 48, 78, 81–82, 85,
    88–89, 97, 99, 101–102, 105–107,
    109, 130, 135–36, 138, 144–46,
    150, 153, 167, 170
Hemingway, Leicester, 6–7, 16, 27, 35,
    80, 96, 99, 102
Hemingway, Madelaine Miller
    (Sunny), 17–18, 33, 40, 65, 81–82,
    87–88, 96–97, 162
Hemingway, Marcelline Sanford, 1–5,
    7–8, 13–15, 26, 39, 65, 126, 146,
    151
Hemingway, Martha Gellhorn,
    119–20, 121–26, 130–35, 142–45,
    147–48, 152, 173 (*Face of War,
    The*, 123), (*Heart of Another, The*,
    137), (*Liana*, 138), (*Love Goes to
    Press*, 144), (*Travels with Myself
    and Another*, 135–36), (*Trouble I've
    Seen, The*, 119, 123), (*What Mad
    Pursuit*, 121)
Hemingway, Mary Welsh Monks (*How
    It Was*), 139–64, 165–72
Hemingway, Patrick, 80, 86, 99,
    101–102, 105–107, 109, 125, 130,
    135–38, 143–46, 150, 153, 156,
    160–64, 167, 170
Hemingway, Pauline Pfeiffer, 57–67,
    75–90, 95–102, 105–11, 113, 115,
    117–18, 122, 124–31, 133–35,
    141–42, 145, 150–51, 156–57,
    159, 161, 170
Hemingway, Tyler, 9

Hemingway, Ursula, 17–18, 40
Hemingway, Valerie Danby-Smith
   (*Running with the Bulls*), 165–68,
   171–72
Herrara, Jose Luis, 146
Hickok, Guy, 86
Hoover, Herbert, 93, 113
Hopkins, Harry, 121
Horne, Bill, 25, 80
Horton Bay, 3, 8–9, 17–18, 25–28, 146,
   151
Hotchner, A. E., 151, 153–54, 156,
   158, 160–61, 163, 166
House UnAmerican Activities
   Committee, 165
Howard, Leland, 160
Hughes, Langston, 39
Hurston, Zora Neale, 39

Idaho, Ketchum, 165–68
Ivancich, Adriana, 152–54, 156–58,
   161, 163, 172
Ivancich, Dora, 154, 158
Ivancich, Gianfranco, 153, 161
Ivens, Joris, 124–25

James, Henry, 23, 51, 54 (*The
   Ambassadors*, 54)
Joyce, James, 139

Kansas City Research Hospital, 80,
   99–100
Kansas City *Star*, 9–10, 17
Kashkin, Ivan, 114
Kazin, Alfred, 131–32
Kert, Bernice, 14, 88, 100, 148, 167
Key West, 79–80, 87–90, 99–102, 104,
   109–10, 113, 115, 119, 121–22,
   124–25, 130, 133–34, 136,
   150–51, 153, 157
Kiki (Alice Prin, *Memoirs*), 87
Klee, Paul (*Construction of a
   Monument*), 98
Kromer, Tom (*Waiting for
   Nothing*), 113
Kubie, Lawrence, 106, 112–13

Lanham, Buck, 143–45, 149, 153

Lardner, Ring, 7
Lausanne Peace Conference, 30
Lavalle, Ramon, 136
Lewis, Sinclair (*Main Street*), 23, 52,
   113 (*It Can't Happen Here*, 113)
Lilly Library Hemingway archives,
   Indiana University, 5
Little Review, The, 46
Loeb, Harold, 49–50

MacLeish, Ada, 57, 60, 67
MacLeish, Archibald, 57, 60, 67, 79,
   84, 113, 120, 125
McAlmon, Robert, 38, 47, 49–50
Maltz, Albert (*Black Pit*), 113
Mann, Thomas, 125
mano a mano, 165
Mason, Alane Salierno, 105
Mason, Grant, 98, 100, 105–106, 117
Mason, Jane, 98–101, 105–107, 109–10,
   112–13, 116–17, 119–20, 128–29
Masson, Andre, 47
Matthews, Herbert, 124, 127
Mayo Clinic, 167, 170
Mencken, H. L., 71
Millay, Edna St. Vincent, 39
Miro, Joan (*The Farm*), 61–62
Mitchell, Billy, 33
Monks, Noel, 145
Montgomery, Constance Cappel, 16–17
Moorehead, Caroline (*Gellhorn*), 124,
   135, 138
Moreira, Peter, 136
Mowrer, Paul Scott, 29, 61, 65, 78, 99,
   107, 109, 139
Murphy, Gerald, 50, 57, 60, 67
Murphy, Sarah, 50, 57, 60, 67
Mussolini, Benito, 29

New Masses, The, 114–15, 133
"New Woman," 70
Nobel Prize for Literature, 160, 170–71
North American Newspaper Alliance
   (NANA), 118–19, 122–23, 133

Oak Park, Illinois, 1–3, 8–11, 13,
   28–29, 32ff, 40–41, 46–47, 80–81,
   85, 90, 96, 126, 140, 170

O'Neil, George, 16, 49
O'Neill, Eugene, 39
Order of Carlos Manual de Cespedes, 160
Ordónẽz, Antonio, 161, 164–66
Ordónẽz, Carmen, 166

Pailthorp, "Dutch," 16
Pamplona, 47, 49, 50–52, 56, 60–61, 78, 86–88, 161, 163
Parker, Dorothy, 59, 88
Parsons, Louella, 157
Pearl Harbor, 135–37
Percival, Philip, 107–109, 161
Perkins, Max, 57–58, 63–64, 69–70, 79, 81–82, 95–98, 104, 114–15, 118–19, 122, 134, 139, 141–42, 151
Pfeiffer, Gus (G. A.), 66–67, 86, 89, 96, 105, 107, 117, 157
Pfeiffer, Jinny, 57, 66–67, 80, 86, 88, 107, 159
Pfeiffer, Mary, 107, 115, 122, 126–27, 129, 134–35, 142, 157
Pfeiffer, Pauline; see Hemingway, Pauline Pfeiffer
Pierce, Waldo, 100
Pilar, 99, 107, 109–10, 113, 115, 117–18, 126, 137, 139, 142, 155, 159, 163
Poetry, 39
Pound, Dorothy, 45
Pound, Ezra, 5, 9, 28, 31, 35, 37, 39, 45–47, 51, 79
Prin, Alice; see Kiki
Prohibition, 87
Pulitzer Prize for Fiction, 136, 160

Querschnitt, Der, 98
Quinlan, Grace, 16, 18
Quintanilla, Luis, 122

Rachmaninoff, Sergei, 23
realism, 34–35
Regler, Gustave, 124–25
Reynolds, Michael, 28, 32, 58
Richardson, Dorothea, 19
Richardson, Dorothy, 22–23
Richardson, Fonnie; see Usher, Fonnie

Richardson, Hadley; see Hemingway, Hadley Richardson
Richardson, James, 20
Richardson, Mrs. James, 19–20
Robin Hood, 7
Robles, Jose, 124
Romaine, Paul, 113
Roosevelt, Eleanor, 119, 121–22, 125
Roosevelt, Franklin Delano, 113, 119, 121, 125
Roosevelt, Theodore, 7–8
Rosenfeld, Paul, 58
Ross, Lillian, 153–54
Rudge, Olga, 5
Russell, Joe, 101

safari, 105–11, 113–14, 160–64
Sanford, Marcelline; see Hemingway, Marcelline Sanford
Scholes, Robert (*Hemingway's Genders*), 75–76, 111
Scribner, Charles, Jr., 151, 153, 155–60
Scribner's, 57, 81, 86, 92–95, 98, 104, 119, 141
Scribner's Magazine, 69–72, 81–82, 86, 110, 122
Shakespeare, William, 71
Shipman, Evan, 122
Sinclair, Upton, 125
Smith, Al, 93
Smith, Bill, 8, 12, 16–19, 50
Smith, Katy Dos Passos, 8–9, 12, 18–19, 21, 82, 88, 110, 113, 151
Smith, Y. K., 18–19, 26, 28
Sojka, Gregory, 37
Spain in Flames (Prudencio de Perada), 122
Spanish Civil War, 112, 118–20, 122–28, 130–31, 133, 165
Spanish Earth, The, 124–25
Spieser, Maurice (Moe), 119
Steffens, Lincoln, 29
Stein, Gertrude, 27–29, 31, 34, 37, 39, 46–48, 51–52, 57–58, 71, 77, 88, 94, 98, 104, 111, 128, 133 (*Autobiography of Alice B. Toklas, The*, 94, 104), (*The Making of Americans*, 49, 51)
Stein, Leo, 52

Stewart, Donald Ogden, 49–52, 61, 72, 88, 98–99
Stoltzfus, Ben, 102–103
Strater, Mike and Maggie, 47, 58, 82, 113
Strindberg, Joan August (*Married*), 23

Tabeshaw, Billy, 33
Tanganyika Guides, 107
Tate, Allen, 88
Tchitcherin, George, 29
Thompson, Charles, 107–109
Thompson, Loraine, 109
Thoreau, Henry David (*Walden*), 116
Toklas, Alice B., 5, 27, 47, 88
Toomer, Jean (*Cane*), 39
Toronto *Daily Star* and *Star Weekly*, 17, 25, 28, 30–31, 39, 46–48
Tracy, Spencer, 160–61
transatlantic review, 48–50
Trilling, Lionel, 134
Turgenev, Ivan (*Sportsman Sketches*), 54–55
Twain (Mark Twain), 110
Twysden, Duff, 50–52, 98

Usher, Fonnie Richardson, 19, 25
Usher, Roland, 19

Vanderbilt, Alfred, 107, 109
Viertel, Jige, 154
Viertel, Peter, 154

Villard, Henry, 12–13
von Blixen, Bror, 108–109
von Clausewitz, Karl, 138
von Kurowsky, Agnes, 12–15, 18, 22, 45, 75, 85, 90, 173

Walloon, Lake (Michigan), 3–4, 16–18
Walpole, Hugh, 23, 71
Walton, Bill, 145
Welsh, Adeline, 149, 156, 163
Welsh, Tom, 149–50, 156–57, 163
Westbrook, Max, 27
Wharton, Edith (*Age of Innocence, The*), 52
Wheeler, Harry, 118
Whitlock, Byra (Puck), 153
Williams, William Carlos, 39
Wilson, Edmund, 78
Woolf, Leonard, 77
Woolf, Virginia (*Jacob's Room, Mrs. Dalloway*) 77–78, 87
World War I, 9–11, 28–31, 39, 114, 125, 127, 133, 136, 170
World War II, 95, 114, 130, 136, 142–45, 150; see Spanish Civil War
Wright, Frank Lloyd, 3
Writers' Congress, 125
Wylie, Eleanor, 58

Yalom, Irving, 45
Yalom, Marilyn, 45
Young, Philip, 159